TEXAS SAMPLER

"Handmade, Homemade...
Recipes You're Bound to Love"

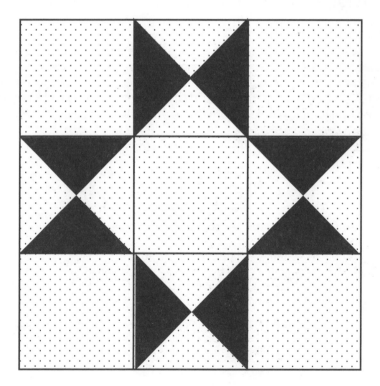

The Junior League of Richardson

The Junior League of Richardson reaches out to women of all races, religions and national origins who demonstrate an interest in commitment to voluntarism.

Who We Are

The Junior League of Richardson is an organization of women committed to promoting voluntarism and improving the community through effective action and leadership of trained volunteers. Its purpose is exclusively educational and charitable.

Organized as the Richardson Service League in 1966, the Junior League of Richardson became a member of the Association of Junior Leagues International, Inc. in 1980 which has over 180,000 members worldwide.

Each year the League provides funds for community projects. Projects are selected based on research into community needs, review of proposals from community agencies and League committees, membership interest and current focus areas. The Junior League of Richardson has contributed more than one million volunteer hours since 1966.

Proceeds from the sale of this book benefit these community and family support projects.

Additional copies may be obtained by writing:
Junior League of Richardson
1131 Rockingham Rd. Suite #1121
Richardson, Texas 75080

First Printing   December 1995   10,000
Second Printing   October 1997   5,000

Printed in the USA by

WIMMER
The Wimmer Companies
Memphis

My neighbor is washing her windows
And scrubbing and mopping her floors,
But my house is all topsy-turvy,
And dust is behind all the doors.
My neighbor, she keeps her house spotless
And she goes all day long at a trot,
But no one would know in a fortnight
If she swept today or not.
The task I am at is enticing...
My neighbor is worn to a rag.
I am making a Quilt out of pieces
I have saved in a pretty chintz bag.
And the Quilt, I know, my descendants
Will exhibit with prideful heart.
"So lovely, my grandmother made it,
An example of patience and art."
But will her grandchildren remember
Her struggles with dirt and decay?
They will not - they will wish
She had made them
A Quilt like I'm making today.

Anonymous

It is not our intent to be competitive in any way with any published works regarding the art of quilting. **TEXAS SAMPLER** simply wants to share the rich history and some small "arm chair adventures" of the people involved in this romantic art as well as the mouthwatering recipes of our talented members and families. We hope we have given the reader ways to bind the past with the present; the present with the future! We believe the final product has indeed accomplished this effectively. To this end we extend grateful acknowledgment to:

Kroger Food Stores

Graphics II - Wichita Falls, TX
North Dallas Photographic
Quilters' Unique
Sarah Bishop - Executive Chef at the Governor's Mansion - Austin, TX
The Outstanding Members of the 1994-1995 and 1995-1996 Cookbook Committees
The Junior League of Richardson Membership & Families

Also:

The Romance of the Patchwork Quilt by Carrie A. Hall and Rose G. Kretsinger
Quiltmaking & Quiltmakers by Marlyn Lithgow
Quilting Manual by Dolores A. Hinson
The Warner Collector's Guide to American Quilts by Phyllis Haders
120 Patterns for Traditional Patchwork Quilts by Maggie Malone
The Quilt; Stories From the NAMES Project by Cindy Ruskin
Jennifer Amor's Flavor Quilts
How Not to Make A Prize-Winning Quilt by Ami Simms
Arkansas Quilts by Arkansas Quilter's Guild, Inc.

and anyone we might have inadvertently left out..............

The Lure of the Quilt

One of the most recognized American art forms, the Quilt, has endured for centuries. It is an art of the people that speaks of love of life, love of work, love of family and love of beauty. Quilts are at the heart of the memories of many Texas families and tell us about their makers with every thread. They are important family links in time when the concept of an extended family is fast fading. As a historical and cultural record, quilts have the capacity to stir people's emotions and memories.

Every quilt pattern has a name. These names are intriguing, and in nearly every instance there is a reason, or at least a suggestion, to the name. Religion, occupations, politics, nature or a great social event all contributed to quilt patches such as the Star of Bethlehem, Job's Tears, The Anvil, The Sawtooth, 54-40 or Fight, Democrat Rose, American Beauty, Morning Glory, Swing-in-Center and Eight Hands Around; the last two being figures and calls for the square dance that finished off many an evening after a quilting bee or a barn raising. Although basic patterns might be the same, every quilt is different in detail from every other quilt. The colors and size vary, the sewing work is individualized by placement of blocks and most assuredly the fabrics utilized are not the same.

Quilts provide us with a bridge to our past, with cultural continuity, and with historical documents of the daily lives of people. Each quilt tells its own story, not in words, but in stitches. The tale, however, is no less compelling:

When a West Texas quilter pieced into her crazy quilt the political ribbon "TURN TEXAS LOOSE!" she was leaving behind a message for future generations;

When Lizzie Tidwell made her son's Oil Patch quilt, she had his comfort in mind, for the heavy, thick quilt would provide him protection as he slept on the ground near the oil wells. Yet today that quilt is symbolic of the wild years of the early Texas Oil Boom days.

All of the beautiful quilts featured in this book were photographed in a restored Victorian farmhouse known as Miss Belle's Place, built in the downtown Richardson area around 1887. In 1902 Margaret Robberson purchased the property for her daughter Virginia Bell, who opened a kindergarten through third grade private school. Known affectionately as Miss Belle, she devoted nearly 36 years stressing to her students the importance of the three R's...reading, 'riting and 'rithmetic. She also instilled in them her love of nature, sense of proper social behavior and interest in civic improvements and beautification of the Richardson community. Through the efforts of the Junior League of Richardson, the house was restored to resemble the 1890 aura of Miss Belle's schoolhouse. The League maintains the home and conducts tours for interested individuals, organizations, schools, etc. As you gaze at the picture of the quilts in the schoolroom you can almost hear a child answering in a crystal clear voice, "Yes ma'am, Miss Belle."

Often called "the national quilt of Texas", the Lone Star quilt had its origins in the biblically named Star of Bethlehem. The "Lone Star" of the quilt refers not to the five-pointed star as displayed on the Texas flag, but to the fact that one star majestically reigns alone on the quilt. The quilt featured on the **TEXAS SAMPLER** cover is an excellent example of the Lone Star at its finest and was donated for our use by Patty and Jerry Nabors. Patty, an interior decorator, commissioned the quilt. She tells us "More and more people are utilizing the warmth and comfort quilts give to the home for aesthetic purposes. We are at the end of a generation that lovingly handstitches quilts; however, there is no shame in commissioning a new quilt for purposes of starting an heirloom. In no time at all that new quilt will become an antique to be treasured. Utilize the craftspeople who presently quilt for the pure enjoyment of it; the church quilting guilds, the elderly (she personally knows some who keep the quiltframe up in their homes just waiting), and others who, for the price of a want ad can still be found." The **TEXAS SAMPLER** thanks the Nabors for sharing their Lone Star.

TEXAS SAMPLER's purpose is twofold. First, to offer mouthwatering family favorites with delicious surprises — all culinary sensations! Second, to reflect back to a time when mothers and grandmothers filled the home with those good ole' home cooked smells. When they wrapped us in sights, sounds, smells and handmade quilts which offered us warmth, security and comforts which ultimately last a lifetime! Use the **TEXAS SAMPLER** "Handmade-Homemade... Recipes You're Bound to Love", to create a special sense of heritage and easygoing hospitality for your family, friends and future generations.

Table of Contents

*Symbols used throughout the book
beside various recipe title names:*

 Family Friendly - loved by all

Holiday Fare - special foods for special times

 Freezes well/can be prepared ahead - foods to
help busy families and friends

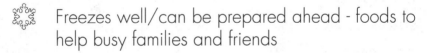 Time Saver - under 40 minutes prep and
cooking time

CHIPS & WHETSTONES

One of the most prevalent and versatile geometric shapes found in pieced quilts, the Triangle, is used in this Charm quilt. Every young child began to quilt pieced work by putting together a series of fabric with no regard to separating the fabric by color and by cutting the pieces into a single size and shape - thus became the One Patch. By the time a one-patch is half finished it is so cumbersome and heavy it has earned the reputation of being a lapful. The small low-seated, high backed, armless rocking chair, known as a sewing rocker, was designed so a woman making a one-patch quilt could spread part of the quilt on the floor to ease the burden of its weight.

Bea Orgish raided "many a scrap bag" from families and friends to produce the pictured quilt containing 1,280 pieces, with no two pieces cut from the same fabric. She and her sister living in Colorado, true to the pioneer woman fashion, traded scraps. They proceeded to collect the same materials always recognizing that their quilts would still not be the same. The variation is achieved through clever positioning of colors across the face of the quilt. Her quilt received Honorable Mention in the 1990 Dallas Quilt Show.

While this Charm quilt looks perfectly at home in Miss Belle's kitchen in Richardson, Texas, it is equally at home in Bea's kitchen, for it is as the old saying goes, the heart of the home is the kitchen. The TEXAS SAMPLER thanks Bea Orgish for sharing something from the heart!

Summer Peach Tea at the Governor's Mansion

Sarah Bishop, Executive Chef of the Texas Governor's Mansion

Tea

        6 cups water
        3 family-size (1-ounce) tea
           bags
        2 cups fresh mint, loosely
           packed
        1 6-ounce can frozen
           lemonade concentrate
        1 32-ounce bottle Peach
           Nectar
    ½-1 cup simple syrup
        1 liter ginger ale
        1 liter club soda
Simple syrup
        2 cups sugar
        1 cup water

■ Bring water to a boil and add tea and mint. Remove tea bags after 10 minutes, but let mint continue to steep.

■ When water has cooled to room temperature, strain into 2-gallon container.

■ To make simple syrup: combine sugar and water and boil slowly until clear - about 4 minutes.

■ Add lemonade, peach nectar, and simple syrup to taste.

■ Chill thoroughly and pour into punch bowl

■ Add chilled ginger ale and club soda just before serving.

Vanilla-Almond Tea

Cheryl Mokrzecky

        3 heaping tablespoons
           instant unflavored tea
        2 cups hot water
        1 12-ounce can frozen
           lemonade
    ½-1 cup sugar, depending
           upon taste
        2 tablespoons vanilla
           extract
        2 tablespoons almond
           extract
           mint sprig (garnish)
           orange slice (garnish)

■ Dissolve tea in hot water.

■ Add the lemonade, sugar, vanilla, and almond extract.

■ Fill to 1 gallon with water.

■ Serve with a mint sprig or orange slice.

Indian Tea

Robin Kelly

Prepare ahead

2 cups sugar
4 cups water
juice of 4 lemons
2 cups strong tea from 2
family size tea bags
1 tablespoon vanilla
1 tablespoon almond
extract
32 ounces ginger ale

■ Mix together first 3 ingredients and boil 3 minutes.

■ Cool mixture completely.

■ Add remaining ingredients and freeze.

■ Thaw about 1 hour before serving. Serve slushy.

Serves 8

Enjoy on a warm day!

Mint Tea

Charlotte Sullivan

4 mint tea bags
1 container sugar free
lemonade drink mix
1 cup orange juice

■ Steep tea bags in 1 quart of water.

■ Add lemonade and enough water to make a total of 2 quarts.

■ Add orange juice.

■ Serve cold.

Serves 12

Orange Blush

Susan McCombs

1 6-ounce can frozen
orange juice, thawed
1 cup cranberry juice
4 tablespoons sugar
1 pint club soda

■ Combine undiluted orange juice, cranberry juice and sugar. Chill thoroughly.

■ Just before serving stir in club soda.

■ Serve over crushed ice in old fashion glasses or wine glasses.

Serves 6

Great beverage for a brunch!

10

Orange Smoothie

Sue Woods

6 ounces frozen orange
  juice concentrate
1½ cups water
½ cup milk
⅓ cup sugar
1 teaspoon vanilla
  extract
2 cups ice
1 cup vanilla ice cream
  (optional)

■ Mix all ingredients together in blender for 30 seconds.

Serves 4 (12 ounces)

Cloved Caffe Frappe

Kathy Tuthill

¼ cup espresso
1½ teaspoons sugar
  dash of ground cloves
2 cups crushed ice
¼ cup water

■ Blend all ingredients.
■ Serve in tall chilled glasses.

Serves 2 (10-ounce servings)

Almond Iced Espresso

Jennifer Hurst

1 2-ounce espresso
1 cup milk
¼ teaspoon vanilla extract
⅛ teaspoon almond extract
½ teaspoon sugar
  (optional)
  ice cubes
  pinch of ground
  cinnamon

■ Combine the espresso, milk, extracts and sugar.
■ Pour over ice in a tall glass.
■ Sprinkle lightly with ground cinnamon.

Serves 1

Iced Caffe Latte

Kathy Tuthill

1 cup milk
ice cubes
1 2-ounces espresso
ground chocolate,
optional

■ Pour cold milk over ice in a tall glass.
■ Pour one shot of espresso over milk.
■ Garnish with ground chocolate.

Iced Cappuccino - Make as above, substitute ½ cup milk and ½ cup frothed milk for 1 cup milk.

Serves 1

Margarita

Pat Lawler

3 ounces tequila
4 ounces fresh squeezed
lime juice (4 large limes)
6 ounces triple sec

■ Stir all ingredients together.
■ To rim glass with salt: Run cut lime around the rim of glass and put in plate filled with salt.
■ Pour over ice or chill and serve straight up in glasses with salt rim. (optional)

Serves 3

Bellini

Anne Koval

1 cup champagne
⅓ cup rum
⅓ cup peach schnapps
2 tablespoons sugar
½ cup peach nectar
½ cup fresh peaches,
without skin and cut up

■ Mix in blender. Add lots of ice and mix until smooth.

Serves 4

Pink Lady

Stephanie Nowacki

1 6-ounce can pink
   lemonade
1 8-ounce can rum or
   vodka
2 tablespoons honey

■ Combine all ingredients in blender. Add ice to fill. Blend slightly.

■ Serve in long stem wine glasses.

Serves 10-12

Can also add 3 cans of water, freeze overnight in large plastic bag. Remove and thaw to slush.

Pink, being an easily obtainable and rather colorfast fabric during the late 1800's and early 1900's was so popular a color scheme, that these fabrics have also acquired names. Some of these included double pink, bubble gum, seaweed, Pepto-Bismol, strawberry and Merrimack pink, named after the textile mill along the Merrimack River in New England that printed thousands of variations for many years.

Pi Ti

Pam Clarke

12 ounces pineapple juice
 2 ounces lime juice
 4 ounces passion fruit
   juice
 4 ounces light rum
 4 ounces dark rum

■ Mix all ingredients in quart container.

■ Fill with ice and stir to chill.

Serves 4 (8 ounces)

Colorado Bulldog

Cissy Holloway

1 ½ ounces coffee-flavored
    liqueur
1 ½ ounces vodka
  2 ounces milk
  ½ ounce cola

■ Pour coffee-flavored liqueur
and vodka into tall glass.
■ Fill with ice and stir in milk.
■ Top with cola.

Serves 1 (12 ounces)

Bloody Mary's by the Gallon

Cissy Holloway

5 tablespoons celery salt
3 tablespoons pepper
2 tablespoons prepared
  horseradish
¼ cup Worcestershire
  sauce
½ cup lime juice
3 quarts tomato juice
1 fifth vodka
  celery ribs

■ Mix celery salt and pepper.
Set aside.

■ Mix horseradish, Worcestershire sauce and lime juice.

■ In gallon container, add both
mixtures, tomato juice and vodka,
stirring well.

■ Serve over ice and garnish
with celery.

Serves 16 (12 ounce servings)

**May be prepared ahead, omitting vodka, and
refrigerated.**

Mock Champagne Punch

Janie Trantham

2 quarts ginger ale
1 quart apple juice
  lemons, sliced
  limes, sliced
  mint leaves

■ Chill ingredients in refrigerator
the day before opening.
■ Mold ice ring with slices of
lemon, limes and mint.
■ Combine ginger ale and apple
juice and enter mold in punch
bowl.

Serves 30

For 300 people use 20/10 ratio.

Champagne Punch

Mary Moore

Prepare ahead

- 1½ ripe pineapples
- ½ pound powdered sugar
- 1 cup lemon juice
- ¼ cup dark rum
- ¼ cup maraschino cherries
- 1 cup brandy
- 1 cup light rum
- 2 bottles of champagne
  fruit slices
- 1 ring of ice

■ Crush pineapples in bowl. Add powdered sugar. Let stand one hour.

■ Add lemon juice, rum, maraschino cherries, brandy, and light rum. Stir and let stand four hours.

■ Add champagne and pour over ice ring in punch bowl.

■ Garnish with fruit slices.

Serves 25

Christmas Rum Punch

Stephanie Zimmermann

- 1 46-ounces of red fruit
  punch
- 2 tablespoons instant tea
  powder
- 1 cup light rum (optional)
- 2 12-ounce cans orange
  soda
  ice cubes
  lemon slices for garnish)

■ In a punch bowl, combine punch, tea, and rum. Stir until tea is dissolved.

■ Slowly stir in orange soda.

■ Add ice and garnish with lemon slices.

Serves 20

Make an ice ring with extra orange soda or red punch.

Hot Espresso Chocolate

Kathy Tuthill

- 1 2-ounce cup espresso
- 1 cup hot chocolate
- 1 cup whipping cream
- ½ teaspoon sugar
- ½ teaspoon grated orange
  peel
  dash of nutmeg or
  cinnamon

■ Mix espresso and hot chocolate in cup.

■ Whip cream and fold in orange peel and sugar.

■ Top with whipped cream and sprinkle with nutmeg or cinnamon.

Serves 1

"Water Wheel" Punch

Janna Fry

1 quart cranberry juice
1 46-ounce can of
pineapple juice
1 ½ cups sugar
1 teaspoon almond extract
1 quart ginger ale

■ Combine cranberry juice, pineapple juice, sugar, almond extract.

■ Chill.

■ Just before serving add ginger ale. Serve over ice.

Serves 16

From the pages of Texas folklore a custom called "Cat Shaking" was associated with quiltmaking. The ritual was enacted when unmarried girls were among the quilters on hand when a quilt was removed from the frames. The girls were told to hold the corners of the quilt while a cat was placed in the middle. When the quilt was shaken, the cat naturally jumped out. According to superstition, the girl standing nearest the point where the cat jumped out would be the next to marry.

The mother of a recent bride decided to incorporate this party idea into her daughter's bridal shower brunch. She had been working on a quilt to present to her daughter so the centerpiece was still on the frame when the bride, her family and girlfriends all had the party of their lives. She admitted she would have loved to have been able to include the following menu recipes:

Water Wheel Punch & Coffee
Love Apple Tomato Bread
Lazy Daisy Casserole & Lone Star Salsa
Steps to Glory Salad
Catch-Me-if You-Can Coffee Cake
Ben's Guilty Pleasures

Caffe Latte

Kathy Tuthill

1 2-ounce cup of espresso
1 cup hot steamed milk

■ Pour espresso into a tall glass.

■ Fill glass with steamed milk and top with thin layer of foam from steamed milk.

Serves 1

Cappuccino

Kathy Tuthill

1 2-ounces espresso
1 2-ounces steamed milk
1 2-ounces frothed milk
   ground cinnamon, to garnish

■ Pour above ingredients in glass or mug.

■ Garnish with cinnamon if desired.

Serves 1

Variation: Pour equal amounts of cappuccino and hot chocolate over a slice of orange. Top with whipped cream and garnish with grated orange peel and/or cinnamon.

 ## Gluehwein (Mulled Wine)

Martha Welch

1⅓ pints red wine
1 stick of cinnamon
4 cloves
1 piece lemon rind
2-3 ounces sugar

■ Heat ingredients almost to the boiling point. Strain through cheese cloth to remove spices and serve.

Serves 6

Alligator Eye Dip

Judith McPhail

Prepare ahead

- 4-6 large chopped tomatoes
- 1 4-ounce can sliced black olives, drained
- 4 sliced green onions
- 4 chopped jalapeños
- 1½ tablespoons vinegar
- 3 tablespoons olive oil
- 1 teaspoon garlic

■ Combine all ingredients and refrigerate 1-2 hours.

Serves 8

Garlic Chive Dip with Pita Triangles

Lori Anderson

Prepare ahead

Dip

- 1 cup mayonnaise
- 1 cup small curd cottage cheese
- 3 ounces cream cheese
- 1 8-ounce carton sour cream
- 1 package ranch flavored dip mix
- ½ teaspoon garlic salt
- ½ teaspoon pepper
- 3 tablespoons chives, chopped

Pita Triangles

- 2 packages pita bread
- 2 sticks margarine, melted
- 1 cup grated Parmesan cheese

■ Preheat oven to 350°.

■ Mix together dip ingredients and refrigerate 1-2 hours.

■ Split all the pita bread apart. Spread with margarine and sprinkle with Parmesan cheese.

■ Bake 5-7 minutes.

■ Cool on paper towels.

■ Store in air tight bags.

Serves 10-12

ABC Dip

Kathleen Denny

Prepare ahead

- ⅓ cup chipped almonds
- 3 strips of bacon, cooked and crumbled
- 1½ cups grated sharp Cheddar cheese
- ¾ cup mayonnaise
- 1 tablespoon grated onion

■ Preheat oven to 350°.

■ Spread almonds on a cookie sheet and bake at 350° for 5-8 minutes. Caution: Watch almonds closely as they burn easily!

■ Combine all the above ingredients and mix lightly.

■ Place in a small bowl or cheese crock. Refrigerate.

■ Serve with wheat crackers.

Makes 2 cups

Beyond Hot Cheese Dip

Tomi Morriss

Prepare ahead

- 1 pound pasteurized process cheese
- 4 ounces sharp Cheddar cheese
- 2 cups mayonnaise
- 1 medium onion, chopped
- 4 pickled jalapeños, seeded and cut into strips

■ Cube cheeses. When cheese is at room temperature, place in food processor with mayonnaise.

■ Alternate mixing in onions and jalapeños. (You may add juice.)

■ Refrigerate.

Serves 8-10

Mixture gets hotter and better with time!

Hell on Red Shrimp Dip

Kathleen Stephens

Prepare ahead

- 1 8-ounce package of cream cheese, softened
- 1 8-ounce carton of sour cream
- ⅓ cup ketchup
- ½-¾ pound shrimp, deveined, cooked and chopped
- 1 jar of Hot Picadily Red or Hell on Red hot sauce chopped onion, to taste

■ Mix all ingredients together. Chill at least 2 hours.

Serves 10-12

Dip is tastier if refrigerated overnight.

Gourmet Shrimp Dip

Peggy Nolan

- 1 cup cooked and finely chopped shrimp
- 1 8-ounce package cream cheese, softened
- ¼ cup chopped onions
- ¼ cup chopped stuffed olives
- ¼ cup mayonnaise
- ¼ teaspoon salt
- ¼ teaspoon white pepper

■ Blend together and chill. Serve with crackers.

Serves 8

Horseradish Shrimp Spread

Brenda Brandon

- 1 8-ounce package cream cheese
- ½ stick unsalted butter
- 1 tablespoon horseradish
- 1 tablespoon minced onion
- 1 tablespoon lemon juice
- 2 cups cooked chopped shrimp

■ Cream together cream cheese and butter.

■ Add remaining ingredients.

Serves 10-12

Can be molded and frozen.

Chilled Crab Dip

Anne Koval

Prepare ahead

- 2 8-ounce packages of cream cheese
- 4 chopped green onions
- 1 large tomato, chopped
- 12 ounces of fresh or canned crab meat, drained
- ¼ cup picante sauce
- 4 drops of hot pepper sauce
- 1 jalapeño pepper, chopped, seeds removed
- 1 clove of garlic, crushed salt and pepper, to taste

- ■ Mix all ingredients together.
- ■ Heat slowly in a double boiler, stirring frequently until well blended.
- ■ Refrigerate.
- ■ Serve with crackers or vegetables.

Serves 10-12

■ ■ ■ *"Handy-Andy" Tip: Place limp celery in deep pitcher or jar; fill with cold water. Place in refrigerator. Celery will become very crisp.*

Hot Dip Crab Casserole

Kathy Tuthill

- 1 3-ounce package cream cheese, softened
- 1 6-ounce can crab meat, drained
- 1 tablespoon lemon juice
- ½ cup mayonnaise
- ¼ cup minced onion
- ⅛ teaspoon hot pepper sauce
  Parmesan cheese

- ■ Preheat oven to 350°.
- ■ Beat cream cheese until smooth.
- ■ Stir in remaining ingredients except Parmesan cheese.
- ■ Pour into a 1 quart casserole dish.
- ■ Sprinkle top with Parmesan cheese. Bake at 350° until bubbly.

Makes 1 cup

Hot White Crab Meat Dip

Kim Hext

1 8-ounce package of
  cream cheese
1 stick butter
1 pound white lump crab
  meat, drained
1 small white onion, finely
  chopped
  dash of hot pepper
  sauce
  dash of garlic powder

■ Melt cream cheese and butter
in a double boiler.

■ Add remaining ingredients.

■ Serve in a chafing dish with
wheat crackers.

Serves 6-8

Parmesan Artichoke Dip

Laura Garretson

2 14-ounce cans artichoke
  hearts, drained and
  chopped
1 cup grated Parmesan
  cheese
1 cup mayonnaise
  dash of Worcesteshire
  dash of hot pepper
  sauce
  pinch of garlic salt
  pinch of fresh or dried
  parsley

■ Preheat oven to 350°.

■ Combine all ingredients except
parsley, stirring thoroughly.

■ Spoon into a 1-quart casserole
dish, and bake at 350° for 20
minutes.

■ Sprinkle with parsley. May be
served hot or cold.

Serves 12

Serve with crackers.

Texas Caviar

Dana Bell

2 15-ounce cans black-
  eyed peas with
  jalapeños, drained
1 4-ounce can chopped
  green chilies
1 8-ounce jar of sharp
  pasteurized process
  cheese spread

■ Heat together and serve with
corn chips.

Serves 8

Sinful Stuff

Annette Weindenfeller

1 round of French or Sour Dough bread
1½ cups sour cream
2 cups cheddar cheese
1 8-ounce package cream cheese
⅓ cup chopped green chilies
⅓ cup green onions, chopped
⅓ cup ham, chopped
Worcestershire sauce, to taste
2 loaves of the same type of bread, cubed for dipping

■ Preheat oven to 350°.

■ Cut top and hollow out round of bread, reserving top.

■ Mix remaining ingredients omitting the bread cubes, with mixer.

■ Fill bread round with mixture and replace top of bread. Wrap entire bread round with foil.

■ Bake at 350° for 30 minutes or until hot.

Serves 12

"Three Cheers" Queso

Martha Welch

1 pound pasteurized process cheese
2 ounces grated Cheddar cheese
2 ounces grated Monterey Jack cheese
½ medium onion, chopped
1 tomato, finely chopped
3 cloves garlic, finely chopped
¼ bunch cilantro, chopped
1 teaspoon cumin powder
1 teaspoon chili powder
1 teaspoon black pepper
½ cup half-and-half

■ Cut pasteurized processed cheese into ½ inch slices.

■ Place on top of double boiler with all other ingredients.

■ Place over low heat and stir occasionally until melted.

■ Serve with tortilla chips.

Serves 12

Southwestern Eggplant Caviar Salsa   *Brenda Brandon*

Prepare ahead

- 1 large eggplant (about 1½ pounds), unpeeled and diced
- 1 medium onion, diced
- 1 large green pepper, diced
- 1 8-ounce can tomato sauce
- 3 large cloves garlic, pressed
- 2 tablespoons sugar
- 4 teaspoons cumin powder
- ¼ teaspoon cayenne pepper
- ⅛ teaspoon salt
- 1 tablespoon to ¼ cup water
- ¼ cup minced fresh cilantro

■ Place eggplant, onion, green pepper, tomato sauce, garlic, sugar, cumin, cayenne pepper and salt in a 12-inch non-stick skillet. Stir to combine.

■ Cover and cook over medium heat until eggplant is soft (about 35 minutes), stirring frequently and adding water as needed.

■ Cool and refrigerate overnight in an air-tight container.

■ Before serving, add chopped cilantro and adjust seasonings. Serve cold.

Makes 4 cups

Can be served as dip, topping for potatoes or relish with meat!

■ ■ ■ *"Handy-Andy" Tip: Texans are familiar with a fresh herb called cilantro. It is also known as coriander on the spice shelf.*

"Lightning" Black Bean Salsa   *Brenda Brandon*

- 1 16-ounce can black beans, drained
- 1 12-ounce jar salsa
- ¼ cup chopped fresh cilantro
- ¼ teaspoon cumin powder
- 2 tablespoons freshly squeezed lime juice

■ In a food processor, roughly chop beans, being careful not to puree beans. Stir in salsa, cilantro, cumin, and lime juice.

■ Refrigerate overnight or serve immediately.

■ Serve with chips or vegetables.

Makes 3 cups

Avocado Pico DeGallo

Lori Anderson

Prepare ahead

        4 large tomatoes,
            chopped
        1 large red onion,
            chopped
        4 cloves garlic, crushed
        6 avocados, chopped
            pinch red pepper
    3-4 cups salsa
    1-2 tablespoons salt

■ Mix all ingredients together
and refrigerate overnight.

■ Serve with tortilla chips.

Makes 8 cups

■ ■ ■ *"Handy-Andy" Tip: To slice or chop an avocado; cut avocado in half
and remove seed. Using a sharp knife either slice or chop while still in shell
... without cutting the shell. Then turn the shell inside out to remove the
avocado.*

Gazpacho Dip

Linda Youngblood

Prepare ahead

        3 tablespoons oil
    1½ tablespoons cider
            vinegar
        1 teaspoon garlic powder
        1 teaspoon salt
      ¼ teaspoon pepper
        1 4-ounce can chopped
            black olives, drained
        1 4-ounce can chopped
            green chilies, drained
        3 large tomatoes, finely
            chopped
        5 green onions, chopped
        4 avocados, diced
            lemon juice

■ Mix all ingredients together,
except avocados and chill
several hours.

■ Sprinkle avocados with lemon
juice to prevent browning. Add
avocados just before serving.

■ Serve with tortilla chips.

Makes 5 cups

Festive Corn Salsa

Julie Robinson

Prepare ahead

2　17-ounce cans whole kernel corn, rinsed and drained
1　4-ounce can chopped green chilies, drained
1　4-ounce can sliced black olives, drained
1　large tomato, chopped
3　tablespoons white vinegar
⅓　cup oil
½　teaspoon salt
1　tablespoon chopped fresh cilantro
¼　cup chopped jalapeños

■ Combine all ingredients in a large glass jar with a lid.

■ Cover and chill for 2 or more hours. Shake often.

■ Serve with tortilla chips or as a relish.

Makes 6 cups

■ ■ ■ *"Handy-Andy" Tip: Run glass jars through dishwasher on rinse cycle and heat dry to get hot.*

 # "Spinning Ball" Hot Sauce

Gina Banister

Prepare ahead

1　pound green jalapeño peppers, seeded, stems removed
2　large onions
5　pods garlic
2　tablespoons sugar
1　cup vinegar
6　8-ounce cans tomato sauce
　　salt and pepper, to taste

■ Grind peppers, onions, and garlic. Mix in other ingredients.

■ Cook 15 minutes at a slow boil.

■ Pour in scalded, hot jars and seal.

Makes 10 cups

Excellent gift idea.

"Lone Star" Salsa

Lisa Matchett

Prepare ahead

    4 cups chopped ripe
      tomatoes
    5 chopped fresh jalapeño
      peppers, seeded
    2 medium to large yellow
      onion, chopped
    ½ green bell pepper,
      seeded and chopped
      (optional)
    1 cup canned tomato
      sauce
    1 teaspoon salt
    1 large clove garlic,
      chopped
    ⅓ cup red wine vinegar
      chopped fresh cilantro,
      to taste
      ground cumin, to taste
      black pepper, to taste
      juice of 1 lemon
      juice of 1 lime

■ Mix all ingredients together.

■ Store overnight in a covered plastic container in the refrigerator.

Serves 8

Can be pureed to make picante sauce.

Will keep three months in refrigerator.

■ ■ ■ *"Handy-Andy" Tip: Chop large quantities of onions and green peppers. Store in plastic bags in freezer. When needed, a thump on the counter will separate pieces and permit desired amount to be poured from bag.*

Black Bean Spirals

Lori Anderson

Prepare ahead

- 1 14-ounce can black beans
- 4 ounces of cream cheese, softened
- ¼ cup sour cream
- ½ cup shredded Monterey Jack cheese
- ¼ cup chopped jalapeños
- 1 teaspoon onion salt
- 8 large flour tortilla

■ Mash beans in a food processor. Add cream cheese and sour cream.

■ Mix in Monterey Jack cheese, jalapeño, and onion salt.

■ Spread on flour tortilla shells and roll up.

■ Wrap each roll in plastic wrap. Refrigerate for several hours.

■ Slice when ready to serve.

80 bite-sized slices

Serve with salsa!

Mexican Cheese Rolls

Nancy Marston

Prepare ahead

- 1 8-ounce carton of sour cream
- 1 8-ounce package cream cheese, softened
- 1 4-ounce can chopped green chilies
- 1 4-ounce can chopped black olives, drained
- 1 cup grated Cheddar cheese
- 4 green onions, chopped
- ¼ teaspoon garlic powder
- 5 large fresh flour tortillas or 10 small fresh flour tortillas

■ Fold together first seven ingredients.

■ Spread mixture on flour tortillas.

■ Roll each tortilla into a log. Wrap each roll in foil or plastic.

■ Chill several hours or overnight.

■ Cut into pinwheel slices or 2-inch sections.

■ Serve chilled.

Makes 50 pinwheel slices if large tortillas are used - 25 pinwheel slices if small tortillas are used.

Best served with fresh salsa and guacamole on the side.

Quesadillas

Lori Anderson

2 onions, chopped
4 tablespoons margarine
4 chicken breasts, cooked, shredded
1½ teaspoons salt
5 teaspoons cumin
2 4-ounce cans chopped green chilies
1-1½ cups chicken broth
2 10-ounce cans diced tomatoes
½ teaspoon red pepper
cayenne pepper
2 packages small sized flour tortillas (40 total)
Monterey Jack cheese
Cheddar cheese
jalapeño pepper slices

■ Preheat oven to 375°.

■ Sauté onion in margarine in large skillet. Add shredded chicken, salt, cumin, green chilies, chicken broth, tomatoes, red pepper and cayenne. Simmer 30 minutes.

■ Spread chicken mixture (thin layer) on a flour tortilla. Sprinkle with both cheeses and top with another tortilla. Sprinkle with both cheeses again. Garnish with jalapeño slices.

■ Bake at 350° for 10 minutes or until bubbly. Slice into 6-8 triangles.

Serves 10-12

Freezes well. Makes a great entrée.

Party Cheddar Mold

Joan Wright

Prepare ahead

1 pound shredded sharp Cheddar cheese
1 cup mayonnaise
1 cup chopped green onions
1 cup chopped pecans

■ Line a small ring mold with plastic wrap and spray with non-stick cooking spray.

■ In a food processor, put ½ cup of cheese, process until smooth. Add the remaining cheese and process until smooth.

■ Mix cheese with the remaining ingredients.

■ Press into ring mold. Chill 8 hours.

■ Remove from mold and serve with crackers. Center can be filled with strawberry preserves.

Serves 10-12

Italian Cheese Ball

Gina Banister

1 12-ounce container of
  soft cream cheese
1 packet Italian dry
  dressing seasonings
  seasoned pepper, to
  taste

■ Mix Italian seasonings into
cream cheese and roll into a
ball.

■ Sprinkle pepper on waxed
paper.

■ Roll cheese ball on the waxed
paper.

Serves 10-12

 Smoked Wine and Cheese Logs

Martha Welch

Prepare ahead

2 8-ounce packages of
  cream cheese, softened
2 cups shredded smoked
  Cheddar cheese
½ cup butter or margarine,
  softened
¼ cup dry red wine
1 tablespoon finely
  snipped chives
2 teaspoons prepared
  horseradish
1 cup finely chopped
  walnuts

■ In a large bowl, combine
cream cheese, cheddar cheese,
butter, wine, chives and horseradish.

■ Beat with an electric mixer until
fluffy.

■ Cover and chill, slightly.

■ On waxed paper, shape
mixture into logs about 1½
inches in diameter.

■ Roll logs in chopped walnuts.

■ Serve with crackers.

Serves 12-14

Can be frozen.

■ ■ ■ *"Handy-Andy" Tip: A dull warm knife works best for slicing cheese.*

Mushroom Basil Baked Brie

Kim Hext

1 box of pastry sheets
6-8 large sliced mushrooms
2 tablespoons chopped shallots
2 tablespoons butter
2 tablespoons chopped fresh basil
garlic to taste
1 8-ounce round of Brie cheese, cut in half lengthwise
1 egg, beaten

■ Preheat oven to 350°.

■ Thaw pastry sheets. Roll pastry sheets on a non-stick surface to 12x12 inches.

■ Sauté the mushrooms and shallots in butter until tender. Add basil and garlic.

■ Drain liquid from mixture.

■ Place half of the Brie on the center of the rolled pastry sheet. Spoon half of the mushroom mixture evenly on the Brie. Place the other half of the Brie on top of mushrooms. Spoon remaining mushroom mixture evenly on top of second half of Brie.

■ Bring together corners of the pastry sheet to cover Brie. Seal any openings.

■ Brush with beaten egg. Bake at 350° for 20 minutes or until golden brown.

Serves 20

Before baking this can be frozen. Thaw to room temperature before baking.

An unusual idea was carried out in the quilting for a prospective bride's hope-chest. The future bride asked her future husband to draw a design of her favorite flower. Every stitch was set by the bride and the result was much admired and never copied because it was understood that they did not wish for any other couple to have this special design...but who is to say that the idea cannot be copied?

Roasted Parmesan Garlic

Brenda Brandon

4 whole garlic heads
4 tablespoons of olive oil
4 tablespoons grated
Parmesan cheese
½ teaspoon saffron threads
salt and pepper, to taste

■ Preheat oven to 275°.

■ Slice the top half-inch from 4 whole heads of garlic

■ Remove some of the papery skins from the outside, keeping the head intact. Place in covered oven-proof dish.

■ Drizzle each head with 1 tablespoon olive oil and sprinkle with salt and pepper. Cover and bake 1 hour.

■ Uncover, baste with the oil in the dish, and sprinkle each with 1 tablespoon grated Parmesan cheese and a few saffron threads.

■ Cover and bake 1 hour more or until tender.

■ Serve warm by squeezing garlic cloves out of the skins onto crackers or sliced bread and spreading with a knife.

Serves 4-6

I see well loved, she only sees used.
I call it priceless, she calls it cheap.
She declares "throw away!", I say "forever keep"
The name above the store to us both reads "ANTIQUES"!

Janie Trantham

Apricot-Brie Gems

Ann Hobbs

1 box pastry sheets
8 ounces Brie cheese, cut into 18 one-inch cubes
18 teaspoons apricot preserves

■ Preheat oven to 325°.

■ Remove pastry sheets from freezer and thaw.

■ Cut each pastry sheets into nine equal squares.

■ Place one cube of Brie and one teaspoon of apricot preserves into the center of a pastry square.

■ Fold pastry square in half, diagonally, and seal. Repeat with remaining squares.

■ Place on baking sheet and bake at 325° approximately 20 minutes or until golden brown.

Serves 6-8

Cheesy Shrimp Tartlets

Stefani Fink

1 loaf thin white sandwich bread, crust removed
⅓ cup melted butter
1 4¼-ounce can tiny shrimp, drained and chilled
¾ cup mayonnaise
⅓ cup Parmesan cheese
⅓ cup grated Swiss cheese
¼ teaspoon Worcestershire sauce
⅛ teaspoon hot pepper sauce
paprika

■ Preheat oven to 400°.

■ Rinse shrimp and place in ice water for 20 minutes. Drain well.

■ Roll bread to ¼ inch and cut with a daisy shaped cookie cutter. Brush bread with melted butter on both sides.

■ Place in mini-muffin tins.

■ Bake at 400° for 8 minutes.

■ Combine shrimp with mayonnaise, Parmesan cheese, Swiss cheese, Worcestershire sauce, and hot pepper sauce.

■ Spoon evenly into shells and sprinkle with paprika.

■ Bake at 400° for 8-10 minutes until bubbly.

Makes 22 tartlets

Ritzy Cocktail Meatballs

Kathy Whipple

1 egg, slightly beaten
1 pound bulk sausage
¼ pound ground round
½ cup finely crushed Ritz crackers
⅓ cup milk
½ teaspoon sage
½ cup water
¼ cup ketchup
1 tablespoon soy sauce
2 tablespoons brown sugar
¼ cup barbecue sauce

■ Preheat oven to 325°.

■ Combine egg, sausage, ground round, crackers, milk, and sage stir until well mixed.

■ Shape into meatballs and brown in a small amount of oil in a large skillet.

■ Drain meatballs and place in baking dish.

■ Combine remaining ingredients in a bowl. Stir until well blended.

■ Pour sauce over meatballs and bake at 325° for 30 minutes.

Serves 8-12

Hawaiian Meatballs

Martha Welch

Prepare ahead
Meatballs:

2-3 slices of bread
¾ cup milk
1 pound ground beef
2 tablespoons finely chopped onion
1 teaspoon salt
½ teaspoon pepper
2 tablespoons flour
2 tablespoons butter

Sauce
¼ molasses
¼ cup ketchup
¼ cup sherry

■ Soak 2-3 slices of bread in milk.

■ Mix milk/bread mixture with meat, onion and spices. Refrigerate 2-4 hours.

■ Roll meat mixture into balls. Roll meatballs in flour. Lightly brown meatballs in butter.

■ Mix together molasses, ketchup and sherry in a bowl. Add sauce to meatballs and simmer 20 minutes or until they are glazed.

■ Serve in a chafing dish.

Serves 20

This can be frozen!

Spinach Stuffed Mushrooms
Nancy Burton

24 large fresh mushroom
caps
2 tablespoons oil
10 ounces, frozen chopped
spinach, cooked and
drained
10 ounces Boursin cheese,
softened
seasoned bread crumbs

■ Preheat oven to broil.

■ Brush mushroom caps with oil. Place on baking sheet, round side up, and broil for 1 minute.

■ Adjust oven temperature to bake. Preheat oven to 375°.

■ Blend spinach with cheese and fill mushroom caps.

■ Sprinkle with bread crumbs and bake on a greased baking sheet at 375° for 10 minutes or until bubbly.

■ Serve immediately!

Serves 8

May be frozen and baked unthawed.

Blue Cheese Shrimp Mushrooms
Audrey Beasley

24 large mushrooms
1 onion, chopped
¼ cup butter
½ pound shrimp, cooked,
peeled and chopped
4 ounces blue cheese
½ teaspoon basil

■ Remove stems from mushroom, reserving ½ of the stems. Chop reserved stems and sauté with onion in butter.

■ Add shrimp, blue cheese and basil, mixing well.

■ Stuff mushroom caps with shrimp mixture and broil for 5 minutes or until cheese bubbles.

Serves 8

Pizza Twists

Lisa Johnson

1 11-ounce package refrigerated breadsticks

24 thin pepperoni slices (1½-inch diameter)

2 tablespoons grated Parmesan cheese

½ teaspoon Italian seasoning

¼ teaspoon garlic powder

½ cup pizza or spaghetti sauce

■ Preheat oven to 350°.

■ Separate and unroll breadsticks.

■ Place 3 pepperoni slices in a single layer over half of each breadstick. Fold remaining half of breadstick over top and seal end with a twist.

■ Place on ungreased cookie sheet.

■ Combine cheese, Italian seasoning and garlic powder. Sprinkle evenly over each breadstick.

■ Bake at 350° for 15-20 minutes or until golden brown.

■ Serve with warmed pizza or spaghetti sauce.

Serves 16

As all college graduates have the inclination to do, my daughter came home with a trunkload of assorted student activity T-Shirts that were, for the most part, still in good condition. I took the various emblems, designs, slogans, etc. and pieced them into blocks that I quilted. When she moved into her first "home", which at this point happened to be a rather cheap, drafty apartment, I presented her with this quilt that no doubt had some treasured memories of an exciting and positive time in her life stitched into the warmth.

Sausage Pinwheels

Susan Bynum

Prepare ahead

- 1 pound medium or hot bulk sausage
- 1 package of crescent rolls (8 in a package)

■ Preheat oven to 350°.

■ Unroll crescent rolls and flatten together.

■ Spread uncooked sausage over rolls. Roll crescent rolls and sausage lengthwise in a jelly roll style.

■ Freeze in wax paper for 8 hours. Slice into ¼ inch pieces.

■ Cook on ungreased cookie sheet at 350° for 20 minutes. Serve hot.

Serves 16

After freezing, refrigerate a few hours before slicing.

Forget Me Knots

Charlotte Sullivan

- 1 pound ground beef
- 1 pound ground pork
- 16 ounces pasteurized process cheese, diced
- 1 teaspoon oregano
- 2 tablespoons Worcestershire sauce
- ½ teaspoon garlic salt
- ½ teaspoon Italian seasonings
- 1 pound party rye slices

■ Preheat oven to 350°.

■ In frying pan, brown beef and pork.

■ Add cheese, oregano, Worcestershire sauce, garlic salt, and Italian seasonings.

■ Cook over low heat, stirring frequently, until cheese is melted.

■ Spread on bread and bake at 350° for 10 minutes or until bubbly.

Serves 10

May be prepared ahead and frozen before baking.

Yummy Coated Nuts

Renee Tucei

10 ounces giant pecans
3 12-ounce cans of mixed nuts without peanuts
2 6-ounce cans of cashews
1 cup sugar
1 egg white
¼ teaspoon salt
½ pound of butter

■ Preheat oven to 250°.

■ Roast all nuts in a 9x11 cake pan for 30 minutes at 250°, set aside.

■ Increase oven temperature to 350°.

■ Beat egg whites until stiff. Add sugar and salt. Add roasted nuts and stir.

■ Melt butter and pour into 9x13 cake pan. Place roasted nuts and egg white mixture in pan. Coat nuts with butter by stirring.

■ Place in a 350° oven for 30 minutes, stirring occasionally.

Makes 6 cups

As nuts are cooling, stir occasionally to prevent sticking.

When my sister-in-law took her leave from teaching to have her baby, her entire second grade class participated in a project. A plain fabric was chosen and cut into the appropriate size blocks. Each child's handprint was traced in chalk. The children signed their names and the room mother embroidered the handprints. The blocks were quilted together and presented to her at her baby shower from her entire class. That precious little bundle of joy never did get to gurgle in that quilt, however, my sister-in-law to this day proudly displays that quilt on the wall of her bedroom.

A more elaborate idea for a crib quilt, created as a school project by the teacher herself, was done by children who signed their own squares. It featured baskets done in crayon with appliquéd flowers in the primary colors. The entire design was separated by a green and white printed material, which reflected the school colors.

BREAD BASKET

In the early days, the Album quilt, known by such other names as Friendship, Bride's, Autograph as well as Presentation, were usually quilts made by friends and then presented as a gift to some fortunate recipient. Such quilts were usually made for special occasions and filled with symbols which were meaningful between the gift giver and the receiver, the meanings of which are sometimes lost to us today.

The Texas Album quilt pictured was handmade by Ruth Young and took over 4½ years to complete. The message is clearly depicted in each appliquéd patch so indicative of Texas, right down to the patch with the Capitol Building in the center.

Appliquéd quilts made during the early days were a symbol of affluence since it was considered wasteful to cut up new cloth when they had the bountiful contents of the scrap bags. In appliquéd quilts the design is formed by pieces cut from whole cloth that are laid on a plain background cloth and stitched down. The appliquéd quilts are considered to be so difficult an accomplishment that they are considered a masterpiece - evidence that a lady is truly an expert needlewoman. We appreciate Ruth Young for sharing her effort of love with the TEXAS SAMPLER...and who says you can't see Texas in a day!

Oma Kuhlmann's Bread

Janie Trantham

2 cups scalded milk
½ cup shortening
½ cup sugar
1 teaspoon salt
1 package active dry yeast
6 cups flour

■ Stir first four ingredients in large, deep pan until shortening melts. Remove from heat and cool.

■ Sprinkle yeast over cooled mixture and stir rapidly to dissolve.

■ Slowly add 6 cups of flour, stirring with spoon until too stiff to stir. Knead in remaining flour for 8 to 10 minutes.

■ Grease a large bowl and put dough in. Turn dough over so greased side is facing up.

■ Place bread in cold oven on the top rack. On lower rack, place a pan of very hot water. Close oven door. Do not open oven door for one hour. Dough should be double in size.

■ Punch down and place dough in greased loaf pans. Let rise again with the same method for one hour or until dough has doubled in size.

■ Bake in 350° oven for 30-45 minutes.

2 loaves.

This recipe can be frozen before dough rises or after baking.

■ ■ ■ *"Handy-Andy" Tip: If an indentation remains when you press your finger into bread dough, the bread has risen enough to proceed to the next step.*

Beer Bread

Kathy Tuthill

3 cups self-rising flour
2 tablespoons sugar
1 12-ounce can beer,
  room temperature
  butter

■ Preheat oven to 350°.

■ Mix all ingredients, except butter and put in greased 9x5-inch loaf pan.

■ Bake at 350° for 25 minutes.

■ Take bread out of oven and brush with butter.

■ Bake bread 25 minutes longer.

Onion Cheese Bread

Pat Lawler

1 cup chopped onion
4 tablespoons margarine,
  divided use
2 eggs, well beaten
1 cup milk
3 cups biscuit mix
1½ cups grated Cheddar
  cheese, divided use
1 tablespoon poppy seed

■ Preheat oven to 400°.

■ Cook onion in 2 tablespoons margarine. Set aside.

■ Combine eggs, milk and biscuit mix. Stir until blended.

■ Add onion and one cup cheese.

■ Spread dough in a small greased bundt pan. Sprinkle top with remaining cheese, poppy seed.

■ Melt remaining margarine and brush over top of dough.

■ Bake at 400° for 30 to 40 minutes or until done.

One ring.

Delicious hot or makes a sandwich more exciting.

No Knead Refrigerated Rolls

Bonnie Post

¼ cup soft shortening
2 package dry yeast
2 cups lukewarm water
½ cup sugar
1 teaspoon salt
6½-7 cups sifted flour
1 egg

■ Dissolve yeast in warm water. Add sugar, salt and about half the flour. Beat 2 minutes.

■ Add egg and shortening. Gradually mix in remaining flour until smooth.

■ Cover with damp cloth and store in refrigerator. Occasionally punch holes in dough.

■ About 2 hours before baking, cut off desired amount of dough and shape into rolls.

■ Preheat oven to 400°. Place rolls on greased baking sheet; brush with melted butter.

■ Let rise.

■ Bake 12 to 15 minutes at 400°.

24-30 rolls.

■ ■ ■ *"Handy-Andy" Tip: If unsure of the freshness of the yeast, dissolve yeast in water according to the recipe and add a pinch of sugar; set aside to become frothy. If it foams and bubbles in 10 minutes you know the yeast is alive and active.*

Refrigerator Rolls

Cathy Freidrickson

¾ cup hot water
½ cup sugar
1 tablespoon salt
3 tablespoons shortening
1 cup warm water (115°)
2 packages yeast
1 egg, beaten
6 cups flour

■ Mix hot water, sugar, salt and shortening in the pan used to heat the water and cool to lukewarm.

■ Mix 1 cup warm water and yeast together. Combine mixtures.

■ Add the egg and 3 cups flour to mixture and beat until smooth.

■ Add the remaining 3 cups flour and mix with hands. Place in a greased bowl.

■ Brush top with shortening. Cover with foil and store in refrigerator. This will keep one week.

■ Preheat oven 375°.

■ Form rolls. Let rolls rise about 1 hour if dough is cold; about 30 minutes if not.

■ Brush tops with melted butter that has cooled.

■ Cover with dish towel and let rise.

■ Bake in 375° oven for 15-20 minutes.

24 rolls.

The groom's mother, used an interesting bit of history and incorporated the idea into her gift to her son. She sent all his relatives a square and asked them to design a patch using something from their "memory banks" to express their sentiments. She then had the patches quilted and presented his quilt to the bride and groom. The quilt started out as their bedcover when they were newlyweds and now serves as their darling baby girl's coverlet for her bed.

Hot Herbed Bread

Eileen Diggins

1 loaf French bread
Butter Spread
   1 cup butter
   ½ tablespoon rosemary
   ½ tablespoon thyme
   ½ tablespoon snipped
      parsley
   1 teaspoon chopped
      onion
   2 garlic cloves, pressed
      salt to taste
      coarsely ground pepper
      to taste

■ Preheat oven to 350°.

■ To make the butter spread: in a saucepan, mix all ingredients. Heat until bubbly.

■ Cut bread into ½ inch slices. Lightly coat with butter mixture.

■ In foil, reform bread into loaf. Cover and bake at 350° for 10 minutes. Uncover, fan bread and broil for 2 minutes or until golden brown.

Serves 6

Focaccia Bread

Susan Yarbro

1 package refrigerated
   pizza crust
4 cloves garlic, chopped
3 teaspoons oregano
3 teaspoons olive oil
2 cups shredded
   mozzarella cheese
3 ounces grated Romano
   cheese
5 firm Roma tomatoes,
   thinly sliced

■ Preheat oven to 325°.

■ Roll dough into a 12 x16 inch rectangle and place on pizza pan or baking stone.

■ Combine olive oil, oregano and garlic.

■ Brush olive oil mixture on top of dough.

■ Sprinkle ½ of Romano cheese and ½ of mozzarella cheese over crust. Spread tomatoes over top. Sprinkle remaining cheese on top.

■ Bake at 325° for 25-30 minutes.

Pizza Jalapeño Bread

Shannon O'Brien

1 loaf French Bread, split
12 ounces grated Cheddar cheese
1 stick margarine, softened
½ cup mayonnaise-type salad dressing
¼ cup chopped green olives
¼ cup chopped black olives
¼ cup chopped jalapeño
garlic powder to taste

■ Preheat oven to 325°.

■ Mix all ingredients together and spread over bread.

■ Bake at 325° for about 10 minutes or until hot and bubbly.

Although considered to be inedible, both the red and yellow varieties of the tomato plant were grown in flower gardens for their ornamental value. It was thought that the tomato stimulated love, hence the name love apple, and the origin of the old quilt design, which usually was made up in red and yellow with realistic tomato leaves.

"Love Apple" Tomato Bread

Gina Banister

4 Kaiser rolls, sliced in two
4 large tomatoes, sliced
1 8-ounce package shredded mozzarella cheese
1 stick butter
2 teaspoons oregano leaves
2 teaspoons paprika
1½ teaspoons garlic salt

■ Preheat oven to broil.

■ In a saucepan; melt butter, add oregano, paprika and garlic salt and simmer 10 minutes.

■ Brush cut side of rolls with butter mixture. Lay on tomato slices and top with cheese.

■ Broil until cheese is melted and starts to brown.

Serves 8

Serve with a tossed salad.

Spoon Bread

Janie Trantham

1 ½ cups boiling water
1 cup corn meal
1 tablespoon butter
3 egg yolks
1 cup buttermilk or sour cream
1 teaspoon salt
1 teaspoon sugar
1 teaspoon baking powder
¼ teaspoon soda
3 egg whites, beaten to hold soft peaks

■ Pour water over cornmeal. Stir until cool to keep from lumping.

■ Add butter and egg yolks, stirring until eggs are blended.

■ Stir in buttermilk.

■ Blend in salt, sugar, baking powder and soda.

■ Fold in egg whites.

■ Pour into a greased 9-inch square baking pan.

■ Bake in 375° oven for 45-50 minutes.

■ Serve immediately.

Serves 6 - 8.

Jalapeño Cheese Corn Bread

Kathy Whipple

1 ½ cups corn bread mix
¾ cup milk
1 egg
½ cup green onion, chopped
½ cup creamed corn
¼ cup chopped jalapeños
¾ cup grated cheese
bacon, to taste
pimientos, to taste
garlic to taste
1 tablespoon sugar
2 tablespoons vegetable oil

■ Preheat oven to 425°.

■ Cream together sugar and oil.

■ Add corn bread mix, milk, and egg.

■ Mix in green onion, creamed corn, jalapeños cheese, bacon, pimientos, and garlic.

■ Pour into buttered 8x8 inch baking dish and bake at 425° for 25 minutes.

Bobbie's "Tree of Temptation" Muffins   *Julie Robinson*

1 cup vegetable oil
1½ cups sugar
3 eggs
2 teaspoons vanilla
2¼ cups flour
1 teaspoon baking soda
1 teaspoon baking powder
1 teaspoon nutmeg
1 teaspoon cinnamon
dash of salt
3 baking apples-peeled, cored and grated

■ Preheat oven to 350°.

■ Cream together oil and sugar. Add eggs and vanilla.

■ Sift together dry ingredients. Add to sugar mixture.

■ Stir in apples.

■ Pour into greased and floured muffin cups to ½ full. Bake at 350° for 20-25 minutes.

Makes 3 dozen

Banana Nut Bread   *Lisa Matchett*

1 cup sugar
1 stick butter
2 eggs
1 tablespoon vanilla
2 cups flour
1 teaspoon soda
½ teaspoon salt
3 mashed bananas
1 cup chopped pecans

■ Preheat oven to 325°.

■ Cream butter and sugar together. Add eggs and beat slightly. Add vanilla.

■ Mix together flour, soda, and salt. Add to butter mixture.

■ Stir in bananas and nuts.

■ Pour into a well-buttered 8x4-inch loaf pan. Bake at 325° for 1 hour and 20 minutes. Let stand in pan 5 minutes before cutting.

Makes one loaf.

■ ■ ■ *"Handy-Andy" Tip: Freeze over-ripe bananas mashed with a little lemon juice and use later in bread or cake.*

Pumpkin Cheese Bread

Debbie Bradshaw

2½ cups sugar
1 8-ounce package cream cheese
½ cup margarine
4 eggs
1 16-ounce can pumpkin
3½ cups flour
2 teaspoons baking soda
1 teaspoon salt
1 teaspoon cinnamon
½ teaspoon baking powder
¼ teaspoon cloves
1 cup of pecans or walnuts

■ Preheat oven to 350°.

■ Cream together sugar, cream cheese and margarine. Add eggs, mix. Add pumpkin, mix. Add dry ingredients. Mix until moistened. Fold in nuts.

■ Pour into two greased and floured 9x5 inch pans.

■ Bake at 350° for 1½ hours.

Makes 2 loaves.

Freezes well!

Fat Free Pumpkin Spice Bread

Becky Newsom

3½ cups flour
½ teaspoon baking powder
2 teaspoons baking soda
1 teaspoon cinnamon
1 teaspoon cloves
1 teaspoon nutmeg
1½ cups sugar
1¼ cups egg substitute
2 cups canned pumpkin
⅔ cup liquid butter substitute
⅓ cup light corn syrup
1 cup raisins

■ Preheat oven to 350°.

■ Mix together dry ingredients. Add remaining ingredients and mix just until blended.

■ Pour into two 8x5 inch loaf pans that have been coated with non-stick vegetable spray.

■ Bake at 350° for 30-40 minutes or until done.

Makes 2 loaves

Strawberry Bread with Spread

Char Ankeney

3 cups flour
1 teaspoon baking soda
1 teaspoon salt
1 teaspoon cinnamon
2 cups sugar
1¼ cups vegetable oil
4 eggs, lightly beaten
20 ounces frozen strawberries, thawed, drained, reserving juice

Spread

½ cup reserved strawberry juice
1 8-ounce package cream cheese, softened

■ Preheat oven to 350°.

■ In large bowl, mix flour, baking soda, salt, cinnamon, and sugar. Make a hole in center and add oil, eggs and strawberries. Stir thoroughly by hand.

■ Line two 8x4 inch pans with foil and pour in batter.

■ Bake at 350° for 1 hour or until done.

■ For spread; mix all ingredients in blender.

Serves 12

Bread may be prepared ahead and frozen.

 ## Zucchini-Chocolate Bread

Janny Strickland

3 eggs
1 cup vegetable oil
2 teaspoons vanilla
2 cups sugar
3 cups grated zucchini
2⅓ cups flour
½ cup unsweetened cocoa
2 teaspoons baking soda
1 teaspoon cinnamon
1 teaspoon salt
¼ teaspoon baking powder
½ cup chopped nuts (optional)
1 cup chocolate chips

■ Preheat oven to 350°.

■ Mix eggs, oil, vanilla, sugar and zucchini.

■ Combine flour, cocoa, soda, cinnamon, salt and baking powder. Stir in nuts and chocolate chips. Add to zucchini mixture and stir together.

■ Pour into two greased 9x5 inch loaf pans.

■ Bake at 350° for 45 minutes.

Makes 2 loaves.

Freezes well!

Honey Zucchini Bread

Lisa Johnson

3 cups flour
1 teaspoon baking soda
1 teaspoon baking powder
1 teaspoon salt
1 tablespoon cinnamon
1 cup chopped pecans
2 cups grated zucchini, about 2 large
2 eggs, slightly beaten
1½ cups sugar
¾ cup honey
1 cup vegetable oil
2 teaspoons vanilla

■ Preheat oven to 350°.

■ Combine first five ingredients, stir in pecans.

■ Combine zucchini and remaining ingredients; add to flour mixture, stirring just until dry ingredients are moistened.

■ Spoon batter into two 9x5 inch greased and floured loaf pans.

■ Bake at 350° for 65 minutes or until a wooden toothpick inserted in center comes out clean.

■ Cool in pans 10 minutes; remove from pans and let cool on wire racks.

Makes 2 loaves

 # Blueberry Morning

Lori Anderson

Crust

2 cups biscuit baking mix
⅓ cup sugar
¼ cup margarine
⅓ cup chopped pecans

Filling

1 8-ounce package softened cream cheese
½ cup sugar
1 egg
3 tablespoons lemon juice
1 teaspoon lemon peel
1 cup blueberries

Topping

½ cup biscuit baking mix
½ cup sugar
½ stick margarine

■ Preheat oven to 350°.

■ Combine crust ingredients. Cut margarine in with pastry knife. Press in greased 9x9 pan. Bake for 15 minutes.

■ Beat together filling ingredients except blueberries. Pour over baked crust. Sprinkle with blueberries.

■ Mix together topping ingredients. Sprinkle over top.

■ Bake 35 to 40 minutes.

Serves 8

Cool before cutting.
Can be prepared the night before.

"Catch-Me-If-You-Can" Coffee Cake   *Dawn Murphy*

Cake

    1½ cups sugar
    1½ sticks margarine
     1 pint sour cream
    1½ teaspoons vanilla
     3 eggs
    2½ cups flour
    2½ teaspoons baking
       powder
    1½ teaspoon baking soda

Filling

    ¾ cup brown sugar
    2 teaspoons cinnamon
    1 cup nuts

■ Preheat oven to 350°.

■ In large bowl, cream together sugar and margarine.

■ Add sour cream, vanilla. Add one egg at time.

■ In separate bowl sift together flour, baking powder and baking soda, add to batter a little at a time.

■ Combine filling ingredients. Sprinkle half of filling mixture in well-greased tube or bundt pan.

■ Pour half of batter on top of filling. Sprinkle with brown sugar, cinnamon and nuts. Cut through with knife. Pour in remaining batter.

■ Bake at 350° for 1 hour.

Serves 12

Cake may be prepared ahead and frozen.

Variation by Julie Robinson: Combine 1 box yellow cake mix, 1 small package vanilla instant pudding, 1 pint sour cream, ½ cup vegetable oil, and 4 eggs in place of above cake recipe. Follow assembly directions above.

Monkey Bread

Kathy Tuthill

1¾ cups sugar, divided
2 tablespoons cinnamon
4 tubes of buttermilk
  biscuits
1 cup chopped pecans
¾ cup butter

■ Preheat oven to 350°.

■ Put ¾ cup sugar and 1 tablespoon cinnamon in a large bowl or plastic bag. Place the 4 tubes of buttermilk biscuits in the mixture. Coat well.

■ Pull apart pieces of the biscuits and drop into a greased bundt or tube pan. Sprinkle with chopped pecans between each tube of biscuits used.

■ Boil 1 cup of sugar, ¾ cup butter, and 1 teaspoon of cinnamon and pour over biscuits.

■ Bake at 350° for 40-45 minutes.

■ Cool 5 minutes. Invert on a plate.

The "Quilting Bee" afforded an excellent means of exchanging the latest bits of gossip and news. During the close confinement of the long winter days the pioneer women spent their spare time piecing and patching quilt tops to replenish the family supply. With the onset of Spring, the blocks were "set together" and sometimes a border was added; then it was ready for quilting. Invitations were sent to the nearest neighbors and preparations were made for the social function, second in importance only to the meetings of religious nature. Guests arrived early, usually around five or six in the morning, and work began at once. The gossipy interchange of news did not interrupt the swift fingers of the quilters. The hostess prepared lunch for all the guests. Recipes for all sorts of pickles and preserves were discussed and exchanged. Then back to the quilt which must be finished before five o'clock, for late in the afternoon the men arrived to share supper. This meal was often very elaborate and was served between five and six o'clock. After the meal the arrival of the fiddlers heralded the beginning of the country dance. Everyone young and old took part in the spirit of the dance which marked the end of a perfect day.

Christmas Morning Cinnamon Rolls   *Carolyn Lesh*

½ cup milk
½ cup butter
½ teaspoon salt
⅓ cup sugar
½ tablespoon dry yeast
2 tablespoons warm water
1 cup flour
1 egg, lightly beaten
1¼ cups flour
6 tablespoons melted
   butter, divided
   red and green cherries

Topping
1 cup sugar
½ cup brown sugar
1 tablespoon cinnamon

■ Preheat oven to 375°.

■ In large saucepan, scald milk and add ½ cup butter to melt. Add salt and ⅓ cup sugar, stirring until dissolved. Remove from heat.

■ Dissolve yeast in water and stir into milk mixture. Blend in 1 cup flour. Add egg and beat for 2 minutes. Gradually blend in remaining flour.

■ Turn out on floured surface and knead lightly 8 times. Place in greased bowl, cover and let rise until doubled.

■ Mix together all of the ingredients for the topping.

■ Roll dough into 20x8 inch rectangle. Spread 1 tablespoon melted butter over dough and sprinkle with ¼ of topping.

■ Using long side, roll jelly roll style and cut into 25 pieces. Spread remaining melted butter in 11x17 inch baking dish. Place rolls, cut side up, in pan. Press on rolls to force butter up. Sprinkle with remaining topping. Press again. Allow to rise until doubled.

■ Bake at 375° for 20 minutes. Arrange rolls to form Christmas tree. Garnish with red and green cherries.

Serves 12

Must be prepared ahead. May be frozen.

■ ■ ■ *"Handy-Andy" Tip: Dough can rise even in a cold kitchen if the bowl is placed on a heating pad set on medium.*

Emmy's Big Buns

Amy Kelly

1 package yeast
2 tablespoons warm water
4 tablespoons margarine, melted
¼ cup dry instant mashed potatoes with 1½ cups warm water
½ cup sugar
1 teaspoon salt
½ cup non-fat dry powdered milk
4 eggs, lightly beaten
4-5 cups flour

Filling

2 tablespoons margarine, melted
1 cup sugar
½ cup brown sugar
1 tablespoon cinnamon

Glaze

1½ cups powdered sugar
2 tablespoons butter, softened
1 tablespoon water

■ Preheat oven to 375°.

■ Grease 10x10 or 9x13 inch baking pan.

■ Dissolve yeast in 2 tablespoons warm water.

■ When foamy, add 4 tablespoons margarine, potato water, sugar, salt, non-fat dry powdered milk, eggs, and 4 cups of flour.

■ Mix until a ragged dough begins to form, adding flour as needed.

■ Turn dough onto a floured board and knead 5 minutes, adding flour as needed to make a smooth, silky dough.

■ Roll dough into a ball, place in greased bowl, cover and let rise 1-2 hours until double in bulk.

■ Turn dough onto floured board. Knead 1 minute.

■ Roll into rectangle ½ inch high and brush with remaining 2 tablespoons melted margarine.

■ Combine sugars and cinnamon and sprinkle onto buttered dough.

■ Roll like a jelly roll and cut into 6 slices placing cut side up in greased pan. Cover loosely and let rise until nearly double (approximately 45 minutes).

■ Bake risen rolls at 375° for 35-40 minutes.

■ Make glaze with powdered sugar, 1 tablespoon water and margarine.

■ Glaze rolls while rolls are still warm.

Serves 6

53

Blueberry Tea Muffins

Leslie Rippamonti

½ cup butter, softened
1 cup sugar
2 eggs
1¾ cups flour
1 teaspoon baking powder
¾ teaspoon baking soda
¼ teaspoon nutmeg
⅛ teaspoon cloves
¾ cup buttermilk
12 ounces canned blueberries, drained
¼ cup butter, melted

Topping

1 tablespoon grated orange peel
⅓ cup sugar

■ Preheat oven to 375°.

■ With mixer, cream ½ cup butter and 1 cup sugar. Add eggs, 1 at a time, beating well after each addition.

■ Sift flour, baking powder, baking soda, salt, nutmeg and cloves.

■ Add to butter mixture alternately with buttermilk, beating well after each addition. Fold in blueberries.

■ Line miniature muffin tin cups with paper liner and fill ⅔ full. Bake at 375° for 20 minutes or until done.

■ For topping; mix orange peel and sugar together. Dip muffins in melted butter then in topping mixture.

Makes 4 dozen

May be prepared ahead. May be frozen.

The Beggar Clock was a design of many small pieces that probably arose from the neighborly custom of begging friends for scraps from frocks or for old neckties to sew a quilt.

Raisin Muffins

Martha Welch

2 cups raisins
2 cups sugar
1 cup vegetable oil
2 cups HOT water
2 teaspoons allspice
2 teaspoons cinnamon
½ teaspoon salt
2 cups flour, white
2 cups flour, whole wheat
2 teaspoons baking soda
1 teaspoon baking
   powder
½ cup chopped nuts
   and/or chopped pitted
   dates (optional)

■ Preheat oven to 350°.

■ Mix in a saucepan, the raisins, sugar, oil, water, allspice, cinnamon, and salt. Boil gently for 5 minutes. Remove from the heat and cool.

■ Sift together flours, soda, and baking powder.

■ When well sifted together, hand beat the dry ingredients into the cooled raisin mixture.

■ Add ½ cup nuts and or chopped dates.

■ Pour into muffin pans that have been lined with paper bake cups.

■ Bake at 350° for 25 minutes.

Makes 2 dozen muffins

Home Builders didn't begin by building a home, they had to learn how to build them. Certainly the first home builder had to learn as well. Building homes is by trial and error, planning and dreaming, learning and doing. These same components are a part of gardening, parenting, friendships, cooking, quiltmaking and ...LIFE.

Chocolate Muffins

Linda Youngblood

1 stick of margarine
1 square of unsweetened chocolate
1 cup sugar
¾ cup flour
2 eggs
½ cup chopped pecans
1 teaspoon vanilla

■ Preheat oven to 325°.

■ Melt margarine in a saucepan. Stir in chocolate squares. Add: sugar and flour.

■ Mix well. Then add eggs, pecans, and vanilla.

■ Pour into greased and floured miniature muffin pans.

■ Bake at 325° for 12-16 minutes.

Makes 2 dozen miniature muffins

Drizzle icing on top for added richness! Can be frozen.

The quilt that took 47 years, 2½ months, was started by my mother in 1947. Material was used which began as flour sacks, later taking the form of dresses for my grandmother and my mother as very young girls. Even a square or two contained material from my great-grandmother. As this kind of handiwork was not something that she naturally enjoyed, the quilt patches were soon relegated to an old shoebox she pushed around; always resisting the urge to "toss it" due to her practical nature of not wishing to "waste anything".

Easter of 1994 she asked me if I had any desire to complete the quilt...in this I am my mother's daughter. I did not hesitate a moment in telling her she should engage the quilting services of my family church's Women's Quilting Guild to complete the quilt.

Armed with the exiting knowledge that I would truly treasure something that she had always considered a "waste of her time" as a young girl, she and my aunt finished the piecing of the quilt and promptly delivered it to the Quilter's Guild. The quilt that might never have been was presented to me June 1994. In 2½ months she completed a family treasure with threads that will link us in enduring ways, uniting the past with the future generations.

GOOSE IN THE POND

In colonial days one of the main parts of a little girl's education was the one or two hours each day she spent learning to sew. She had to make each stitch extremely consistent in length. To do this she counted the threads in the material as she sewed. Three years old was considered the perfect time to begin learning to sew. By the time the child became a woman, practice had perfected her sewing into almost machine-like regularity but with a finesse that put any machine sewing to shame.

Even in our grandmother's day there existed quilts considered too fine for common use. These were used only when very special guests were entertained. Charlotte Fowler, however, remembers covering up as a little girl with the pictured Fan quilt. Her mother, Maurine McCarty, was presented with this quilt in the early 1930's.

Although the sewing machine was never used in the making of a quilt back then, it was indeed a sign of status. Pioneer women who owned sewing machines often moved them onto the front porch of their home when entertaining. Early pictures show complete families posing, smiling and preening as any teenager might with his prized first car.

TEXAS SAMPLER appreciates Charlotte Fowler for sharing her cherished quilt. One can almost see the smile of the woman as she gazes at two of her most sought-after possessions - the sewing machine which enabled her to complete her domestic chores quicker and allowed her to pursue the art she so loved - her quilting!

Roasted Red Pepper Soup

Olga Ruff

5 large red peppers
3 tablespoons olive oil, divided
2 cups chopped onion
2 cloves garlic, crushed
1 10-ounce can condensed chicken broth
1 can water
½ teaspoon salt
½ teaspoon cumin (optional)
5 whole peppercorns sour cream, chopped parsley, green onions or chives, garnish

■ Preheat oven to broil.

■ Prepare peppers: cut in half, remove seeds and place cut side down on large ungreased cookie sheet. Brush lightly with 1 tablespoon olive oil.

■ Broil 10 minutes, skins should be charred and blistered.

■ Place peppers in paper bag immediately, crease bag securely. Let stand 10 minutes.

■ Scrape away the blackened skins and rinse well. Slice peppers into strips.

■ Heat 2 tablespoons olive oil in stockpot, add onions and garlic. Cook over medium to high heat for 5 minutes.

■ Add roasted peppers, cumin, salt, peppercorns, broth and water. Simmer for 20 minutes. Remove from heat, puree soup with hand blender.

■ Top bowls of soup with sour cream, chopped parsley, green onions or chives.

Serves 4-6

A Cigar Ribbon quilt is an example of a Curiosity quilt in which everyday material is put to imaginative use. The quilt top is made from hundreds of yellow silk ribbons that were used to lift cigars from the boxes. Cigar quilts are quite rare, and therefore, quite valuable today.

Shrimp and Corn Bisque

Brenda Brandon

Seasoning Mixture

    2 teaspoons dry mustard
1½ teaspoons salt
1½ teaspoons paprika
1½ teaspoons garlic
      powder
1¼ teaspoons onion
      powder
  ½ teaspoon white pepper
  ½ teaspoon dried thyme
      leaves
  ½ teaspoon dried basil
      leaves
  ¼ teaspoon black pepper
  ¼ teaspoon cayenne
      pepper
  ¼ teaspoon dried oregano
      leaves

Creamy Mixture

    2 cups evaporated skim
      milk
    6 tablespoons nonfat dry
      milk
  ¼ cup nonfat mayonnaise
  ¼ cup nonfat cream
      cheese

Base

1½ cups chopped onion
      (divided use)
    4 cups fresh cut corn
    2 cups apple juice
      (divided use)
    1 cup chopped celery
    1 teaspoon minced fresh
      garlic
1½ cups shrimp or fish stock
      (divided use)
1½ pounds medium shrimp,
      peeled
    2 tablespoons minced
      fresh parsley

■ Seasoning mixture: combine mustard, salt, paprika, garlic powder, onion powder, white pepper, thyme, basil, black pepper, cayenne and oregano in a small bowl. Set aside.

■ Creamy mixture: place evaporated skim milk, nonfat dry milk, mayonnaise and cream cheese in blender. Mix well, until smooth and creamy. Set aside.

■ Puree 1 cup onion, 2 cups corn, ½ cup apple juice and 1 tablespoon of the seasoning mix in blender or food processor.

■ Preheat a heavy 5-quart pot, preferably a non-stick, over high heat for about 4 minutes.

■ Stir pureed ingredients into pot and add 1 tablespoon of seasoning mix.

■ Cook, scraping occasionally, for about 12 minutes until a brown crust forms on the bottom and the volume is reduced.

■ Add celery, garlic, ½ cup apple juice, ½ cup stock and remaining onions, corn and seasoning mix.

■ Stir and add remaining apple juice, scraping the bottom of the pot. Cook for 15 minutes, stirring occasionally.

■ Add the shrimp and cook 3 minutes.

(Continued on next page)

(Shrimp and Corn Bisque, continued)

■ Stir in creamy mixture and remaining stock. Mix well and bring to a gentle boil.

■ Remove from heat, stir in parsley and serve.

Serves 6

 # Creamy Mushroom Soup   *Kim Hext*

¼ cup butter
¾ cup chopped green onions, including tops
2 cups chopped fresh mushrooms
2 tablespoons flour
1 cup half-and-half
1 cup chicken broth
¼ teaspoon salt
⅛ teaspoon pepper

■ In large skillet cook green onions in butter over low heat for 5 minutes or until tender.

■ Add mushrooms and cook mixture, stirring for 2 minutes.

■ Add flour and cook for 3 minutes.

■ Remove pan from heat and add chicken stock and half-and-half in a steady stream, whisking.

■ Bring soup to a boil over moderate heat.

■ Simmer, stirring, for 5 minutes.

■ Add salt and pepper.

Serves 4.

This is better if made ahead and reheated.

🕐 Potato Soup

Stephanie Zimmermann

8 ounces fresh sliced mushrooms
1 onion, chopped
3 tablespoons butter
3 tablespoons flour
2 cups milk
salt, to taste
red or black pepper, to taste
3 cups chicken broth
2 cups raw potatoes, diced
1 teaspoon Worcestershire sauce
2 tablespoons fresh parsley, chopped
1 teaspoon lemon juice
1 pound sausage or bacon, cooked, cut in bite size pieces
shredded Cheddar cheese, for garnish

■ Brown mushrooms and onion in butter.

■ Stir in flour.

■ Slowly pour in milk and broth. Add potatoes, lemon juice, Worcestershire sauce and seasonings.

■ Cook over low heat until potatoes are tender.

■ Add sausage or bacon.

■ Top with cheese before serving.

Serves 4

Picante Cheese Soup

Lisa Matchett

1 10-ounce can cheddar cheese soup
1 10-ounce can golden mushroom soup
1 8-ounce package pasteurized processed cheese, cubed
1 soup can milk
2 tablespoons cumin powder
2 tablespoons butter
¼ cup picante sauce
salt and pepper, to taste
½ cup sour cream

■ In double boiler melt cheese with soups and milk.

■ Add picante sauce, butter and seasonings.

■ Remove from heat and add sour cream.

■ Add small amount of milk if soup is too thick. Stir frequently.

Serves 4

Crab-Broccoli Soup

Jane Greer

6-8 ounces frozen Alaska King Crab or 7½-ounce can, drained
⅓ cup chopped onion
3 tablespoons butter
2 tablespoons flour
2 cups milk
2 cups half-and-half
2 chicken bouillon cubes
½ teaspoon salt
⅛ teaspoon black pepper
⅛ teaspoon cayenne pepper
¼ teaspoon thyme
10 ounces frozen broccoli, cooked, drained, reserving liquid

■ Thaw and slice crab.

■ Cook broccoli according to package directions.

■ Sauté onion in butter and blend in flour.

■ Add milk and half-and-half, stirring and cooking until thickened and smooth.

■ Dissolve bouillon cubes in hot soup and add salt, black pepper, cayenne pepper, thyme, crab and broccoli.

■ Add reserved broccoli liquid if needed to achieve the correct consistency. Heat thoroughly.

Serves 4-6

Serve with crusty bread.

■ ■ ■ *"Handy-Andy" Tip: Chill onions before chopping to prevent watery eyes.*

French Onion Soup

Lisa Matchett

Prepare ahead

6 tablespoons margarine
4-6 onions, sliced thin
6 tablespoons flour
2 14½-ounce cans chicken broth
3 14½-ounce cans beef broth
4 pieces toast
4 slices mozzarella cheese

■ Sauté onions in butter until limp and transparent.

■ Melt in flour.

■ Add chicken broth, beef broth and salt.

■ Simmer for 2-3 hours.

■ Serve in bowl with toast floating on it covered by slice of mozzarella cheese.

Serves 4.

Black Bean Soup

Nancy Marston

Prepare ahead - Soak beans in water overnight!

1 pound black beans
2 quarts water
½ pound thick sliced bacon cut into 1-inch pieces
1½ cups chopped onion
1½ cups chopped celery
1½ cups diced carrots
1 tablespoon minced garlic
1 bay leaf
1 teaspoon thyme
3 tablespoons ground cumin, divided use
½ tablespoon oregano
10 cups chicken broth
2 ham hocks
1 teaspoon cayenne pepper
4 tablespoons fresh lime juice
 salt and pepper, to taste
 sour cream, garnish

■ Soak beans in 2 quarts of water overnight. Drain.

■ Sauté bacon until crisp in heavy saucepan.

■ Add onions, celery and carrots. Sauté 5 minutes on medium heat, or until onion is clear.

■ Add garlic, bay leaf, thyme, 1 tablespoon cumin and oregano. Cook for 5 minutes.

■ Add broth, ham hocks and beans. Bring to a boil and cook 2 to 2½ hours uncovered until beans are soft.

■ Remove ham hocks and bay leaf. Remove ham from bone and add ham back to soup.

■ Add cayenne, remaining of cumin, lime juice and salt and pepper.

■ Serve with a dollop of sour cream on top.

Serves 8

Texas quilters named their mistakes. A knot showing on the quilt top was sometimes called a "rooster tail" while an overly large quilting stitch was dubbed a "toenail hanger."

Tortilla Soup

Charlotte Fowler

6 chicken breast halves
2 tablespoons oil
1 onion, chopped
1 green bell pepper, chopped
2 garlic cloves, minced
1 14-ounce can whole kernel corn, drained, reserving liquid
1 14-ounce can pinto beans, drained reserving liquid
1 14½-ounce can stewed tomatoes
1 4-ounce can chopped green chilies
1 tablespoon Worcestershire sauce
1 teaspoon cumin powder
1 teaspoon chili powder
2 teaspoons salt
½ teaspoon black pepper
¼ teaspoon red pepper
tortilla chips
grated Monterey Jack cheese
black olives (optional)

■ Cook chicken in water, chop up chicken and reserve broth.

■ In large stock pot sauté onion, bell pepper and garlic in oil until tender.

■ Combine reserved liquid from corn, beans and broth to make 6 cups.

■ Add to sautéed vegetables along with tomatoes, corn, beans, green chilies, Worcestershire sauce, and seasonings.

■ Simmer for 2 hours adding chicken last ½ hour.

■ To serve, ladle soup into bowl and top with chips, cheese and olives.

Makes 4 quarts

■ ■ ■ *"Handy-Andy" Tip: An excellent thickener for soups is a little oatmeal. It will add flavor and richness to almost any soup.*

Tortilla Rice Soup

Janny Strickland

3 corn tortillas, cut in 2x2½-inch strips
½ cup + 2 tablespoons vegetable oil, divided use
⅓ cup sliced green onions, including tops
2 cups cooked rice
1 10-ounce can diced tomatoes with green chilies, undrained
1 cup cooked chicken breast cubes
1 4-ounce can chopped green chilies, undrained
4 cups chicken broth salt to taste
1 tablespoon lime juice
½ cup chopped tomato
½ cup avocado, cut in small cubes
4 lime slices, for garnish cilantro sprigs, for garnish

■ Heat ½ cup of oil to 350°.

■ Fry tortilla strips until golden brown and drain on paper towels.

■ In a large saucepan or Dutch oven cook onions until tender in 2 tablespoons of oil.

■ Add rice, tomatoes with green chilies, chicken, chilies and broth.

■ Cover and simmer for 20 minutes.

■ Stir in salt and lime juice.

■ Just before serving pour into soup bowls and top with tortilla strips, tomato and avocado.

■ Garnish with lime slices and cilantro sprigs.

Serves 4

One can draw many parallels between the time, effort, expense, planning and the preservation of both a quilt and a marriage. We labor over the details, some aspects are exciting and others just plain boring with the sameness of it all...we continue, however, because we know it's for the good of the whole.

Butternut Squash and Apple Soup

Dorothy Cheairs

2 slices bacon
½ cup chopped onion
1 large leek, chopped fine, white and pale green parts
1 large clove garlic, minced
½ bay leaf
1¼ pounds butternut squash, seeded, peeled and cut into 1-inch pieces (3 cups)
1 medium Granny Smith apple, peeled, cored, and chopped
2 cups chicken broth
½ cup water
2 tablespoons sour cream

■ In skillet, cook bacon until crisp and drain. Reserve 1½ tablespoons fat. Crumble bacon.

■ In heavy saucepan cook onion, leek, garlic, and bay leaf with salt and pepper to taste in reserved fat over moderate heat, stirring often until vegetables are softened.

■ Add squash, apple, broth and ½ cup water.

■ Simmer covered till squash is tender (about 15 minutes). Discard bay leaf.

■ In blender or food processor, puree mixture in batches. Transfer to saucepan. Add water to reach desired consistency.

■ Whisk in cream, salt and pepper, to taste. Heat but do not boil.

■ Serve garnished with bacon.

Serves 6.

■ ■ ■ *"Handy-Andy" Tip: To keep vegetables and fruits fresh longer, line refrigerator food crisper with 2 layers of paper towels. Towels will absorb the moisture, keeping vegetables and fruits crisper and tastier longer.*

Italian Chicken and Vegetable Soup   *Sheridan Oates*

1 pound diced chicken
1 teaspoon olive oil or
   non-stick vegetable
   cooking spray
1 medium to large onion,
   diced
1 garlic clove, diced
3 14½-ounce. cans of
   ⅓ less salt chicken broth
3 cross-cut sliced celery
   stalks
1 medium bell pepper -
   any color, diced
2 cups diced carrots
2 cups new potatoes
1-2 cans of pasta ready
   tomatoes
2 teaspoons Greek
   seasoning
1 bay leaf
   salt, to taste
   pepper, to taste

■ Spray a 4½-quart stew pot or Dutch oven with cooking spray or use olive oil. Sauté chicken, onion and garlic.

■ Add 2 cans of chicken broth, celery, bell pepper and carrots.

■ Add tomatoes, potatoes, bay leaf and Greek seasoning.

■ Add additional can of chicken broth as needed.

■ Bring to a boil for about ten minutes stirring occasionally.

■ Reduce heat, and simmer on medium until carrots are done.

■ Add additional water or chicken broth to get desired soup or stew consistency.

■ Add additional Greek seasoning or salt and pepper to taste.

■ Adjust seasoning only after simmering at least 30 minutes to allow time to blend all flavors.

Serves 6

Serve with cornbread muffins and tossed salad with Italian or Caesar dressing.

■ ■ ■ *"Handy-Andy" Tip: Boiled soup is spoiled soup. Cook soup gently and evenly.*

If soup tastes too salty, a raw piece of potato placed in the pot will absorb the salt. Discard the potato when the flavor is right.

Fagioli Soup

Gina Banister

1 pound ground beef or mild Italian sausage
2 medium onions, diced
2 tablespoons butter
1 clove garlic, minced
2 large celery stalks, diced
2 carrots, sliced
½ green pepper, sliced
1 tablespoon dried parsley
1 28-ounce can whole tomatoes, pureed
8 ounces water
1½ cups beef broth
1 15-ounce can pinto beans, undrained
1 teaspoon salt
¼ teaspoon pepper
1 teaspoon basil leaves
¼ teaspoon oregano
¼ teaspoon thyme
⅛ teaspoon cloves
2 bay leaves
2 dashes hot pepper sauce
4 ounces bow-tie pasta

■ Brown meat and drain. Set aside.

■ Sauté onion and garlic in butter. Add all the other vegetables. Sauté until slightly cooked.

■ Add tomatoes, water, beef broth, beans and all spices. Add sausage.

■ Simmer on low for 2 hours.

■ Add pasta and cook until done. Serve immediately.

Serves 6-8

A husband commissioned a quilt to be made in memory of his wife. His church's women's quilting guild lovingly completed the quilt for display during the Easter season each year.

 Too Busy To Cook Soup

Pat Lawler

1 pound ground beef
1 cup chopped onions
4 cups hot water
1 cup sliced carrots
1 cup chopped celery
1 cup chopped potatoes
2 teaspoons salt
½ teaspoon pepper
1 teaspoon beef bouillon
1 teaspoon
    Worcestershire sauce
1 bay leaf
    pinch basil
1 can tomatoes

■ Brown beef and onions. Drain.
■ Add remaining ingredients and cook until vegetables are done.
■ Can be eaten in 30 minutes.

Serves 6.

"Help for Harried Housewives" - For pity's sake, don't let the laundry problem get you down. Does the very thought of doing the washing bring visions of sloshing about mournfully in huge tubs of water, or working the clouds of strong, steamy odors: of lifting pails of water; of struggling with an antiquated washer or heaven forbid, of rubbing on a washboard with a sketchy luncheon, a cross family and a generally upset household?

Needlecraft Magazine, September 1938

1995 Advice:
Say "BAG IT"! Come on down to your favorite quilt shop and take a class.

Corn Chowder

Sabrena Neely

10 new potatoes
4 cups chicken broth
6-7 pieces bacon
1 onion, chopped
4 tablespoons butter
6 tablespoons flour
3 cups half-and-half
1 11-ounce can Mexicorn, drained, reserving liquid
1 11-ounce can corn, drained, reserving liquid
salt and pepper, to taste
¼ cup sugar
6 slices pasteurized processed cheese

■ Cook potatoes in chicken broth until done.

■ Cook bacon until crisp, reserve grease.

■ Sauté onion in bacon grease, add crumbled bacon to onion.

■ Add butter and flour, stirring well.

■ Add half-and-half and stir until well blended.

■ Pour mixture into potato broth.

■ Add Mexicorn and corn, stir in salt and pepper, add reserved liquid from corn as needed to achieve desired consistency.

■ Add sugar and processed cheese.

■ Simmer on low for 20 minutes, until cheese has melted.

Serves 6-8

With the early years of the marriage comes the buzz of excitement and we tell all who will listen about the wonderfulness of it all. It's later, when the cold blast of reality hits, that you wrap yourself up in your marriage and treat it with renewed respect and appreciation for the security and warmth it gives...so it is for the heirloom quilt.

Mom's Chicken Chowder

Gina Banister

4 medium potatoes, quartered
1 medium onion, diced
1 large stem celery, diced
½ medium green peppers, diced
½ medium red pepper, diced
2 chicken bouillon cubes
1 raw chicken breast, diced
½ cup frozen corn
1 cup water
½ teaspoon salt
⅛ teaspoon pepper
½ teaspoon curry powder
1 tablespoon butter or margarine
¼ cup shredded cheese (American or pasteurized processed cheese)
1 can evaporated milk

■ Bring to a boil potatoes, onion, celery, green pepper, red pepper, bouillon cubes, chicken, corn, water and salt.

■ Reduce heat and simmer until potatoes are very tender, mash mixture slightly (there may still be lumps).

■ Add pepper, curry powder, butter or margarine, cheese and evaporated milk.

■ Add more milk if mixture is too thick.

■ Heat but do not boil.

Serves 4

Green Chili Stew

Lisa Matchett

1 pound ground turkey
1 cup beef broth or hot water
1 cup chopped onions
1 28-ounce can stewed tomatoes
1 4-ounce can chopped green chilies, mild
1 teaspoon garlic salt

■ Brown ground turkey and drain grease.

■ Add broth or water, onions, stewed tomatoes, green chilies and garlic salt.

■ Simmer 1 to 2 hours.

Serves 4

Serve with pinto beans and cornbread.

White Chili

Lieschen Bibby

Prepare ahead- Soak beans overnight!

1 pound dried Great Northern white beans, rinsed and picked over
2 pounds skinless, boneless chicken breasts
1 tablespoon olive oil
2 medium onions, chopped
4 cloves garlic, minced
2 4-ounce cans chopped green chilies
2 teaspoons ground cumin
1½ teaspoons dried oregano, crumbled
¼ teaspoon ground cloves
¼ teaspoon cayenne pepper
6 cups chicken stock or canned broth
3 cups grated Monterey Jack cheese, divided use
salt and pepper, to taste
sour cream
salsa
fresh chopped cilantro

■ Place beans in heavy large pot, add enough cold water to cover by at least 3 inches and soak overnight. Drain beans.

■ Place chicken in heavy large saucepan, add cold water to cover and bring to simmer.

■ Cook until tender, about 15 minutes, drain and cool. Cut into cubes.

■ Heat oil in same pot over medium high heat, add onions and sauté until translucent, about 10 minutes.

■ Stir in garlic, then chilies, cumin, oregano, cloves and cayenne and sauté 2 minutes.

■ Add beans and stock and bring to a boil, reduce heat and simmer until beans are very tender, stirring occasionally, about 2 hours.

■ Add chicken and 1 cup cheese to chili and stir until cheese melts.

■ Season to taste with salt and pepper.

■ Ladle into chili bowls, serve with remaining cheese, sour cream, salsa and cilantro.

Serves 8

Beans can be prepared 1 day ahead of time, covered and refrigerated. Bring back to a simmer before adding chicken and cheese.

 ## Chili a la Char

Charlotte Fowler

3 pounds ground sirloin
2 onions, chopped
1 green pepper, chopped
3 cloves garlic, minced
1 15 ounce can pinto beans with liquid
1 14½ ounce can chili style chunky tomatoes
1 14-ounce can Mexican style stewed tomatoes
½ can beer (drink left over!)
3 tablespoons chili powder
1 teaspoon cumin
1 tablespoon sugar
2 teaspoons salt
1 tablespoon Worcestershire sauce
1 teaspoon black pepper
grated Cheddar cheese

■ Brown meat and drain.

■ Add onion, green pepper and garlic.

■ Cook until tender.

■ Add pinto beans with liquid, chunky tomatoes, Mexican style stewed tomatoes, beer, chili powder, cumin, sugar, salt, Worcestershire and black pepper.

■ Simmer 1 hour.

■ Serve in bowls and top with grated cheese.

Serves 6-8

Freezes well.

"Drunkard's Path" Turkey Chili

Nancy Temple

2 pounds ground turkey
salt, to taste
pepper, to taste
1 small onion, chopped
1 small green bell pepper, chopped
1 28-ounce can tomatoes
1 8-ounce can tomato sauce
2 15-ounce cans kidney beans, drained
1 tablespoon honey
1 "slug of beer"
2 packages chili mix (mild or spicy)

■ Brown ground turkey and drain fat.

■ Salt and pepper to taste.

■ In large pot add onion, green pepper, tomatoes, tomato sauce, kidney beans.

■ Add honey and pour in "slug of beer", stir in chili mix.

■ Add ground turkey and simmer (approximately. 30-45 minutes).

Serves 6-8

The longer it simmers, the better.
Works great in a crockpot.

Chicken and Black-Eyed Pea Chili

Pat Lawler

Prepare ahead

2 teaspoons olive oil
½-1 pound boneless, skinless chicken breasts, diced
½ cup onion, chopped
3 cloves garlic, chopped
¾ pound tomatillas, chopped
1 14½-ounce can tomatoes
1 10½-ounce can chicken broth
1 7-ounce can diced green chilies
½ teaspoon oregano
½ teaspoon coriander
½ teaspoon cumin
2 15-ounce cans black-eyed peas
   juice of one lime
⅓ cup chopped cilantro
   salt and pepper, to taste
   grated Monterey Jack cheese
   chopped avocado
   chopped cilantro

■ In a large saucepan, heat olive oil and lightly brown chicken. Remove from pan.

■ Add onion and garlic to pan; sauté until softened.

■ Stir in tomatillas, tomatoes with liquid, chicken broth, green chilies, oregano, coriander and cumin. Bring to a boil; reduce heat and simmer about 20 minutes.

■ Return chicken to pan with drained black-eyed peas; simmer about 5 minutes.

■ Add lime juice, cilantro, salt and pepper.

■ Serve in bowl with grated Monterey Jack cheese, chopped avocado and chopped cilantro for garnish.

Serves 4.

Tastes best if cooked 24 hours in advance and reheated.

Even Martha Washington named her quilts as is testified by a medallion quilt displayed in the museum at Mt. Vernon named "Penn's Treaty with the Indians."

Zuni Stew from the Governor's Mansion

Sarah Bishop, Executive Chef of the Texas Governor's Mansion

1 ¼ cups pinto beans, soaked overnight and drained
1 bay leaf
1 teaspoon dried oregano
1 teaspoon salt
2 tablespoons corn or vegetable oil
2 yellow onions, cut in ¼ inch pieces
2 cloves garlic, finely chopped
2 tablespoons red chili powder, or more, to taste
1 teaspoon ground cumin
½ teaspoon ground coriander
1 pound fresh tomatoes, peeled, seeded, and chopped (drain if canned)
2 ancho chilies, deveined and seeded and cut in narrow strips
1 pound mixed summer squash, cut in 1-inch pieces
4 ears corn, kernels cut from cob (about 2 cups kernels)
8 ounces fresh green beans, cut in 1-inch pieces
4 ounces Monterey Jack cheese, grated
½ bunch fresh cilantro, roughly chopped

■ Place beans, bay leaf, and oregano in a saucepan, cover with plenty of water, and cook over medium heat for 1 ½ to 2 hours. Remove from heat when beans are soft but not mushy. Add salt. Drain beans, saving broth.

■ Heat oil in large skillet and sauté onions over high heat for 1 to 2 minutes.

■ Lower heat, add garlic and spices, and stir. Add a little bean broth so chili powder doesn't scorch.

■ Cook until onions begin to soften, about 4 minutes, then add tomatoes and cook for 5 minutes.

■ Stir in chilies and remaining vegetables, along with cooked beans and enough broth to make a moist stew.

■ Cook at a high simmer until vegetables are done, about 20 minutes.

■ Stir in cheese and chopped cilantro and garnish with whole leaves of cilantro.

Serves 6.

Serve with cornbread or tortillas.

Football Lover's Stew

Marcia Otte

½ pound bacon, cut up
¼ cup flour
1 teaspoon salt
½ teaspoon pepper
2½ pounds stew meat, cut
  into 2-inch cubes
¼ cup olive oil
3 cups chopped onion
2 large cloves garlic,
  chopped
1½ cups orange juice
1 cup dry red wine
¾ cup canned tomato
  puree
1 teaspoon sugar
2 beef bouillon cubes
¼ teaspoon nutmeg
2 bay leaves
4 medium potatoes,
  peeled and cut into
  chunks
5 medium carrots, peeled
  and cut into chunks

■ In large kettle or heavy saucepan sauté bacon until golden.

■ Combine flour, salt and pepper and dredge meat into flour mixture.

■ Brown meat in bacon fat.

■ Add olive oil, onion and garlic and sauté.

■ Add orange juice, wine, tomato puree, bouillon, salt, pepper, nutmeg, sugar and bay leaves.

■ Reduce heat and simmer 30 minutes.

■ Add vegetables, cover and cook 1 hour. (May cook longer over very low heat, stirring occasionally.)

■ Serve over noodles if desired.

Serves 4-6

 ## Cadillo (Mexican Stew)

Martha Welch

3 pounds cubed beef
1½ cups diced onions
  bacon drippings
3 cups diced tomatoes
1½ cups sliced canned
  green chilies
½ cup beef stock
½ cup chicken stock
2 teaspoons salt
2 teaspoons pepper
2 teaspoons garlic salt
2 teaspoons cumin
2 pounds potatoes, cubed

■ Sauté beef and onion in bacon drippings.

■ Add tomatoes, green chilies, stocks and seasonings.

■ Cook over low heat until meat is tender.

■ Add cubed potatoes during last 30 minutes.

Serves 6-8

Cadillo may be frozen.

No Peek Stew

Robin Kelly

Prepare ahead

2 pounds stew meat
1 package dry onion soup mix
1 8-ounce can cream of mushroom soup
1 4-ounce can mushrooms
⅔ soup can of water

■ Preheat oven to 300°.

■ Cut meat into bite size pieces and put in large roasting pan with lid.

■ Add soup mix, mushroom soup, mushrooms and water, mixing well.

■ Cook covered for 3 hours at 300°, and DO NOT PEEK!

Serves 8

Serve over wide egg noodles or rice with sour cream.

■ ■ ■ *"Handy-Andy" Tip: One tablespoon of vinegar added to the cooking water will tenderize meat.*

Cajun Shrimp and Sausage Gumbo

Suzette Bryan

Prepare ahead

½ cup olive oil
½ cup plus 2 tablespoons flour
2 large red onions, chopped
1 large bell pepper, chopped
2 stalks celery, chopped
1 hot pepper, chopped
2 cups chicken broth
1 cup wine
5 cloves garlic, chopped
1 pound of sausage
2-3 pounds shrimp, peeled and deveined
Creole seasonings to taste
salt to taste
fresh parsley
chopped green onions

■ Mix oil and flour. Stir over medium heat until it is the color of a pecan shell.

■ Add onions, bell pepper, celery, and hot pepper. Sauté until tender.

■ Add chicken broth, wine, and garlic. Allow mixture to simmer for 1-1½ hours.

■ Broil sausage to remove fat. Add sausage to roux mixture. Cook an additional 30-45 minutes.

■ Add shrimp and cook for 15 minutes more. Season with salt and Creole seasonings.

■ Serve over rice and garnish with fresh parsley and green onions.

Serves 8

GARDEN MAZE

The revival of quilt making is a boon to many who now find themselves in the enviable position of having more time on their hands. Grandmothers who have raised their families can now appreciate the pleasure of creating something and passing it down for generations to enjoy.

In an article in *Woman's Day Magazine* on American Needlework, Rose Wilder Lane expressed the following sentiments regarding machine-made quilts: "I know how the Pilgrim women would have welcomed the machine, incredulously, admired its swiftness and its perfect stitches and thanked God for easing women's work. Whether your tool is a needle or tamed electricity, your patchwork is you own; you express yourself in patterns and colors and way of working."

Making a quilt by machine presents a whole new realm of challenges as can be testified to by Rea Terry. She sewed the pictured Americana Sampler for her twelve year old grandson in 1995. Sampler quilts combine as many different pattern blocks as possible in one quilt. She chose the red, white and blue colors and symbols for patriotic reasons. Her grandson, who has slept underneath the quilt since it was presented to him, approves of her choice. The TEXAS SAMPLER appreciates Rea Terry for sharing this "binding of love for one generation with another"!

The Amish Children Sampler was loaned by twenty one year old Amanda Stanger. Her grandmother, Martha Colston bought the Amish quilt in Pennsylvania and gave the quilt to Amanda for her first birthday. Amanda had already incurred three surgeries and her grandmother saw the "moxy" her granddaughter displayed in the exuberant play of the children. When Amanda was young the quilt was displayed; it has now been safely tucked away for Amanda's enjoyment in the future with a child of her own. The charm and appeal of these smiling children can't help but evoke a smile from the viewer and the TEXAS SAMPLER thanks Amanda Stanger for reminding us that everything truly important is really all defined in the smiles of…our children…our future!

Texas Fruit Salad

Charlotte Sullivan

Prepare Ahead

- 1 20-ounce can pineapple chunks, drained
- 2 11-ounce cans mandarin oranges, drained
- 4 bananas, sliced
- 8 ounces frozen strawberries, thawed
- 1 21-ounce can peach pie filling
- 1 cup whipping cream, optional

■ In a large bowl, mix all fruit together.

■ Pour peach pie filling over fruit and gently stir.

■ Chill and serve.

■ To serve as dessert, top with whipped cream.

Serves 15

■ ■ ■ *"Handy-Andy" Tip: Use confectioners' sugar to sweeten whipped cream in order for it to remain firm longer.*

"Fruit Basket" Salad

Jane Greer

Prepare ahead

- 1 15½-ounce can peaches, drained and cut bite sized
- 1 16-ounce can pineapple, drained and cut bite sized
- 1 15½-ounce can pears, drained and cut bite sized
- 10 ounces frozen strawberries
- 1 3.4-ounce package instant vanilla pudding

■ Put all fruit in bowl.

■ Sprinkle pudding on top of fruit. (Do not stir).

■ Place frozen strawberries on top and put in refrigerator overnight.

■ Stir before serving.

Serves 10

"Snow Crystals" Salad

Reba Pennington

Prepare ahead

- 2 8-ounce cartons sour cream
- ¾ cup sugar
- 2 tablespoons lemon juice
- 1 8-ounce can crushed pineapple
- 2 diced bananas
- ¼ cup cherries, chopped
- ¼ cup pecans, chopped
- dash of salt

■ Mix together sour cream, sugar and lemon juice.

■ Add the remaining ingredients and pour into a mold and freeze.

Serves 8

 ## Blueberry Fruit Gel

Robin Kelly

Prepare ahead

- 2 small packages raspberry gelatin
- 1¼ cups boiling water
- 1 15-ounce can crushed pineapple, drained
- 1 16-ounce can blueberry pie filling mix

Topping

- 1 8-ounce package cream cheese
- ½ cup sugar
- 1 8-ounce container sour cream
- 1 teaspoon vanilla

■ Dissolve gelatin in boiling water.

■ Add crushed pineapple and blueberry pie filling mix to gelatin mixture. Allow to congeal in refrigerator.

■ Mix topping ingredients together and put on top of gelatin after congealed.

Serves 12

Fresh Cranberry Salad

Candy Brown

Prepare ahead

1 16-ounce bag of
   cranberries
1½ cups sugar
1 package of unflavored
   gelatin
½ cup orange juice
1 cup celery, chopped
1 cup nuts, chopped
1 unpeeled apple,
   chopped

■ Grind cranberries in food
processor. Add sugar and let
stand 15 minutes.

■ Soften gelatin in orange juice
for 5 minutes. Place in pan of hot
water and cook, stirring until fully
dissolved.

■ Mix gelatin with cranberries,
celery, nuts and apples.

■ Pour into a 8-cup mold and
chill overnight.

Serves 8-10

Pretzel Fruit Salad

Sharon Newbold

Prepare ahead

2 cups crushed pretzels
1¼ cups sugar, divided use
¾ cup melted butter
1 8-ounce package cream
   cheese, softened
1½ cups frozen whipped
   topping, thawed
2 cups pineapple juice
6 ounces strawberry
   gelatin
20 ounces frozen
   strawberries

■ Preheat oven to 350°.

■ Mix pretzels, ¼ cup sugar and
butter. Press into 13x9-inch
baking dish.

■ Bake at 350° for 10 minutes.
Cool.

■ With mixer, blend cream
cheese and 1 cup sugar. Fold in
whipped topping.

■ Spread over crumb mixture and
set aside.

■ In saucepan, heat pineapple
juice, add gelatin and stir until
dissolved. Pour into large bowl,
mix in strawberries and refrigerate until partially congealed.

■ Spread over cream cheese
mixture and refrigerate until set.

Serves 12

Toasted Pecan Asparagus Salad

Gina Banister

Prepare ahead

2 envelopes of unflavored gelatin
½ cup hot water
½ cup sugar
½ cup vinegar
1 cup water
1 cup celery, chopped
½ cup toasted pecans, chopped
1 15-ounce can asparagus spears, bite sized pieces
1 small jar pimientos, cut in strips
1 tablespoon onion, finely chopped
pinch of salt
juice of ½ of lemon

■ Dissolve gelatin in hot water.

■ Combine sugar, vinegar, 1 cup of water and salt. Bring to a boil.

■ Boil 5 minutes. Remove from heat and add gelatin, stirring until dissolved. Cool.

■ Combine remaining ingredients and add to liquid mixture. Pour into a mold and chill until firm.

Serves 6 to 8

Pretty at Christmas!

 # Caesar Salad

Eunice Gerard

Salad

3 large heads Romaine lettuce, torn into pieces
½ cup salad oil
croutons
grated Romano cheese

Dressing

2 garlic cloves, pressed
1 tablespoon Worcestershire sauce
¾ teaspoon salt
½ teaspoon cracked pepper
⅓ cup lemon juice
1 egg, room temperature

■ For dressing: whisk all ingredients together.

■ Toss lettuce with salad dressing.

■ Add oil and toss again.

■ Garnish with croutons and Romano cheese.

Serves 8

Wilted Lettuce

Liz Jackson

Salad

- 1 head lettuce, torn into pieces
- 1 egg, hard boiled and sliced
- 4 green onions, chopped

Dressing

- 2 tablespoons bacon drippings
- ¼ cup plus ¾ teaspoon vinegar
- ½ teaspoon salt
- ½ tablespoon sugar
- 3 tablespoons water

■ For dressing: mix all ingredients in small saucepan and bring to a boil.

■ Toss all salad ingredients.

■ Add warm dressing and lightly toss.

■ Serve immediately.

Serves 6

Lisa's Spinach Salad

Dede Jackson

Prepare ahead

Salad

- 1 bag fresh spinach, washed and stemmed
- 4 hard cooked eggs, chopped
- 8 strips bacon, crumbled

Dressing

- 1 cup vegetable oil
- 5 tablespoons red wine vinegar
- ¼ cup sour cream
- 1½ teaspoons salt
- ½ teaspoon dry mustard
- 2 tablespoons sugar
- 2 teaspoons parsley
- 2 cloves garlic, crushed

■ Mix dressing ingredients together, chill 6 hours before serving.

■ Combine spinach, eggs and bacon.

■ Toss with dressing just before serving.

Serves 6

Spinach Salad

Laura Garretson

Salad

- 5-6 cups spinach, washed, stems removed
- 1 avocado, peeled, sliced
- ¼ pound fresh mushrooms, sliced

Dressing

- 3 tablespoons wine vinegar
- 6 tablespoons salad oil
- ½ teaspoon salt
- ½ teaspoon pepper
- ¼ teaspoon dry mustard
- 2 tablespoons chopped parsley
- 1 tablespoon chopped anchovy, optional
- 1 clove garlic, cut in ½

■ Combine all dressing ingredients and let stand 20 minutes. Remove garlic halves.

■ Combine salad ingredients.

■ Immediately prior to serving, toss salad with dressing.

Serves 6.

 ## "Christmas Star" Salad

Janie Trantham

- 2 bunches broccoli flowerettes
- 1 head cauliflowerettes
- 1 purple onion, cut in rings
- ½ cup diced green onion tops
- 2 cups halved cherry tomatoes
- 1 cup mayonnaise
- ½ cup sour cream
- 1 tablespoon vinegar
- 2 tablespoons sugar salt and pepper, to taste

■ Combine broccoli, cauliflower, onions, tomatoes.

■ Stir together mayonnaise, sour cream, vinegar, sugar.

■ Toss together.

■ Sprinkle with salt and pepper.

■ Chill 3 to 4 hours. Will keep several days.

Serves 6-8.

Looks great at Christmas!

"Steps to Glory" Salad

Pat Collins

Prepare ahead

- 3 cups lettuce, shredded
- 2 medium summer squash, ¼ inch slices
- 1 small red onion, sliced & separated
- 1 10-ounce package frozen peas and carrots, thawed
- 1 8-ounce can water chestnuts, drained
- 1 medium green pepper, cut in strips
- 1 cup celery, ¼ inch slices
- 1 cup mayonnaise
- ½ cup sour cream
- ¼ cup grated Parmesan cheese
- ¼ teaspoon garlic powder
- 1 cup (10-12) slices bacon, cooked crispy and crumbled

■ Layer lettuce, squash, onion, peas and carrots, water chestnuts, pepper and celery in a 3-quart salad bowl.

■ Combine mayonnaise, sour cream, Parmesan cheese and garlic powder.

■ Spread over salad. Sprinkle crumbled bacon over dressing.

■ Cover and chill.

Serves 8-10

Looks beautiful in a clear glass bowl!

Life is like a patchwork quilt
And each little patch is a day,
Some patches are rosy, happy and bright,
And some are dark and gray.

But each little patch as it's fitted in
And sewn to keep it together
Makes a finished block in this life of ours
Filled with sun, and with rainy weather.

So let me work on Life's patchwork quilt
Through the rainy days and the sun -
Trusting that when I have finished my block
The Master may say: "Well done."

Elizabeth Ryan DeCoursey

 ## "Sunflower" Broccoli Salad

Anne Koval

Prepare ahead

Salad

1 large bunch broccoli, broken in small pieces
½ cup red onion, finely chopped
1 cup red or green whole seedless grapes
½ cup sunflower seeds
1 pound bacon, fried crisp and crumbled

Dressing

1 cup mayonnaise
½ cup sugar
2 tablespoons wine vinegar

■ Mix dressing ingredients the night before so the sugar can dissolve completely. Refrigerate.

■ Mix the salad ingredients together.

■ Toss salad with dressing just before serving.

Serves 6

Looks pretty at Christmas!

Green Goddess Pea Salad

Dana Bell

4 cans peas, drained
1 onion, chopped
1 bunch celery, chopped
1 green pepper, chopped
4 hard boiled eggs, chopped
1 can sliced water chestnuts, drained
1 4-ounce jar pimento, drained
1 8-ounce can button or sliced mushrooms, drained
½ pound grated longhorn cheese
1 large bottle Green Goddess salad dressing, chilled

■ Combine all ingredients except salad dressing.

■ Chill.

■ Toss with salad dressing just before serving.

Serves 6-8

Napa Cabbage Salad

Brenda Brandon

Prepare Ahead

- 1 head Napa cabbage, shredded
- 1 bunch green onions, chopped
- 1 stick butter
- 2 packages Ramen noodles, breakup (flavor doesn't matter)
- 1 ounce sunflower seeds
- 1 package slivered almonds

Dressing

- ½ cup sugar
- 2 tablespoons soy sauce
- ¼ cup vinegar
- ¾ cup vegetable oil

■ Mix cabbage and onions in large bowl.

■ Sauté Ramen noodles, sunflower seeds and almonds in butter until lightly brown. Set aside to cool.

■ Combine dressing ingredients in saucepan and boil for 1 minute. Cool.

■ Mix cabbage and noodle mixtures then toss with dressing just before serving.

Serves 6

No Mayo Cole Slaw

Anne Hobbs

Prepare ahead

- ⅓ cup vinegar
- ¼ cup salad oil
- 2 tablespoons sugar
- 2 tablespoons onion flakes
- 1 teaspoon dry mustard
- ½ teaspoon celery salt
- 1 teaspoon salt
- ¼ teaspoon hot pepper sauce
- 4 cups shredded cabbage (green and/or purple)
- 1 carrot, grated
- ¼ cup chopped green pepper

■ Combine vinegar, oil, sugar, onion flakes, dry mustard, celery salt, salt, and hot pepper sauce. Mix well.

■ Add cabbage, carrot, and pepper. Toss to mix.

■ Cover and refrigerate. Toss again before serving.

Serves 6

It's better the next day!

Tomatoes a la Clare

Amy Kelly

Prepare ahead.

6 medium to large
tomatoes, sliced
3 cloves of fresh garlic,
minced
1 bunch green onions,
finely chopped, with
tops
⅓ cup chopped parsley
½ teaspoon salt
coarse ground black
pepper, to taste
⅓ cup corn oil
¼ cup brown cider vinegar
1 tablespoon Dijon
mustard

■ Arrange tomatoes in a shallow
dish or platter.

■ Mix garlic, onions, parsley, salt
and pepper. Sprinkle over
tomatoes.

■ Cover with plastic wrap and
refrigerate 3 to 4 hours.

■ Prepare dressing by combining
oil, vinegar and mustard in a
small jar.

■ At serving time, shake dressing
well and pour over tomatoes.

Serves 6 to 8.

■ ■ ■ *"Handy-Andy" Tip: Fresh lemon juice will remove onion scent from
hands.*

Potato Salad Italiano

Lori Anderson

Prepare ahead

10-12 new red potatoes,
cooked, cut into
quarters
¼ cup chopped chives
¼ cup chopped parsley
¼ cup ripe olives
½ cup prepared oil-free
Italian dressing

■ In a large bowl, combine hot
potatoes, chives, parsley and
olives.

■ Pour dressing over hot potato
mixture. Toss gently to coat.

■ Refrigerate 1-2 hours before
serving.

■ Toss again just before serving.

Serves 8.

Fourth of July Potato Salad

Pat Knott

Prepare ahead

- 6 large potatoes
- 4-5 eggs, hard boiled and coarsely chopped
- 4 celery ribs, coarsely chopped
- 3 tablespoons chopped onion
- 4 tablespoons sweet relish
- salt to taste
- 1 cup salad dressing
- 1 cup sour cream
- 1 tablespoon vinegar
- 1-2 tablespoons sugar
- 1 tablespoon prepared mustard
- 1 tablespoon celery seed
- paprika

■ Boil potatoes until done, drain. Cool, peel and cube.

■ Mix potatoes with eggs, celery, onion, relish and salt. Set aside.

■ In separate bowl, blend salad dressing, sour cream, vinegar, sugar, mustard and celery seed. Pour over potatoes and mix thoroughly.

■ Cover and refrigerate for 24 hours. Sprinkle with paprika before serving.

Serves 8

Must be prepared ahead 24 hours.

The simple pleasures of the every-day life of the colonists and their close touch with nature are reflected in their quilt-patch names. Great-grandmother had no movies, no automobiles, no airplanes, no radios; is it any wonder she wove her pleasure into patchwork quilts?

Sherrie A. Hall and Rose G. Kretsinger,
The Romance of the Patchwork Quilt

■ ■ ■ *"Handy-Andy" Tip: A few drops of lemon juice in potato water will whiten boiled potatoes.*

Black Bean, Corn and Poblano Pepper Salad

Brenda Brandon

Prepare ahead

- 1½ cups dried black beans, rinsed and picked over
- 4 teaspoons salt, divided use
- 4 poblano peppers
- 1 tablespoon cumin seeds
- ¼ cup sherry wine vinegar
- 1 tablespoon Dijon mustard
- 2 teaspoons freshly ground black pepper
- ½ cup olive oil
- 2 cups corn, fresh or defrosted
- 18 cherry tomatoes, cut in half
- 3 scallions, thinly sliced

■ In a large bowl, combine beans with enough cold water to cover by at least 3 inches. Soak overnight.

■ Drain beans and add enough fresh water to cover by at least 3 inches. Bring to a boil over high heat. Reduce heat and simmer, partially covered, for 30 minutes. Stir in 2 teaspoons salt. Continue cooking until beans are just tender, 35-45 minutes; drain.

■ Roast poblano peppers until skins are lightly charred. Seal in a paper bag for 10 minutes. Rub away charred skin. Stem and seed the peppers. Cut into ¾ inch squares.

■ In a small skillet, toast cumin seeds over moderately high heat, tossing until fragrant and golden brown, about 1 minute. Grind in a spice mill or finely chop on a cutting board.

■ In a small bowl, whisk together vinegar, mustard, cumin seeds, black pepper and remaining 2 teaspoons of salt. Slowly whisk in oil.

■ In a large bowl, combine beans, poblano peppers and corn. Pour dressing over salad. Toss well. (Can be prepared to this point up to 24 hours ahead. Cover and refrigerate. Let return to room temperature before proceeding.)

(Continued on next page)

(Black Bean, Corn and Poblano Pepper Salad, continued)

■ Add tomatoes and scallions to the salad, toss well and season with additional salt and pepper to taste.

■ Serve at room temperature.

Serves 4-6

■ ■ ■ *"Handy-Andy" Tip: Corn that has been husked soon loses its flavor and dries out. Always buy corn with the husk still intact.*

Open Sesame Salad   *Joan Wright*

Salad

2 cups chicken, diced
2 cups cooked ham, diced
2 cups cooked small
  macaroni shells
1 cup Swiss cheese, diced
½ cup sesame seeds,
  toasted
½ cup slivered almonds,
  toasted
½ cup green onions, sliced
  (about 3 bunches)
½ cup green peppers,
  finely chopped
½ cup celery, finely
  chopped

Dressing

¾ cup cider vinegar
¾ cup peanut oil
¼ cup dark sesame oil
¼ cup honey
2 tablespoons Dijon
  mustard
1 teaspoon dry mustard
½ teaspoon garlic powder

■ Mix dressing ingredients together.

■ Combine all other ingredients.

■ Toss with dressing.

Serves 8

Chicken Caesar Salad

Lisa Johnson

- 1 pound boneless, skinless chicken breast halves
- 3 tablespoons white wine vinegar
- 1 teaspoon Dijon mustard
- ½ teaspoon Worcestershire sauce
- 1½ teaspoons lemon pepper
- 1 teaspoon garlic powder
- ¼ cup olive oil
- 1 1 pound head Romaine lettuce, torn into bite sized pieces
- 1 cup garlic croutons
- ¼ cup grated Parmesan cheese

■ Cook chicken, cut into ¼ inch strips. Brown if desired. Set aside.

■ In a small bowl, combine vinegar, mustard, Worcestershire, lemon pepper and garlic powder. Gradually whisk in olive oil.

■ Place lettuce in a large bowl. Add chicken. Toss with oil mixture.

■ Serve topped with croutons and cheese.

Serves 8

Chicken Fruit Pasta Salad

Barb Wood

Prepare ahead

- 2 cups shell macaroni
- 3 cups cubed, cooked chicken
- 2 tablespoons onion, finely chopped
- 1 teaspoon salt
- 1½ cups sliced celery
- 1½ cups seedless green grapes
- 1 11-ounce can mandarin orange segments, drained
- ½ cup slivered almonds, toasted
- 1 cup salad dressing or mayonnaise
- 1 cup whipping cream, whipped

■ Cook macaroni to desired doneness as directed on package. Drain; rinse in cold water.

■ In large bowl, combine all ingredients except whipping cream.

■ Cover; refrigerate 3 hours to blend flavors.

■ Just before serving, fold in whipped cream.

Serves 12 (1-cup)

Cheesy Hot Chicken Salad

Susie Hatley

6-8 chicken breasts
3 hard boiled eggs, sliced
1 can undiluted cream chicken soup
2 cups diced celery
1 cup mayonnaise
1 cup sour cream
1 4-ounce can sliced mushrooms
½ cup slivered almonds
2 tablespoons minced onions
1 teaspoon salt
2 tablespoons lemon juice
1½ cups grated American cheese, divided use

■ Preheat oven to 375°.

■ Clean and skin chicken breasts. Simmer 1 hour. Debone and dice.

■ Mix remaining ingredients with ½ cup cheese.

■ Put into a casserole dish (9x13). Top with remaining cheese.

■ Bake at 375° for 30 minutes.

Serves 12

Chicken Cashew Salad

Debbie Bradshaw

Prepare ahead

12 chicken breast halves, cooked
2 cups celery, chopped
2 8-ounce cans sliced water chestnuts, drained
1 16-ounce can pineapple chunks, drained
2 cups mayonnaise
2 tablespoons soy sauce
2 teaspoons curry powder
2 cups whole cashews
lettuce
croissants or pita bread

■ Remove chicken from bone and cut into bite sized pieces. Chill.

■ Combine celery, water chestnuts, pineapple and chicken.

■ Stir together mayonnaise, soy sauce, curry powder. Add to chicken mixture. Toss and chill.

■ Add cashews prior to serving. Serve on lettuce with croissant or pita bread.

Serves 12

Make Ahead Wild Rice Tuna Salad

Charlotte Sullivan

Prepare ahead

1 package long grain &
    wild rice
2 7-ounce cans tuna
½ cup sour cream
4 tablespoons onion,
    chopped
1 cup cashew nuts
1 cup mayonnaise
½ cup celery, chopped

■ Cook rice mix according to package directions and chill.

■ Drain tuna in a colander and pour hot water over.

■ Mix rice and tuna.

■ Combine sour cream, onion, cashew nuts, mayonnaise and celery. Add to tuna and rice mixture.

■ Cover and refrigerate.

Serves 6-8

Make several days before serving. The longer it sits, the better it tastes!

 # Taco Salad

Stella Daniel

1 pound hamburger meat
1 head lettuce, torn into
    bite-size pieces
1 large tomato, chopped
2-3 green onions, chopped
    (optional)
16 ounces grated Cheddar
    cheese
1 can ranch style beans,
    drained
1 large bottle of spicy
    French salad dressing
1 bag plain Mexican-style
    chips, crushed

■ Brown hamburger meat, drain and set aside.

■ In large bowl, combine lettuce, tomato, green onions, cheese, beans, and meat.

■ Add ½ to ¾ bottle of salad dressing (more if you wish). Toss.

■ Add crushed chips.

Serves 4-6

Cowboy Taco Salad

Anne Koval

1½ pounds ground beef
1½ cups diced onion
1 cup diced celery
1 cup diced bell pepper
3 diced garlic buds
1 teaspoon salt
2 teaspoons chili powder
¾ teaspoon ground cumin
1 pound pasteurized processed cheese
1 can diced tomatoes with chilies
1 large head of lettuce, torn in pieces
2 fresh firm tomatoes, cut in chunks
1 package corn chips

■ Sauté meat in a small amount of oil until cooked but not brown. Add all chopped vegetables and simmer together until soft. Season with salt, chili powder, and cumin.

■ Melt cheese and add canned tomatoes.

■ Put lettuce and tomato in large serving bowl.

■ Add crushed corn chips and meat mixture. Toss again.

■ Pour hot cheese mixture on top and serve immediately.

Serves 6-8 as main dish;
16 as buffet

Artichoke Rice Salad

Stella Daniel

Prepare ahead

1 6-ounce package chicken rice vermicelli mix
1 7-ounce jar marinated artichoke hearts
¼ teaspoon curry powder
⅓ cup mayonnaise
12 green olives, chopped
½ green pepper, chopped
4 green onions, sliced thin

■ Cook rice and seasoning packet according to package directions, omit butter.

■ Drain artichokes, reserving the liquid. Chop artichokes.

■ Combine the reserved liquid, mayonnaise and curry powder. Blend well.

■ Add chopped artichokes, vegetables and mayonnaise mixture to rice.

■ Mix thoroughly and chill.

Serves 6

93

Ham and Rice Salad

Trish Barker

Prepare ahead

- 2 cups cooked white rice (cooked 48 hours in advance & refrigerated)
- 2 cups diced low-fat ham
- 1 bunch green onions, diced
- ½ cup green or red bell pepper, chopped
- ½ cup celery, chopped

Dressing

- ½ cup lite cole slaw dressing
- 1 teaspoon soy sauce
- 1 tablespoon champagne vinegar

■ Mix together all dressing ingredients.

■ Mix together rice, ham, green onion, bell pepper, and celery.

■ Combine dressing and rice with ham mixture.

■ Refrigerate for 24 hours.

Serves 6

This recipe is also great with shrimp!

Artichoke Pasta Salad Supreme

Dolores Spence

- 2 12-ounce packages tortellini
- 1 8.5-ounce can artichoke hearts, quartered and drained
- 1 tomato, cubed
- 1 cup Feta cheese
- ½ cup chopped walnuts
- ½ cup ripe olives, chopped
- ¼ cup white wine vinegar
- ¼ cup green onion, chopped
- 3 cloves garlic, chopped fine
- 1 tablespoon dried basil, crumbled
- 1 teaspoon dried dill weed
- ½ cup olive oil

■ Cook tortellini according to package to directions.

■ In a large bowl, mix together tortellini, artichokes , tomato, cheese, walnuts, and olives. Set aside.

■ In a small bowl, whisk together, vinegar, green onions, garlic, basil, and dill. Whisk while pouring olive oil in slow steady stream

■ Combine pasta mixture and dressing. Toss gently.

■ Serve at room temperature.

Serves 8-10

Fiesta Pasta Salad

Lisa Matchett

Prepare ahead

- 1 pound spiral noodles, cooked and drained
- ⅔ cup cider vinegar
- ¼ cup safflower oil
- 8 green onions, chopped
- 1 2-ounce jar pimientos
- 4 dashes Worcestershire sauce
- 4 dashes hot pepper sauce
- 2 tablespoons green chilies, drained and chopped
- 1 teaspoon salt
- 1½ teaspoons pepper
- 1 16-ounce can black eyed peas, drained
- 1 16-ounce can corn, drained
- 1 4-ounce can ripe olives, drained and chopped
- 1½ cups mayonnaise
- 2 tablespoons picante sauce

■ Mix all ingredients together.
■ Refrigerate for at least 24 hours.

Serves 20-25

"The vast majority of quilts from the past are scrap quilts and it's that practice of making quilts from small pieces of cloth left over from other sewing that has given quiltmakers their unbeatable reputation as frugal recyclers. We'll never know whether, given the choice of plenty of yardage, a nineteen century quilter would have stuck to quilts combining only a few fabrics."

Quilts from America's Heartland

Southwestern Pasta Salad

Sherry McMenamy

Prepare ahead

    8 ounces elbow macaroni
    1 6-ounce package deli thin sliced ham, chopped
    ½ cup sweet yellow pepper, diced
    ½ cup sweet red pepper, diced
    1 cup peeled, seeded and chopped tomato
    ¼ cup purple onion, diced
    1 tablespoon plus 1½ teaspoons minced cilantro
    1 clove garlic, minced
    1 small jalapeño pepper, seeded and minced
    1 tablespoon olive oil
    1 tablespoon red wine vinegar
    ¼ cup Feta cheese
    2 tablespoons pine nuts, toasted

■ Cook macaroni according to directions. Drain and set aside.

■ Combine ham and next 9 ingredients in a large bowl.

■ Stir in macaroni.

■ Cover and chill at least 2 hours.

■ Top with cheese and pine nuts.

Serves 4 to 6

■ ■ ■ *"Handy-Andy" Tip: To seed a tomato, cut in half, squeeze, and shake seeds out.*

Why not join the computer generation as the participants in the border swap quilts from GEnie Online Quilters II Guild have done. The five ladies live across the country from California to Washington, D.C. and most have never met except by computer. The center block was created by one and the other four added the borders.

Warm Chicken Pasta Salad

Terri Brezette

2 cups fresh asparagus (¾ pound) julienne strips OR 2 cups small thin pieces broccoli

16 ounce pasta, curly rotini (rainbow)

2 cups chicken breasts, cooked and cut into thin strips

1 tablespoon minced shallots

2 tablespoons grated lemon rind

6 tablespoons balsamic vinegar

½ teaspoon salt

2 teaspoons ground black pepper

½ cup olive oil

½ cup fresh grated Parmesan cheese

■ Cook pasta according to directions on package. Drain and rinse under warm water.

■ Microwave asparagus or broccoli on high for 6 minutes, covered. Let stand for 5 minutes.

■ Mix remaining ingredients together and toss with pasta, chicken and asparagus or broccoli while still warm.

■ Sprinkle with Parmesan cheese and serve.

Serves 6

■ ■ ■ *"Handy-Andy" Tip:* **Acini de Pepe** *is a tiny peppercorn-shaped pasta that is great in soups or salads.*

Al dente *pasta cooked until tender but slightly firm.*

Farfalle*, meaning "butterfly" in Italian, is also called bow-tie pasta.*

Lumache*, also known as "little shells", is available in small and medium sizes.*

Orzo *is a tiny barley-shaped pasta, also known as rosamarina, and is terrific in soups and salads.*

Pesto *is an Italian sauce made from basil, garlic and olive oil.*

Radiatore *pasta is shaped like a car radiator. This small ruffly pasta is an excellent choice for salads.*

Tip*: Depending on the pasta's size and shape, two ounces of dried pasta yields about 1 cup of cooked pasta or one serving.*

Penne with Roasted Garden Vegetables

Brenda Brandon

Lowfat

- 1 each red, green, and yellow bell pepper, cut into ½ inch strips
- 2 red onions, cut into ½ inch slices
- 2 yellow squash, cut into 1-inch slices
- 1 small eggplant, cut into 1-inch cubes
- 6 large garlic cloves, peeled and halved
- 3 tablespoons olive oil
- ¼ cup chopped parsley
- 2 teaspoons fresh thyme leaves
  salt and pepper
- 1 pound penne pasta
- ⅓ cup grated Parmesan cheese

■ Preheat oven to 400°.

■ Divide vegetables and garlic between 2 large, flat roasting pans. Add olive oil and toss vegetables to coat evenly. Sprinkle with parsley and thyme.

■ Bake stirring frequently, until browned and tender, about 40 minutes. Season with salt and pepper.

■ Cook pasta. Ladle out ½ cup of the pasta cooking liquid and reserve. Drain pasta.

■ Toss with the vegetables, reserved cooking liquid and Parmesan cheese.

■ Sprinkle with additional Parmesan cheese, if desired.

Serves 6-8.

A very good friend of mine is a marathon runner. Her mother has recently taken the T-shirts that she has accrued over the years and retrieved the logos from each event to turn into a patchwork quilt. My friend has a lovely quilt, made with love, that she now enjoys while she makes her long runs to the refrigerator during the commercials of her TV shows.

This idea could also be incorporated into a sports trivia quilt idea. How many of you have dozens of sports T-shirts from your children's sports years? Using the same idea as above, why not utilize their logos (dirt and all) and make yourself something to keep you warm in the cold winters ahead. As you warm yourself by the fire while your children freeze their toes off watching their kids play their sports in the dead of winter, you can smile with the memory.

Linguine Verde

Brenda Brandon

16 ounces fresh spinach
   linguine
 1 cup sun-dried tomatoes,
   soak in warm water to
   soften
 ½ cup olive oil
 2 teaspoons minced garlic
20 mushrooms, sliced
 1 cup chicken broth
 4 tablespoons fresh basil,
   cut in thin strips
   salt and pepper to taste
 ½ cup pine nuts
 ½ cup butter
 1 tablespoon lemon juice
 ¼ cup grated Parmesan
   cheese

■ Cook pasta according to direction; drain and reserve.

■ Drain softened sun-dried tomatoes.

■ Heat olive oil in a large skillet and add sun-dried tomatoes, garlic and mushrooms; sauté for 1 to 2 minutes.

■ Add broth, basil, salt, pepper and pine nuts. Cook about 2 minutes longer, until mushrooms are wilted.

■ Add pasta and toss to combine with ingredients. Remove from heat.

■ Stir in butter, lemon juice and Parmesan cheese, tossing to combine. Serve immediately.

Serves 4

To reduce fat braise tomatoes, garlic and mushrooms in white wine or broth. Add remaining broth and complete recipe. Reduce amount of butter added at end to 1-2 tablespoons.

■ ■ ■ *"Handy-Andy" Tip: Add 2 teaspoons olive oil to boiling water before adding rice, noodles, macaroni and spaghetti to make foods glisten and separate.*

Linguine with Tomatoes and Basil
Brenda Brandon

Prepare ahead

> 4 ripe tomatoes, cut into ½ inch cubes
> 1 pound Brie cheese, rind, removed, torn into irregular pieces
> 1 cup cleaned fresh basil leaves, cut into strips
> 3 garlic cloves, finely minced
> 1 cup plus 1 tablespoon best quality olive oil, divided use
> 2½ teaspoons salt, divided use
> ½ teaspoon freshly ground black pepper
> 1½ pounds linguine freshly grated Parmesan cheese, optional

■ Combine tomatoes, Brie, basil, garlic, 1 cup olive oil, ½ teaspoon salt and pepper in a large serving bowl. Prepare at least 2 hours before serving and set aside, covered at room temperature.

■ Bring 6 quarts water to a boil in a large pot. Add 1 tablespoon olive oil and remaining salt. Add linguine and boil until tender.

■ Drain pasta and immediately toss with the tomato sauce. Serve at once.

■ Add grated Parmesan cheese on top if desired.

Serves 4-6

Can be served as a side dish.

Alexandra's Favorite Pasta
Stacy Stout

> 1 28 ounce can plum tomatoes, undrained
> 2 teaspoons olive oil
> 2 cloves garlic, minced
> 16 ounces spaghetti or fettucine, uncooked
> 7 ounces mozzarella cheese, cut into ½ inch cubes
> ¼ cup Parmesan cheese
> ⅛ teaspoon red pepper flakes

■ Cube tomatoes. Heat tomatoes with juice over medium heat with garlic and olive oil for 20 minutes.

■ Cook pasta al dente, drain and place in serving bowl.

■ Add tomato mixture, cheeses, and red pepper flakes. Toss.

■ Cover bowl for 5 minutes to allow cheese to melt. Toss before serving.

Serves 6-8

Penne Pasta with Zucchini

Kathy Whipple

2 cups penne pasta
6 unpeeled medium-size firm zucchini
2 tablespoons olive oil crushed red pepper, to taste
½ cup grated Parmesan cheese

■ Fill a large saucepan with water and bring to boil over high heat. Add penne pasta and cook until barely tender.

■ Grate zucchini into a sauté pan; stir over high heat 3 minutes.

■ Add oil and season to taste with red pepper; cook, stirring for 1 minute.

■ Drain pasta into a colander and place in a warm bowl. Pour zucchini and all liquid from pan over pasta.

■ Add grated cheese and toss carefully to mix well.

■ Serve hot.

Serves 4

In 1987 a small group of volunteers in a San Francisco storefront workshop revived the old-fashioned notions of the quilt and the quilting bee. Their determination and courage, and that of hundreds of other quilters across the nation, created what has become the largest community arts project in America: The Quilt.

Nearly 2,000 three-by-six foot individual panels have been designed and sewn into the Quilt. Each one represents the life of someone who has died of AIDS and the love and hope of those who remember them, signifying that death has not come in vain.

Panels continue to arrive from the across the country as friends and family grieve for the loved ones taken by this dreadful disease.

 ## "Mother's Star" Manicotti

Susan McCombs

3 tablespoons Parmesan
cheese
2 eggs, lightly beaten
1 tablespoon dried chives
1 tablespoon finely
chopped parsley
salt and pepper to taste
1 16-ounce container
ricotta cheese
1 10-ounce package
grated mozzarella
cheese
2 large jars of spaghetti
sauce
1 package of manicotti
shells, uncooked

■ Preheat oven to 400°.

■ Combine the Parmesan cheese, eggs, chives, parsley, salt and pepper together.

■ Mix in ricotta and mozzarella cheeses.

■ Fill the uncooked manicotti shells using a teaspoon or small rounded knife.

■ Heat 2 large jars of spaghetti sauce.

■ Pour a little of hot spaghetti sauce in the bottom of 9x13 baking dish. Arrange shells in a single layer side by side. Add remaining spaghetti sauce to completely cover shells.

■ Cover baking dish with foil crimping edges to seal tightly.

■ Bake at 400° for 60 minutes.

Serves 6

When my only child went off to college, I sent him with a cornucopia of childhood and high school memories, all in the form of a cotton quilt. Some 80 friends and family shared good wishes, words of wisdom and memories. He later told me that he would have never survived those long nights of studying and worrying had he not had the comfort of his "love quilt".

Pesto Sauce

Kathy Whipple

2 garlic cloves, peeled
1 cup fresh basil leaves
    (no stems)
1 cup parsley springs
    (no stems)
½-¾ cup olive oil
½ cup grated Parmesan
    cheese
¼ cup pine nuts

■ Put garlic into blender with basil and parsley; puree.

■ Start adding olive oil to this puree a little at a time. Add cheese and pine nuts; puree. Continue adding oil until finished sauce is like creamed butter, adding more oil if too thick.

Makes 1½ cups

This sauce freezes well!

 ## Creamy Tomato and Italian Sausage "Bow Ties"

Lieschen Bibby

2 tablespoons olive oil
1 pound sweet Italian
    sausage, casing
    removed, crumbled
½ teaspoon dried red
    pepper flakes
½ cup diced onion
3 garlic cloves, minced
1 28-ounce can Italian
    plum tomatoes, drained,
    coarsely chopped
1½ cups whipping cream
½ teaspoon salt
12 ounces bow tie pasta,
    cooked al dente,
    drained
3 tablespoons minced
    fresh parsley
    freshly grated Parmesan
    cheese

■ Heat oil in heavy large skillet over medium heat. Add sausage and pepper flakes. Cook until sausage is no longer pink. Stirring frequently, about 7 minutes.

■ Add onion and garlic. Cook until onion is tender and sausage is light brown, Stir occasionally, about 7 minutes.

■ Add tomatoes, cream and salt. Simmer until mixture thickens slightly, about 4 minutes.

■ Add pasta and cook until pasta is heated through and sauce thickens, about 2 minutes.

■ To serve; divide pasta among plates. Sprinkle with parsley. Pass Parmesan cheese separately.

Serves 4

**Meat sauce can be prepared 1 day ahead.
Cover tightly and refrigerate.**

"X-Quisite" Lasagna

Debbie MacDonald

2 tablespoons olive oil
2 tablespoons vegetable oil
¾ pound ground top round
½ pound Italian sausage, skinned and sliced
2 finely chopped onions
2 cloves minced garlic
5 tomatoes, peeled and coarsely chopped, or 1 13-ounce can Italian crushed tomatoes
2 8-ounce cans tomato sauce
3 tablespoons sugar
1 tablespoons salt
1 tablespoon fresh oregano
1 tablespoon fresh basil
¼ teaspoon ground pepper
½ cup grated Parmesan
½ pound lasagna noodles, cooked
1 pound ricotta cheese
1 pound Mozzarella cheese
¼ pound grated Parmesan cheese

■ Heat olive and vegetable oils in heavy saucepan. Add beef and sausage. Sauté until browned.

■ Add garlic and onions, sauté 3 minutes. Add tomatoes, tomato sauce, sugar, salt, oregano, basil, ½ cup Parmesan, and pepper. Mix well. Bring to a boil, reduce heat, and simmer slowly for 2 hours stirring occasionally.

■ In the bottom of a greased 13x9 baking dish, put a thin layer of sauce, then a layer of noodles, then a layer of cheeses. Repeat layers twice, ending with a layer of sauce, and sprinkle with Parmesan cheese.

■ Bake at 350° for 40 minutes. Let stand for 15 minutes before serving.

Spaghetti Pie

Peggy Theis

8 ounces thin spaghetti
2 tablespoons margarine
⅓ cup Parmesan cheese
2 eggs, well beaten
1 pound ground beef
½ cup chopped onion
¼ cup chopped green
   pepper
1 14.5-ounce can stewed
   tomatoes
1 6-ounce can tomato
   paste
1 teaspoon sugar
1 teaspoon oregano
½ teaspoon garlic salt
¼ teaspoon pepper
1 cup cottage cheese
½ cup shredded
   mozzarella cheese

■ Cook spaghetti according to package directions; drain. Stir margarine into hot spaghetti. Cool slightly. Stir in Parmesan cheese and eggs.

■ Form spaghetti mixture into a crust in 2 buttered 10-inch pie pans.

■ Brown ground meat on medium heat; then drain grease. Stir in onion and green pepper and cook until vegetables are tender.

■ Stir in undrained tomatoes, tomato paste, sugar, oregano, garlic salt and pepper. Heat thoroughly.

■ Spread cottage cheese over bottom of spaghetti crust. Fill pie with meat mixture.

■ Bake uncovered at 350° for 20 minutes.

■ Sprinkle with mozzarella cheese on top. Bake 5 minutes longer or until cheese melts.

Serves approximately 12

May be frozen then baked later!

Sausage, Spinach Pasta Toss

Terri Brezettes

1 pound package sliced fresh mushrooms
2 cloves garlic, minced
1 large red bell pepper, julienne
3 tablespoons olive oil
1 pound cooked smoked sausage, sliced
1 10-ounce package frozen spinach chopped, thawed and well drained
1 tablespoon dried Italian seasoning
2 14½-ounce cans chunky Italian seasoned tomatoes, undrained
1 pound penne, cooked freshly grated Parmesan

■ Cook mushrooms, garlic and peppers in olive oil until tender.

■ Add sausage, spinach, Italian seasoning and tomatoes. Cook 10 minutes.

■ Add pasta and toss well.

■ Sprinkle with Parmesan cheese.

Serves 8

Hot Red Pepper Sausage Ziti

Brenda Brandon

1 pound Italian sausage
¼ cup olive oil
2 cloves garlic, pressed or minced
½ teaspoon crushed hot red pepper
2 cups broccoli, parboiled, cut into bite-sized florets
1 pound tomatoes, peeled, coarsely chopped
1 pound ziti, cooked and drained
grated Romano cheese

■ Cut sausage in ½-inch slices. Cook in non-stick skillet until done. Drain on paper towel. Set aside.

■ In saucepan sauté garlic and pepper in olive oil over high heat until garlic begins to brown.

■ Add broccoli, stirring 1 minute to sear on all sides. Add sausage, stir. Add tomatoes, stir 1 minute.

■ Lower heat to simmer. Cook, covered, for 15 minutes or until tomatoes are soft and broccoli well-cooked.

■ Toss pasta with broccoli and sausage mixture. Serve with Romano cheese.

Serves 6

Rigatoni

Anne Koval

2 medium onions, chopped
4 cloves garlic, minced
1½ pounds mild Italian sausage
½ cup Parmesan cheese, divided use
1 6-ounce can tomato paste
6 ounces water
1 8-ounce can tomato sauce
1 15-ounce can whole tomatoes, undrained
1 tablespoon basil
1 tablespoon Italian spices
1 teaspoon salt
½ teaspoon pepper
1 package rigatoni noodles, cooked and drained
12 ounces grated mozzarella cheese

■ Brown onions and garlic in large saucepan at medium heat. Add sausage and brown. Drain.

■ Sprinkle with ¼ cup Parmesan cheese. Brown an additional 30 seconds. Add next seven ingredients and remaining Parmesan cheese. Simmer for 20 minutes.

■ Mix noodles and sauce in large bowl.

■ Pour ½ of mixture in 9x13 pan. Sprinkle on ½ of the mozzarella cheese. Add remaining mixture. Sprinkle remaining mozzarella cheese.

■ Cover with foil and bake at 350° for 25 minutes. Uncover and bake additional 5 minutes.

■ Remove and let it sit for 5 minutes before serving.

Serves 6

Quilt contests began in the nineteenth Century. The most successful contest was held in 1933 when 24,000 contestants entered, lured by the $7,500 in cash prizes in the midst of the Depression.

Fettucine with Grilled Chicken and Sun Dried Tomatoes

Susan McMahon - Clarion Hotel Richardson

3 cloves garlic, chopped
¼ medium onion, chopped
¾ cup green onions, tops only, chopped
1 tablespoon olive oil
2 cups chicken broth
½ cup chardonnay wine
4 boneless, skinless breasts of chicken
1 cup chopped sun dried tomatoes, packed in oil
1 cup chopped fresh basil (plus garnish)
1 pound fettucine, cooked and drained
salt and freshly ground black pepper
¼ cup freshly grated Parmesan cheese

■ Sauté onion in olive oil until transparent.

■ Add garlic, sauté one minute, add white wine to deglaze, add chicken broth. Simmer until reduced to 1 cup liquid.

■ Prepare chicken breast: season with salt and pepper, grill, slice into strips; set aside and keep warm.

■ When sauce is reduced, add basil, green onion, sun dried tomatoes, salt and freshly ground pepper to taste.

■ Warm for 1-2 minutes. If too thin, thicken with 1 teaspoon cornstarch and 1 teaspoon water mixture.

■ Toss pasta and sauce. Add chicken. Garnish with basil, Parmesan cheese and freshly ground pepper.

Life is like a patchwork quilt
Little squares of every hue
Some of silk and calico
Some of pink and gold and blue.

But each piece will do its part
Help to make the pattern fine.
And when at last
The quilt is spread
Lovely is its whole design.

Author Unknown

Chicken Picatta

Stacy Stout

1 small onion, peeled and chopped
1 teaspoon minced garlic
5 green onions, chopped
1 teaspoon olive oil
8 4-ounce boneless, skinless chicken breasts
½ cup flour
½ teaspoon salt
½ teaspoon pepper
2 tablespoons margarine
2 tablespoons sherry
2 tablespoons lemon juice
1 tablespoon chopped capers
2 tablespoons chicken broth
8 thinly sliced lemon slices (optional)
2 tablespoons parsley
16 ounces angel hair pasta, cooked and drained
non-stick vegetable spray

■ Spray skillet with non stick spray. Sauté onion, garlic and green onions in olive oil just until tender; remove from the pan and set aside.

■ Pound chicken breasts flat with a meat mallet.

■ Mix the flour, salt and pepper together, and place in a flat bowl. Dip the chicken slices into the flour mixture.

■ Lightly brown chicken slices in margarine, 2 to 3 minutes per side; add the sautéed onions and garlic.

■ Over high heat, add the sherry, lemon juice, capers and chicken broth.

■ Serve over pasta and garnish with thin slices of lemon and parsley.

Serves 8

The China Clippers brought back one of the oldest superstitions that surrounds quiltmaking. It was said that since only God could produce perfection, if a human produced an object without some flaw, it would call the Devil and misfortune would follow. For this very reason, some expert quiltmakers created their own flaws to offset the evil.

Chicken and Artichoke Pasta

Laura Travis

2 whole boneless skinless chicken breasts cut into 1 inch pieces
6 tablespoons unsalted butter, divided use
2 tablespoons vegetable oil
½ cup chopped onion
½ pound sliced mushrooms
1 cup chicken broth
1 9-ounce package frozen artichoke hearts
1 cup chopped tomatoes
¼ cup tomato puree
1 tablespoon parsley
1 tablespoon basil
1 teaspoon sugar
salt and pepper, to taste
1 pound spinach noodles, cooked

■ Season chicken with salt and pepper. Sauté in 2 tablespoons of butter and oil for 2 minutes. Transfer to plate with slotted spoon.

■ In fat remaining in skillet, cook onion until softened. Add mushrooms. Cook until tender. Add broth and bring to a boil. Add artichoke hearts. Simmer 6-7 minutes or until tender.

■ Stir in tomatoes, tomato puree, parsley, basil, sugar, salt and pepper to taste. Bring mixture to simmer. Add chicken. Cook until chicken is hot.

■ Toss cooked noodles with remaining butter.

■ Place noodles on shallow plate and top with sauce.

Serves 4

Most vintage Log Cabin blocks have a red center square that represents the hearth as the center of the cabin. Yellow centers symbolize candles in the cabin window.

Chicken Tetrazzini

Gayle Ingle

1 package spaghetti, cooked and drained
1 stick of butter
2 10 ounce cans mushroom soup
2 4 ounce cans sliced mushrooms
1 pint sour cream
6 chicken breasts
Parmesan cheese

■ Preheat oven to 300°.

■ Sauté mushrooms in butter for 10 minutes.

■ Cut chicken in bite-sized pieces. Add to the mushrooms and sauté for about 3 minutes.

■ Remove from heat. Cover and let stand for 30 minutes.

■ Add soup, sour cream and remainder of ingredients.

■ Place cooked spaghetti in bottom of greased 9x12 casserole dish.

■ Pour chicken and soup mixture over spaghetti. Sprinkle with Parmesan.

■ Bake at 300° for 45 minutes.

Serves 12

The Star is one of the most popular motifs in the history of American quilting. Over one hundred variations of the basic star pattern have been documented.

Five Pepper Chicken

Brenda Brandon

12 ounces linguine, cook
    and drain
1 egg
½ cup milk
¾ cup bread crumbs
¼ cup Parmesan cheese
    salt and pepper to taste
8 boneless, skinless
    chicken breast halves
    flour
    vegetable oil
1½ tablespoons butter
½ cup thin strips each of
    red, yellow, and green
    bell pepper, poblano
    pepper and
    pepperoncini peppers
½ cup chopped red onion
2 tablespoons olive oil
2 teaspoons chopped
    fresh basil
    cherry tomatoes, black
    olives and parsley for
    garnish

■ Beat together egg and milk; reserve.

■ Combine bread crumbs and Parmesan. Season to taste with salt and pepper.

■ Lightly coat chicken breasts with flour, then dip in milk and egg mixture. Press both sides of chicken breast into crumbs to coat evenly.

■ Spray bottom of skillet with non-stick vegetable oil spray. Add ¼ inch of oil and heat over medium high heat. Sauté chicken breasts, four at a time, until crisp and brown on both sides. Add oil if necessary, before cooking second batch. Keep warm.

■ Drain oil from pan and wipe out excess. Add butter to pan over medium heat. Add peppers and onion, tossing and cooking until crisp-tender, 3-4 minutes.

■ Toss warm linguine with olive oil and basil; season to taste with salt and pepper. Serve chicken breasts on bed of linguine. Arrange sautéed peppers and onions over breasts.

■ Garnish with cherry tomatoes, black olives and parsley.

Serves 8

Pine Nuts, Mushroom and Shrimp Pasta

Brenda Brandon

juice of 1 lemon
1 teaspoon grated lemon rind
4 tablespoons softened butter
2 sticks butter
8 ounces sliced mushrooms
4 teaspoons chopped garlic
1 pound medium shrimp, cleaned and peeled
2 cups (about 4 ounces) fresh spinach leaves
8 teaspoons pine nuts
2 teaspoons salt
2 teaspoons pepper
1 pound vermicelli, cooked al dente, drained
4 teaspoons bread crumbs
lemon slices and parsley for garnish

■ Prepare lemon butter by whipping together the lemon juice and rind and softened butter. Chill.

■ Melt 2 sticks of butter in a large skillet over medium heat. Add mushrooms. Sauté briefly.

■ Add garlic and shrimp. Cook just until shrimp begins to color.

■ Add spinach and pine nuts and stir. Add prepared lemon butter, salt and pepper. Bring to a simmer, cooking just until shrimp is done, about 2 minutes.

■ Pour mixture over pasta. Sprinkle with bread crumbs. Garnish with lemon wheels and chopped parsley. Serve immediately.

Serves 6

Crawfish/Shrimp Fettucini

Anne Hobbs

3 sticks margarine
3 onions, chopped fine
2 celery stalks, chopped fine
2 bell peppers, chopped fine
¼ cup flour
1 pint half-and-half
1 pound pasteurized process cheese, cubed, divided use
2 tablespoons jalapeño relish
2 pressed garlic cloves
3 pounds crawfish tails or fresh shrimp
4 tablespoons parsley, chopped fine
salt, red pepper, black pepper to taste
1 pound fettucini, cooked and drained
Parmesan cheese

■ In a large skillet, melt margarine. Sauté vegetables for 15-20 minutes.

■ Add flour, half-and-half, pasteurized process cheese (reserve some for topping), jalapeño relish, garlic, crawfish or shrimp and seasonings. Cook on low heat 30-35 minutes, stirring often.

■ Add cooked noodles and mix thoroughly. Sprinkle with Parmesan cheese and remaining pasteurized process cheese.

■ Bake at 350° for 15-20 minutes.

Serves 12-16

"Ann Landers-type Recipe"

Take two heaping cups of patience, one heartful of love and two handfuls of generosity. Add a dash of laughter, and a full cup of understanding and two cups of loyalty. Mix well and sprinkle generously with kindness. Spread this irresistible delicacy over a lifetime and serve everybody you meet.

* This recipe was originally seen in the Chicago Tribune in Ann Landers column. It reminds me of the wonderful ladies involved in the Junior League of Richardson.

Sherri Hancock

MORNING-GLORIES

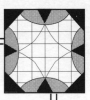

Often a woman displayed only those quilts which she could boast that she had put in every stitch herself. These quilts were laid carefully on the company bed, one on top of the other. They were removed and folded, one at a time, and incidentally admired, by the guest before he or she could retire. It was said that even Martha Washington, an expert needlewoman, kept between fifteen and twenty quilts displayed in this way.

The pictured quilt, while not made with her own hands, will certainly be proudly displayed by Verna Niehaus, who with the price of a raffle ticket became the proud owner of the Flower Basket appliquéd quilt. While she, at 94 years old is still an avid quiltmaker, this one came a little easier than her numerous others, winning it on her 88th birthday.

Baskets - new ones, small ones, old ones, tall ones - all a joy to behold. Baskets have always been a favorite pattern as have been flowers, by far the most profuse design in appliquéd quilts. Is it any wonder that the combining of these ideas gives us the notion that we can almost smell the blooms! The TEXAS SAMPLER thanks Verna Niehaus for sharing her masterpiece "stroke of luck" with us.

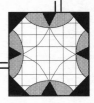

Country French Apple Crescent Casserole

Linda Youngblood

Prepare ahead

> 2 tablespoons sugar
> ½ teaspoon cinnamon
> 1 8-ounce can of crescent dinner rolls
> 1 large apple, peeled, cored, cut in 8 slices

Topping

> ½ cup sugar
> ½ cup whipping cream
> 1 teaspoon almond extract
> 1 egg
> ½ cup sliced almonds
> 1 teaspoon cinnamon

■ Preheat oven to 375°.

■ In small bowl combine 2 tablespoons sugar and ½ teaspoon cinnamon, mix well.

■ Separate crescent rolls into 8 triangles. Sprinkle sugar mixture over each. Press mixture in and flatten slightly.

■ Place 1 apple slice at wide end of each triangle, tuck edges around apple. Roll up starting at wide end. Seal all seams.

■ Place seam side down in ungreased 9-inch round baking dish.

■ Bake for 15-20 minutes or until golden brown.

■ In small bowl whisk first four topping ingredients until well blended. Spoon sauce evenly over partially baked rolls.

■ Sprinkle with sliced almonds and cinnamon.

■ Bake an additional 13 to 18 minutes or until golden brown.

■ Cover pan with foil the last 5 minutes to prevent over browning.

■ Serve warm.

Serves 8

 ## Cinnamon Applesauce Pancakes

Sherri Hancock

1 egg
1 cup flour
½ cup milk
2 tablespoons vegetable oil
1 tablespoon sugar
3 teaspoons baking powder
½ teaspoon salt
½ cup applesauce
¼ teaspoon cinnamon
½ small Granny Smith apple, cut into small chunks (optional)

■ Spray griddle with non-stick spray and heat.

■ Beat egg until fluffy.

■ Beat in remaining ingredients. Add apple to batter (optional).

■ Pour batter onto hot griddle.

■ Cook pancakes until puffed and dry at edge. Turn and cook other side until golden brown.

Makes 7-8 (4- to 5-inch diameter) pancakes.

Add raisins to create a face!

■ ■ ■ *"Handy-Andy" Tip: Pancakes freeze beautifully. Put enough for one serving in a bag and freeze. To serve, thaw before popping in toaster. No time...toast twice.*

Good Morning Granola

Pat Lawler

Prepare ahead

4 cups old-fashioned oats
1 cup pecan halves
1 cup flaked coconut
½ cup wheat germ
½ teaspoon salt
¼ cup cane syrup
¼ cup salad oil
½ cup raisins
½ cup chopped dried apricots
½ cup chopped dried apple slices

■ Place first five ingredients in a 9x13 baking pan.

■ Combine syrup and oil. Pour over all. Mix well.

■ Bake at 375° for 40 minutes. Stirring every 10 minutes.

■ Remove from oven. Cool.

■ Add raisins, apricots and apples.

■ Keep stored in an airtight container.

Makes 8 cups.

Best if made several days in advance.

Asparagus Eggs Amandine

Amy Kelly

2 pounds fresh asparagus
6-8 hard cooked eggs
4 tablespoons butter, divided use
¼ cup minced onion
2 teaspoons powdered curry
2 tablespoons flour
2 cups half-and-half
¾ teaspoons salt
¼ teaspoon Worcestershire sauce
⅛ teaspoon pepper
2 tablespoons minced parsley
½ cup sliced almonds

■ Preheat oven to 225°.

■ Cook whole asparagus spears in salted water to cover until tender but still firm.

■ Drain and arrange in a heat proof service platter.

■ Slice hard cooked eggs and arrange over asparagus.

■ Cover dish with foil and set in oven.

■ In a saucepan, heat 3 tablespoons of the butter and sauté onion.

■ Stir in curry and flour. Cook until bubbly.

■ Gradually stir in half-and-half. Cook, stirring until thickened.

■ Stir in salt, Worcestershire sauce, pepper and parsley. Keep warm.

■ In remaining tablespoon of butter lightly toast almonds.

■ Just before serving pour sauce over asparagus and eggs, sprinkle with almonds.

Serves 4

■ ■ ■ *"Handy-Andy" Tip: Add 1 tablespoon salt to cold water before boiling eggs in order to peel them easier.*

Eggs Creole

Janie Trantham

8 tablespoons butter, divided use
4 tablespoons plus one pinch flour
2 cups milk
½ teaspoon salt
¼ teaspoon pepper
4 tablespoons chopped onion
4 tablespoons chopped green pepper
1 clove garlic, mashed
2½ cups canned tomatoes
½ tablespoon chili powder
8 hard cooked eggs, sliced
1 cup cracker crumbs
4 tablespoons melted butter
1 cup grated pasteurized processed cheese

■ Preheat oven to 350°.

■ Over low heat melt four tablespoons butter and stir in four tablespoons flour. Cook until mixture bubbles.

■ Add milk gradually and stir until the sauce is medium thick. Add salt and pepper and set aside.

■ Prepare tomato sauce by melting four tablespoons of butter and cooking onion and green pepper until soft.

■ Add tomatoes, garlic and chili powder. Cook until medium thick, using a pinch of flour to thicken.

■ Blend white sauce into tomato sauce.

■ Place alternate layers of sauce and sliced eggs in a greased 10-inch casserole.

■ Drizzle melted butter over crumbs. Top with cheese and crumbs.

■ Bake at 350 degrees for 15 to 20 minutes.

■ Serve over rice or Chinese noodles.

Serves 6

If nothing falls off, you're doing OK!

How Not To Make A Prize-Winning Quilt
Ami Simms

Eggs with Tomato Shells

Janie Trantham

4 large ripe tomatoes
  celery salt, to taste
  pepper, to taste
4 eggs
4 slices bacon, broiled
  crisp and crumbled

■ Preheat oven to 375°.

■ Remove the stem of each tomato and carefully scoop out most of the pulp. Chop and retain the pulp.

■ Sprinkle tomato cavity with celery salt and pepper. Break an egg in each cavity.

■ Place chopped pulp on top of egg.

■ Put tomatoes in a baking dish and place a piece of buttered foil on each tomato.

■ Put dish holding the tomatoes into a larger dish filled partially with water and bake tomatoes in oven for 30 minutes at 375°.

■ Serve topped with crumbled bacon.

Serves 4

Egg Cheese Soufflé

Rene Dubois

Prepare ahead

  ½ stick butter
  10 slices of bread, cubed
  8-10 ounces of grated
       Cheddar cheese
  6 eggs, beaten
  2½ cups milk
  1 10-ounce can mushroom
    soup

■ Melt butter in 10x12-inch pan.

■ Mix bread, cheese, eggs and milk and pour into pan.

■ Cover and refrigerate overnight.

■ Set out to reach room temperature (approximately 1½ hours).

■ Spread with mushroom soup, thinned with milk.

■ Bake at 400° for 30 minutes or until browned on top.

Serves 10

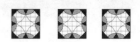

Egg Cheese Shrimp Soufflé

Amy Kelly

Prepare ahead

- 6 slices homemade buttered bread, dried and diced
- 1 can mushrooms, stems and pieces
- ¼ cup stuffed olives, stuffed
- 1 pound tiny frozen shrimp, thawed and patted dry
- ¾ pound shredded sharp Cheddar cheese
- 4 eggs
- 2 cups milk
- ½ teaspoon dry mustard
- ½ teaspoon salt

■ In a 3-quart soufflé or casserole dish, layer in thirds bread, mushroom pieces, olives and shrimp.

■ Sprinkle with cheese.

■ Beat eggs. Add milk, mustard and salt, mixing well.

■ Pour over cheese and cover. Refrigerate overnight.

■ Bring to room temperature, bake covered at 350° for 1 hour.

Serves 6-8

North of the Border Eggs

Annette Weidenfeller

- 12 slices of Canadian bacon
- 12 1-ounce slices of Swiss cheese
- 12 eggs
- 1 cup whipping cream
- ⅓ cup grated Parmesan cheese
  pepper, to taste
  paprika
  chopped parsley

■ Preheat oven to 450°.

■ Place Canadian bacon in a lightly greased 9x13-inch baking dish, top with Swiss cheese.

■ Break eggs into baking dish, spacing evenly.

■ Carefully pour whipping cream over eggs.

■ Bake at 450° for 10 minutes.

■ Sprinkle with Parmesan cheese, pepper and paprika.

■ Bake an additional 8 to 10 minutes, or until set.

■ Sprinkle with parsley, let stand 10 minutes before serving.

Serves 6-8

"Morning Star" Sausage Casserole

Louise Hager

Prepare ahead

6-8 slices of bread, crusts removed, cubed
1 pound fresh sausage, cooked crumbled and drained
½ cup shredded Swiss cheese
½ cup shredded sharp Cheddar cheese
¾ cup half-and-half
1¼ cups milk
6 eggs, beaten
1 teaspoon Worcestershire sauce
1 teaspoon prepared mustard
½ teaspoon salt
⅛ teaspoon pepper

■ Line bottom of greased 9x13-inch pan with bread cubes.

■ Sprinkle cooked sausage over bread and cover with cheeses.

■ Combine half-and-half, milk and eggs.

■ Stir in seasonings and pour over other ingredients.

■ Cover and refrigerate overnight.

■ Bake covered at 350° for one hour.

Serves 10-12

"Lazy Daisy" Breakfast Casserole

Barbara Cass

1 pound sausage (hot or regular)
1 dozen eggs
2 cups grated Cheddar cheese
1 4-ounce can chopped green chilies, drained

■ Preheat oven to 350°.

■ Brown, crumble and drain sausage.

■ Beat eggs and blend in cheese.

■ Mix all ingredients together and place in well greased 9x13 casserole dish.

■ Bake at 350° for 35 to 40 minutes.

Serves 8-10

Huevos Rancheros

Nancy Marston

Salsa

- ½ cup fresh cilantro, chopped
- 3 tomatoes, seeded and chopped
- 1 jalapeño pepper, finely chopped
- ½ medium onion, chopped juice of half a lemon

Eggs

- 4 large eggs
- 1-2 tablespoons milk or cream
- 4 tablespoons sour cream, room temperature
- 4 flour or corn tortillas, warmed butter

■ Mix together all salsa ingredients and set aside.

■ Beat eggs very well with 1 or 2 tablespoons of milk or cream and scramble in a little butter.

■ Use a rubber spatula to turn and cook eggs over a medium low heat.

■ Place two tortillas on each plate.

■ Place eggs in center of each.

■ Spoon salsa over eggs and top with a dollop of sour cream.

Serves 2

■ ■ ■ *"Handy-Andy" Tip: To test an egg for freshness, put in a bowl of water. If the egg floats, it is too old to use.*

A man spoke lovingly of the many quilting bees he attended as a child. He said mothers took their children along and likely as not, the children had as much fun as the women. Two or three quilting frames were always set up on the long L-shaped porch. The children would play while listening to the mothers talk. He said the children never understood the whole conversations though, because just as the ladies got to the interesting parts...they would whisper! Some things indeed never change.

Cheese Chorizo Strata

Pat Lawler

Prepare ahead

¼ pound Chorizo sausage, cooked and drained

¼ cup chopped green chilies

¼ cup minced fresh jalapeño pepper

⅓ pound grated Monterey Jack cheese

3 cups French bread cubes

5 tablespoons butter, melted, divided use

4 eggs

¾ teaspoon cumin

½ teaspoon salt

½ teaspoon pepper

2⅔ cups milk

■ Preheat 300°.

■ Spread sausage evenly in the bottom of a well greased casserole dish.

■ Add, in order, chilies, jalapeños, cheese and bread cubes.

■ Drizzle with melted butter.

■ Whisk eggs in a medium bowl. Add spices and milk to egg mixture and whisk.

■ Pour into casserole dish. Cover and refrigerate overnight.

■ Place the casserole dish in a pan of hot water and bake at 300° for 1 ½ hours, or until it is puffed and set.

Serves 8-10

Serve with your favorite salsa and sour cream.

Mexican Style Eggs

Diane Day

¼ pound sliced bacon

¼ cup diced onions

1 10-ounce can tomatoes with green chilies

⅛ pound grated sharp Cheddar cheese

¼ teaspoon garlic salt black pepper to taste

6 eggs

6 slices toasted bread

■ Cut bacon into small pieces and fry slowly until almost crisp.

■ Add onions and sauté. Add tomatoes, cheese, garlic salt and pepper. Simmer, stirring constantly for 6 minutes.

■ Carefully break eggs onto top of tomato sauce in skillet. Cover and simmer for 3 to 5 minutes to poach eggs.

■ To serve, place an egg on each piece of toast and spoon sauce over eggs.

Serves 6

Avocado Omelet

Bonnie Post

1 avocado, chopped
¼ cup sour cream
2 tablespoons chopped green chilies
1 tablespoon chopped green onion
1 teaspoon lemon juice
¼ teaspoon salt
 dash of hot pepper sauce
2 tablespoons butter
2 corn tortillas, torn into pieces
6-8 eggs
1 cup grated Monterey Jack cheese

■ Preheat oven to 325°.

■ Combine first seven ingredients and set aside.

■ Melt butter in a 10-inch skillet. Add tortilla pieces and cook until soft.

■ Pour in eggs and cook three to five minutes over medium heat, lifting eggs to allow raw ones to flow under.

■ Remove from heat. sprinkle with cheese and place skillet in 325° oven for three to four minutes, or until cheese melts.

■ Spread avocado mixture over half the omelet, and return to oven for five minutes.

■ Fold in half to serve.

Serves 4

■ ■ ■ *"Handy-Andy" Tip: To ripen an avocado, place it in a paper bag with a ripe apple. Poke small holes in the bag to allow the carbon dioxide to escape.*

For fluffier omelets add a pinch of cornstarch before beating eggs.

Chili Egg Puff

Mary Jackson

10 eggs
½ cup flour
1 pint cottage cheese
1 pound shredded Monterey Jack cheese
½ cup butter, melted
1 8-ounce can chopped green chilies, drained
1 teaspoon baking powder
½ teaspoon salt

■ Preheat oven to 350°.

■ Beat eggs until lemon colored.

■ Stir in remaining ingredients, mixing well.

■ Pour into a 9x11-inch baking dish.

■ Bake at 350° for 30 minutes or until done.

Serves 10-12

Serve with salsa on the side.

 ## Chili Rellenos Crescent Pie

Nancy Marston

1 8-ounce can of refrigerated crescent rolls
2 tablespoons cornmeal
1½ cups grated Monterey Jack cheese
1 cup grated Cheddar cheese
1 4-ounce can chopped green chilies
3 eggs, slightly beaten
1 cup sour cream

■ Preheat oven to 350°.

■ Separate dough into 8 triangles and place in ungreased 9-inch pie pan. Press over bottom and up sides to form crust.

■ Sprinkle cornmeal over crust. Press into crust.

■ In bowl, combine cheeses, reserving ½ cup for topping.

■ Add green chilies and sprinkle over crust.

■ Beat eggs and sour cream until smooth. Pour over cheese mixture.

■ Sprinkle with reserved cheese.

■ Bake at 350° for 35-45 minutes or until knife inserted near center comes out clean.

■ Cool 5 minutes before serving.

Serves 6

■ ■ ■ *"Handy-Andy" Tip: Cover edge of crust with foil during first 20 minutes.*

 ## Onion Ring Crab Quiche

Susan Bynum

3 eggs
1 cup sour cream
½ teaspoon Worcestershire sauce
¾ teaspoon salt
1 cup grated Swiss cheese
1 6-ounce can crabmeat, drained
1 3-ounce can of French fried onion rings
1 9-inch deep dish pie crust, unbaked

■ Preheat oven to 325°.

■ Mix eggs, sour cream, Worcestershire sauce, salt, Swiss cheese, crabmeat and onion rings.

■ Pour into crust.

■ Bake at 325° for 1 hour.

Serves 6

May be prepared ahead.

Savory Crustless Quiche

Annette Weidenfeller

8 ounces grated Monterey Jack cheese
12 ounces small curd cottage cheese
⅓ cup cheddar cheese
¼ cup biscuit baking mix
1 teaspoon salt
½ stick butter or margarine (softened)
6 eggs, slightly beaten
4 ounces chopped green chilies, drained
3-4 green onions, chopped
1 6-ounce can sliced mushrooms

■ Preheat oven to 375°.

■ Mix all ingredients and pour into a well greased 9x13-inch baking dish.

■ Bake at 375° for 15 minutes.

■ Lower heat to 325° and continue baking for 40 minutes longer.

■ Let stand 5 minutes before cutting into serving squares.

Serves 12

■ ■ ■ *"Handy-Andy" Tip: Grate an entire block of cheese at one time and freeze in freezer bags to be used as needed.*

Mushroom Quiche

Lisa Matchett

8-12 eggs
1 cup milk
1 tablespoon flour
1 pound Cheddar cheese, shredded
1 pound mozzarella, shredded
4 ounces fresh mushrooms, sliced
1½ pounds hot sausage, cooked, crumbled and drained
sliced jalapeños, to taste (optional)
chopped green onions, to taste (optional)
2 pie crusts

■ Preheat oven to 350°.

■ Mix eggs, milk and flour.

■ Add cheese, mushrooms, and optional fillers.

■ Place sausage in crusts, pour mixed ingredients over sausage.

■ Bake at 350° for 30 minutes.

Makes 2 quiches

Salmon Quiche

Joan Wright

- 1 unbaked 9-inch deep dish pastry shell
- 1 6.5-ounce can red salmon
- 4 slices cooked bacon, crumbled
- 1½ cups cream
- 1 cup Cheddar cheese, grated
- 3 eggs, beaten
- 2 tablespoons parsley, chopped
- 1 tablespoon Parmesan cheese, grated
- ½ teaspoon paprika

- ■ Preheat oven to 450°.
- ■ Drain and flake salmon, reserving liquid. Spread salmon evenly on pastry shell and layer bacon on top.
- ■ Beat together remaining ingredients, adding reserved salmon liquid.
- ■ Gently pour cream mixture over salmon.
- ■ Bake at 450° for 10 minutes, then reduce to 350° and continue baking for another 30-35 minutes or until set.

Serves 4-6

"Triple X" Cheese Casserole

Dede Jackson

- 1 pound pasteurized process cheese, cut in chunks
- 8 ounces grated sharp Cheddar cheese
- 8 ounces large curd cottage cheese
- 4 eggs
- ¾ stick butter
- 2 tablespoons flour

- ■ Preheat oven to 350°.
- ■ Butter a 9x12 casserole dish.
- ■ Mix all ingredients well and place in dish.
- ■ Cook at 350° for 30 minutes or until bubbly and beginning to brown on top.

Serves 8-10

If you want warmth, buy an electric blanket.

How To Not Make A Prize-Winning Quilt
Ami Simms

Egg, Bacon & Ham Brunch Bread

Kathy Tuthill

6 slices bacon, chopped
6 eggs, well beaten
¾ cup milk
1½ cups flour
2½ teaspoons baking powder
½ teaspoon salt
1 cup chopped ham
1 cup cubed Swiss cheese
1 cup cubed Cheddar cheese

■ Preheat oven to 350°.

■ Brown bacon in skillet; drain.

■ Combine eggs, milk, flour, baking powder and salt in bowl, mixing by hand until smooth.

■ Stir in bacon, ham and cheeses. Pour into greased and floured loaf pan.

■ Bake at 350° for 50 to 60 minutes or until bread tests done.

■ Cool in pan on wire rack.

Serves 12

Bread is delicious toasted.

Sausage Bread

Lisa Matchett

1½ pounds hot sausage
1 package hot roll mix
1 pound shredded Cheddar cheese
1 pound shredded mozzarella cheese
1 egg white

■ Cook, drain and crumble sausage.

■ Prepare hot roll mix per package instructions and flatten on counter.

■ Sprinkle sausage, Cheddar cheese and mozzarella cheese in center. Let rise for 30 minutes.

■ Fold dough over sausage and cheese. Drizzle egg white over top of dough.

■ Bake at 350° for 20-25 minutes.

Serves 8-10

Hot Curried Fruit

Julie Robinson

2 17-ounce cans chunky mixed fruits
1 11-ounce can Mandarin oranges
1 16-ounce can pitted black cherries
1 20-ounce can pineapple chunks
2 bananas, cut in 1- to 2- inch chunks
1 4-ounce jar maraschino cherries
½ cup brown sugar
2 tablespoons cornstarch
1 teaspoon curry powder
½ cup melted butter or margarine

■ Preheat oven to 350°.

■ Pour all fruit (except banana) in colander and drain well.

■ Place in 9x13 glass baking dish.

■ Add bananas.

■ Combine all dry ingredients mixing well. Sift over fruit.

■ Pour melted butter or margarine over all and bake at 350° for 40 minutes.

Serves 10-12

Great served with brunch or with chicken, turkey or ham.

Memories stitched into a quilt help you remember and revisit the people, places and events in your life. They afford others the opportunity to utilize a similar window to view part of your journey.

Blintz Soufflé

Linda Youngblood

12 blintzes (from frozen food section)
4 eggs
½ cup sugar
1 teaspoon vanilla
14 ounces sour cream
½ pound margarine

■ Preheat oven to 350°.

■ Place frozen blintzes on bottom of 9x13-inch pan.

■ Mix eggs, sugar, vanilla, sour cream and margarine and pour over blintzes.

■ Bake at 350° until brown for 45 minutes to 1 hour.

Serves 12

Care of your quilt:

1. Do not store in plastic bags or in cedar chests.

2. Use acid-free tissue to wrap the quilts or store them in old pillow cases or soft sheets. Unless the quilt is made of wool, mothballs or other preservatives are not required.

3. Fold your quilt in new ways periodically; this keeps the quilt from getting permanent folds, eventually breaking down the fibers.

4. A quilt should be washed approximately every five years when it is in storage to prevent yellowing. When a quilt is in use it should be washed not more often that twice a year unless absolutely necessary.

5. Use mild soap or detergent in warm, never hot, water. If the machine has a fragile setting, use it.

6. Never wring the water out of a quilt or twist - such treatment breaks the stitches and weakens the quilt.

7. Dry it in a dryer, if possible...this fluffs the cotton filler and makes the quilt look better.

8. Never iron a quilt. This prevents the quilting from standing out, thus spoiling the effectiveness of the whole quilt.

9. If in doubt, it is always advisable to consult a professional.

GOING HOME

Everyone loves the quilt! For centuries it has been an art practiced by the women of many lands. It holds one of the most popular, prominent, and important positions in all needlecraft providing vast fields for displaying individual tastes and self-expression. It is said that women cherished and saved a "nicely bent" needle for they were as fitted to the quilters' fingers as gloves were to one's hands.

While there are literally hundreds of known quilt patterns, with just the slightest rearrangement of the basic elements, there still exist an unlimited number of unique and original patch designs not yet developed. To this end in 1991, Joanna Shampine, a true artisan, designed, pieced and quilted the pictured Tulip quilt. The Tulip is second in popularity only to the Rose, and can closely resemble the real flower or may be more abstract or geometric in design. She based the center and outside borders on the antique pattern Sister's Choice.

As was often the case with the pioneer women, a patch pattern was based on what they were familiar with or what they saw. Joanna designed the center squares based on how tulips would look when viewed from an upstairs window; the border on how tulips would appear when viewed from the side with grass bordering the outside of the bed.

The Tulip quilt displayed won second place in the 1992 Dallas Quilt Show and the Ruth Anderson Special Quilt Award at the 1993 State Fair of Texas. The TEXAS SAMPLER thanks Joanna Shampine for sharing her creative masterpiece vision.

Two Hour Rib Eye Roast

Sherry McMenamy

1 8 to 9 pound rib eye
roast
cracked black pepper
salt

■ Preheat oven to 500°.

■ Rub the rib eye all over with pepper. Place in a shallow pan.

■ Put the roast in hot oven and close door. Do not open the door for 2 hours.

■ Cook meat 6 minutes per pound at 500°.

■ Turn off oven when meat has cooked specified time. From the time you start the roast until it is ready to slice will be 2 hours.

■ Pour part of the fat out of the pan. Add some water and salt for natural gravy.

Serves 8-10

You may want to cook your roast for additional minutes per pound if you don't like your meat quite as pink.

"A Dandy" Rump Roast

Gina Banister

1 4 pound rump roast,
trimmed of all fat
(except layer on bottom)
1 10-ounce can cream of
mushroom soup
salt and pepper, to taste
½ teaspoon bottled brown
bouquet sauce

■ Preheat oven to 350°.

■ Place roast on large sheet of aluminum foil. Season generously with salt and pepper. Spread soup on top.

■ Wrap roast in foil and seal tightly. Repeat foil wrap.

■ Place in pan and bake at 350° for 3 to 3½ hours.

■ Remove from oven. Snip through all foil on a corner. Drain off juices into a medium saucepan. Add bottled brown bouquet sauce and thicken for gravy.

■ Slice roast in about ¼ inch slices.

Elegant Roast Tenderloin

Kathy Whipple

Prepare ahead

    ¼ cup dry white wine
    ¼ cup brandy
    3 tablespoons lemon juice
    2 tablespoons snipped
        chives
1 ½ teaspoons salt
    ¼ teaspoon freshly ground
        pepper
    1 teaspoon
        Worcestershire sauce
    1 2 pound roast
        tenderloin
    2 tablespoons water
    2 tablespoons margarine
    8 ounces mushrooms,
        halved and sautéed in
        butter
    plastic cooking bag

■ For marinade: combine wine, brandy, lemon juice, chives, salt, pepper and Worcestershire sauce.

■ Place meat in plastic cooking bag and place in loaf pan. Add marinade and seal. Refrigerate overnight or let stand at room temperature no more than 2 hours. Press bag occasionally.

■ Preheat oven to 425°.

■ Remove meat from bag and wipe with paper towels, reserving marinade.

■ Place on rack in shallow roasting pan and roast 45-55 minutes at 425°, basting occasionally with half of the marinade.

■ Heat remaining marinade, water and margarine in a small pan until bubbly.

■ Slice meat, arrange on heated platter and spoon sauce over. Garnish with sautéed mushrooms.

Serves 8

People with big chests shouldn't quilt in small cars.

How Not To Make A Prize-Winning Quilt
Ami Simms

Italian Tenderloin of Beef

Mary Pittman

Prepare ahead

 1 7-pound tenderloin, fat
 trimmed
 1 tablespoon soy sauce
 1 tablespoon brown sugar
 ½ cup Italian dressing
 ¼ cup lemon juice

■ Place tenderloin in a 9x13 inch pan. Line pan with foil for quicker clean up.

■ Combine remainder of ingredients and pour over tenderloin. Marinate in refrigerator several hours or overnight.

■ Turn oven to broil. Place pan with tenderloin and marinade in oven on bottom shelf. Broil 20 minutes on each side.

■ Preheat oven to 350°. Then cover and bake at 350° for 10 to 15 minutes.

■ Cut into 12 thick fillets.

Serves 12

Burgundy Sirloin Over Rice

Anne Koval

 2 tablespoon oil
 2 pounds sirloin, cut into
 cubes
 1 10-ounce can beef broth
 ⅓ cup Burgundy wine
 2 tablespoons soy sauce
 2 cloves garlic, minced
 ¼ teaspoon onion powder
 ¼ cup water
 2 tablespoons cornstarch

■ Brown sirloin tips in oil.

■ Add remaining ingredients. Bring to a boil. Reduce heat and simmer 1 hour.

■ Mix cornstarch with water. Add to mixture. Simmer till slightly thickened.

■ Serve over rice.

Serves 6-8

■ ■ ■ *"Handy-Andy" Tip: For ease when slicing or cubing meat, partially freeze meat beforehand.*

Connecticut Supper

Charlotte Sullivan

2 large onions, chopped
2 tablespoons shortening
2 pounds chuck, cut in 1-inch cubes
1 cup water
2-3 large potatoes, cut into ⅛-inch slices
1 can cream of mushroom soup
1 cup sour cream
1¼ cups milk
1 teaspoon salt
¼ teaspoon pepper
1 cup grated Cheddar cheese

■ Brown onions in shortening. Add beef cubes. Brown and then add water. Cover and simmer for 50 minutes.

■ Preheat oven to 350°.

■ Pour meat mixture in a 9x13 pan. Place potato slices on meat.

■ Blend soup, sour cream, milk, salt and pepper. Pour evenly over the top of meat. Sprinkle with cheese.

■ Bake uncovered for 1½ hours.

Serves 6-8

■ ■ ■ *"Handy-Andy" Tip: Rice will be light and fluffy if a teaspoon of vinegar or lemon juice is added while cooking.*

 ## "Texas Treasures" Stroganoff

Kathleen Denny

½ cup minced onion
¼ cup margarine
1 pound ground beef, browned and drained
1 clove garlic, minced
2 tablespoons flour
2 teaspoons salt
¼ teaspoon seasoned salt (optional)
¼ teaspoon pepper
¼ teaspoon paprika
2 4-ounce cans mushrooms
1 10-ounce can cream of chicken soup
1 cup sour cream
parsley

■ Sauté onion in butter until golden, stir in meat, garlic, flour, salt, seasoned salt, pepper, paprika and mushrooms. Sauté 5 minutes.

■ Add soup and simmer 10 minutes.

■ Stir in sour cream.

■ Serve on rice or noodles.

■ Garnish with parsley.

Serves 4-6

Round steak cut into strips can be used in place of ground beef.

Vegetable-Swiss Steak

Dana Bell

¼ cup flour
1½ teaspoons salt
⅛ teaspoon pepper
1½ pounds round steak -
    1-inch thick
1 tablespoon shortening
1 medium onion, chopped
1 20-ounce can tomatoes,
    drain, reserve liquid
1 box frozen mixed
    vegetables

■ Combine flour, salt and pepper in a bag. Add serving size cuts of meat in bag and shake to coat.

■ Melt shortening in a large skillet, add meat and brown on all sides.

■ Add onion and cook until onion is slightly transparent.

■ Add ¼ cup reserved tomato liquid to remaining seasoned flour and stir until smooth.

■ Add tomatoes mixture to meat and bring to a boil. Cover and cook 3 hours.

■ Uncover and add mixed vegetables. Cook 15 minutes or until vegetables are done.

■ Serve with mashed potatoes.

Serves 6

Easy to make before the kids get out of school to serve for dinner that night!

Quilter's Tip

The work of your hands reveals the love that is in your heart. Skill puts the pieces together, but love applies the art.

When skill, by itself is used, the work - alone - may please. But when skill and love work together, expect...a masterpiece!!!

Mary Horner

Mushroom, Beef & Noodle Casserole

Joan Wright

2 onions, chopped
2 cloves garlic, finely chopped
1 bell pepper, chopped
2 tablespoons vegetable oil
2 pounds ground beef
1 29-ounce can chopped tomatoes
½ cup chopped black olives, drained
1 8-ounce can mushrooms
salt and pepper, to taste
1 8-ounce package of medium noodles
8 ounces processed American cheese, shredded

■ Preheat oven to 325°.

■ In a large skillet, sauté onions, garlic and bell pepper in oil until soft, then brown meat and drain.

■ Add the tomatoes, olives, and mushrooms, salt and pepper.. Cover and simmer slowly for about 15 minutes.

■ Cook noodles according to package directions. Drain and add to meat mixture.

■ Add cheese, stirring until it melts. Transfer from skillet to casserole dish(es) and bake at 325° for 30 minutes.

Serves 8-10

Italian Rice

Robin Kelly

1 cup rice
¼ cup salad oil
1 pound ground beef
1 onion, chopped
1 clove garlic, minced
½ teaspoon salt
¼ teaspoon pepper
3 cups tomato juice
2 cups water
1 teaspoon sugar
1 cup grated Cheddar cheese

■ Heat oil in a skillet, add rice and cook stirring constantly about 10 minutes until lightly browned.

■ Add meat, onions, garlic, salt and pepper. Cook stirring frequently about 10 minutes.

■ Add tomato juice, water and sugar. Simmer over low heat 15 to 20 minutes, or until rice is tender. Add more water, if needed.

■ Add grated cheese, stir until cheese is melted.

Serves 6

"Noon and Night"Meatloaf

Laura Garretson

1 ½ pounds ground beef
1 cup cracker crumbs
2 eggs, beaten
½ cup chopped onion
2 tablespoons chopped
  green pepper
1 ½ teaspoons salt
2 tablespoons
  Worcestershire sauce
1 4-ounce can tomato
  sauce

Sauce:

½ cup ketchup
⅓ cup brown sugar
1 ½ tablespoons
  Worcestershire sauce
½ teaspoon mustard

■ Preheat oven to 350°.

■ Mix ingredients in order given and shape into loaf.

■ Bake in a 1 ½ quart loaf pan for 1 ¼ hours at 350°.

■ Mix together ingredients for the sauce.

■ Drain meat and pour sauce over top.

■ Return to oven for 15 minutes.

Serves 6

■ ■ ■ *"Handy-Andy" Tip: Meatloaf won't crack when baking if it's rubbed with cold water before going into the oven.*

Nancy's Golden Meat Loaf

Tomi Morriss

1 ½ pounds lean ground
  beef
2 eggs
⅔ cup milk
2 teaspoons salt
¼ teaspoon pepper
3 slices bread, crumbled
1 chopped onion
½ cup grated carrot
1 cup grated Cheddar
  cheese

Topping:

¼ cup ketchup
¼ cup brown sugar
1 tablespoon prepared
  mustard

■ Preheat oven to 350°.

■ Combine the first nine ingredients. Shape into a loaf. Put in an 8x8 baking pan.

■ Bake at 350° for 45 minutes.

■ Mix topping ingredients together. Spread on meat loaf.

■ Return to oven and bake for 15 minutes.

■ Let stand for 10 minutes before serving.

Serves 6

This freezes great!

 Tator Tot Casserole

Janette Williams

1 pound ground beef
1 medium onion, chopped
1 teaspoon salt
1 teaspoon pepper
1 10-ounce can cream
  of mushroom soup
  (or chicken)
⅔ can of water
1 cup Cheddar cheese,
  grated
1 32-ounce bag of tator
  tots

■ Preheat oven to 350°.

■ Brown meat mixture with onion and drain. Add salt and pepper.

■ Mix soup and water in meat mixture.

■ Place in 3-quart casserole. Top with cheese.

■ Line tator tots across top of casserole.

■ Bake at 350° until the tots are brown and casserole is heated.

Serves 4-6

Ropa Vieja (Old Clothes !!)

Cuqui Levine

2 pounds flank steak
1 onion
1 green bell pepper
2 garlic cloves, chopped
⅓ cup olive oil
1 10-ounce can tomato
  sauce or stewed
  tomatoes
1 teaspoon salt
¼ teaspoon pepper
½ cup white sauterne
  cooking wine
1 bay leaf

■ Boil the meat until done. Let it cool. Separate into long strips and set aside.

■ Cut the onion in fine rings and separate. Cut the bell pepper in long strips.

■ Sauté the garlic in oil with onion and bell pepper, until onion is lightly brown.

■ Add all remaining ingredients. Cook slowly for 15-20 minutes, covered. Stir every 5 minutes to prevent sticking.

■ Serve with white rice and a mixed salad.

Serves 6-8

■ ■ ■ *"Handy-Andy" Tip: Inexpensive cuts of meat can be tenderized by cooking in tea instead of water.*

Salpicon (Shredded Meat)

Martha Welch

Must be prepared ahead!

8 pounds top sirloin or
    eye of round
2 cloves garlic
1 bay leaf
1 12-ounce can tomatoes
¼ cup fresh cilantro
    salt and pepper to taste
1 bottle Italian salad
    dressing
1 cup cooked garbanzo
    beans, drained
½ pound Monterey Jack
    cheese, cut in ½-inch
    squares
1 cup chopped green
    chilies
2 avocados, cut in strips
1 bunch parsley, garnish

■ Place beef in heavy-duty stew pot; cover with water and add garlic, bay leaf, tomatoes, cilantro, salt and pepper. Cook over medium heat about 5 hours.

■ Drain and cool meat. Cut into 2-inch squares. Shred and arrange into a 9x11 inch casserole dish.

■ Cover beef with salad dressing and allow to marinate overnight in refrigerator.

■ Before serving, arrange in layers over the beef: beans, cheese, chilies, avocados. Garnish with parsley.

Serves 16

Texas Brisket

Jill Herod

1 7 to 9 pound brisket
    celery salt
    onion salt
    garlic salt
½ bottle liquid smoke
    barbecue sauce

■ Preheat oven to 250°.

■ Generously salt brisket with celery, onion, and garlic salts. Pour ½ bottle of liquid smoke over brisket.

■ Cover with foil and bake 5-6 hours (fat side down) at 250°.

■ When tender, uncover and pour off juices. Pour your favorite barbecue sauce over brisket. Bake uncovered an additional 20 minutes.

■ Slice and serve.

Serves 10-12

Brisket slices easier after being refrigerated.

 ## South of the Border Fiesta

Julie Robinson

Great for a Party!

1 large onion, chopped
2 pounds ground beef
2 teaspoons chili powder
2 teaspoons oregano
2 teaspoons cumin
(ground or seeds)
2 teaspoons salt
2 teaspoons seasoned salt
flavored enhancer
(optional)
3-4 tablespoons sugar, add
to taste
2 cloves garlic, chopped
or pressed
2 8-ounce cans tomato
sauce
5⅓ cans water
3 6-ounce cans tomato
paste
Condiments:

chopped onion
sliced green onions
chopped bell peppers
shredded lettuce
chopped tomatoes
can of kidney beans or
pinto beans, drained
sliced black olives
sliced jalapeños
avocados, chunks or
guacamole
sour cream
grated Cheddar cheese
salsa or picante sauce
small corn chips

■ Brown ground beef and onion together. Drain well.

■ Combine all other ingredients and simmer on low flame 1 ½ to 2 hours.

Serves 6-8. May be doubled, tripled, etc., as needed!

To serve the supper: Each person ladles the sauce over a pile of small corn chips. Then garnish with all of the condiments!

My Very Best Taco Casserole
Julie Robinson

1 pound ground beef
½ cup chopped onion
1 package taco seasoning
1 15-ounce can kidney beans
1 6-ounce can tomato paste
½ cup water
1 6-ounce can sliced ripe olives (optional)
½ cup sour cream
½ cup tortilla chips, slightly crushed
1 cup grated cheese (Monterey Jack or Cheddar)

■ Preheat oven to 350°.

■ Cook onion and ground beef in large skillet until beef is brown and onion is tender. Drain.

■ Add taco seasoning, kidney beans with liquid, tomato paste and water. Simmer for about 10 minutes.

■ Pour into 9-inch square baking dish or equivalent. Top with olives. Spread sour cream over top. Add crushed tortilla chips and cheese.

■ Bake at 350° for 15-20 minutes or until heated through and cheese is melted.

Serves 6

Can be made ahead up to the sour cream stage and refrigerated. Remove from refrigerator and bring to room temperature. Add chips cheese, then bake.

Serve with salsa

"Stepping Stones" Enchiladas

Dana Bell

1 pound ground meat
1 large onion, diced
1 10-ounce can mushroom soup
1 10-ounce can cream of chicken soup
1 10-ounce can enchilada sauce (mild or hot depending upon taste)
1 6-ounce can green chilies, chopped
1 pound longhorn cheese, grated
6 corn tortillas

■ Preheat oven to 350°.

■ Brown meat and onion together. Drain off excess liquid.

■ Add both soups, enchilada sauce, and chilies to the meat mixture. Simmer approximately 20 minutes.

■ Grease 9x13 casserole dish. Tear tortillas into pieces placing them in bottom of casserole dish.

■ Pour ½ of meat mixture over tortillas. Add ½ of cheese. Repeat layers.

■ Bake at 350° for 30 minutes or until bubbly.

Serves 4-6

"In the early days of our state's history, quilting was work born out of necessity. Scraps of cloth were salvaged and pieced together to produce items that provided warmth. Yet despite their functional nature, many of these early quilts included intricate patterns and designs that reflected a keen eye for the exacting standards of fine workmanship - precise stitching, symmetry of pattern, and a strong sense of color - all hallmarks that have elevated the craft to be a form of artistic expression.

Over the years, these standards of excellence have become a part of the tradition itself; traditional art forms, have come to symbolize those aspects of our heritage that we most treasure. Quilters no longer pursue their craft out of necessity. Instead, they recognize the importance and value of preserving and passing on the best..."

Bill Clinton
State of Arkansas
Office of the Governor

Enchilada Pie

Christine Power

2 pounds ground beef
2 onions, sliced
3 bell peppers, red, green, or a combination, sliced
2 cloves garlic, minced
1 teaspoon salt, divided use
½ teaspoon pepper, divided use
1 28-ounce can tomatoes, drained
1 tablespoon red wine vinegar
2 teaspoons cumin
1 teaspoon oregano
6 flour tortillas
¾ cup grated Cheddar cheese
¾ cup grated Monterey Jack cheese
2 fresh jalapeño peppers, sliced

■ Preheat oven to 350°.

■ Cook ground beef in a large skillet until no longer pink. Remove meat with a slotted spoon.

■ Add onions, bell peppers, garlic, ½ teaspoon salt and ¼ teaspoon pepper and cook until soft, about 15 minutes. Remove with a slotted spoon and return meat to pan.

■ Add vinegar, cumin, oregano, ½ teaspoon salt , ¼ teaspoon pepper. Break up tomatoes. Simmer 10 minutes.

■ Line bottom and sides of a 2 quart baking dish with 4 tortillas. Put in ½ of the meat mixture and top with ½ of the onion mixture. Cover with 2 tortillas. Repeat layering of meat mixture and onion mixture.

■ Top with cheeses and sprinkle with jalapeño peppers.

■ Cover loosely with foil. Bake at 350° for 20 minutes.

■ Uncover and bake an additional 10 minutes.

Serves 6

If it doesn't fit, pull on it or cut it off.

How Not To Make a Prize-Winning Quilt
Ami Simms

 ## Mamma's Favorite Deep Dish Pizza   *Louanne Grimes*

Prepare ahead

Pizza Crust:

    2¼ teaspoons dry yeast
        (1 package)
    1 cup warm water
    3½ cups flour
    ½ teaspoon salt
    ½ teaspoon sugar
    ⅓ cup corn oil
    2 tablespoons olive oil

Pizza Sauce:

    3 8-ounce cans tomato
      sauce
    2 teaspoons olive oil
    ½ teaspoon oregano
    ½ teaspoon basil
    ¼-½ teaspoon garlic powder
      pepper to taste
    1 tablespoon Romano or
      Parmesan cheese
      (optional)

Toppings:

    mozzarella cheese
    meats
    vegetables

■ Preheat oven to 400°.

■ Dissolve yeast in warm water. Set aside.

■ Mix all dry ingredients together. Make a well in dry ingredients and pour water and oils into well. Stir from inside out. Mix well by hand or with dough hooks.

■ Cover dough with plastic wrap. Put bowl in a warm place for 1 hour.

■ Deflate dough then divide in 3 greased 10-inch pans.

■ Cover again with plastic wrap. Let dough rise for 1 hour. Deflate again. Spread dough out with fingers.

■ For pizza sauce, mix ingredients together. Spread approximately 8-ounces per pizza.

■ Layer pizza crust with cheese, then add favorite meats and/or vegetables, spread the pizza sauce on top.

■ Bake at 400° for 30 minutes.

Makes 3 10-inch pizzas

"Hunter's Star" Chicken Fried Backstrap *Barron Hobbs*

1 venison backstrap
⅓ cup milk
vegetable oil
¾ cup flour
1 tablespoon creole seasoning (or to taste)
2 teaspoons pepper (or to taste)
1 teaspoon salt (or to taste)
1 teaspoon red pepper (or to taste)
1 egg, well beaten

■ Pour generous amount of oil into cast iron skillet/pot for frying on medium high heat.

■ Cut backstrap into medallions. Cover with plastic wrap. Pound till flat.

■ Beat egg and milk together in a bowl.

■ Combine flour and seasonings in shallow plate.

■ Dip venison in egg/milk mixture. Dredge through flour mixture. Repeat in egg/milk and flour mixture.

■ When oil is hot enough for frying, place battered venison in skillet and fry until brown. Turn and fry other side. Drain venison on paper towels.

Serves 4

Serve with mashed potatoes and black-eyed peas!

■ ■ ■ *"Handy-Andy" Tip: Barron says, "While your wife is not looking, sneak into the garage and get a claw hammer. Beat the venison medallions until flat. I promise it's the hammer that makes the recipe."*

⏱ Southwest Blackened Pork Chops

Amy Kelly

Heat up outdoor grill

- 4 boneless pork loin or rib chops, ½ inch thick
- 1 teaspoon vegetable oil
- 1½ tablespoons chili powder
- 1 teaspoon crushed fennel seed
- ½ teaspoon cumin
- 1¼ cups salsa
- 2 small oranges, peeled, segmented and coarsely chopped
- ¼ cup sliced green onion

■ Rub both sides of pork chops with oil.

■ Combine chili powder, fennel seed and cumin. Put seasoning mixture onto both sides of each pork chop.

■ Over medium hot coals, grill pork 5 minutes on each side or until no longer pink in center.

■ In a medium bowl, combine salsa, oranges and green onions. Mix well. Serve with pork chops.

Serves 4

Grilled Coriander Pepper Chops

Kellye Price

Heat up outdoor grill

- 2 cloves garlic, crushed
- 1 tablespoon crushed coriander seeds
- 1 tablespoon coarsely ground black pepper
- 1 tablespoon brown sugar
- 3 tablespoons soy sauce (low sodium)
- 4 boneless pork chops, about 1 inch thick

■ Combine all ingredients except pork chops. Place chops in shallow dish and pour marinade over them. Marinate 30 minutes.

■ Drain pork, discarding marinade.

■ Grill chops over indirect medium hot heat for 12-15 minutes, turning once.

Serves 4

Marinated Pork Tenderloins

Mary Wylie

Prepare ahead

- 3 pork tenderloins
- 2 cloves garlic
- 1 tablespoon ground pepper
- ½ cup soy sauce
- 3 tablespoons sugar
- 2 tablespoons oil
- ½ cup sesame seeds

■ Preheat oven to 375°.

■ Mix together all of the ingredients except pork tenderloins.

■ Trim any fat and pour marinade over tenderloins. Marinate at least 3 hours in refrigerator.

■ Bake uncovered for 45 minutes at 375°.

■ To serve; cut into thin strips and pour any remaining marinade over pork.

Serves 6

Pozole

Karen Washington

Prepare ahead

- 2 cups hominy
- 6 cups water
- 1 pork roast or 2 tenderloins
- 2 teaspoons salt
- 2 cloves garlic, chopped
- 2 teaspoons oregano
- 1 teaspoon saffron, optional
- 1 onion, chopped
- 4 dried red chili pods

■ Combine all ingredients except chili pods. Cook in crock pot on low all day or until done.

■ Boil chili pods in water until soft. Put into blender with water and blend to paste or sauce consistency. Pour over meat when ready to serve. Use cautiously!

Serves 6

Mustard - Sauced Pork Chops

Stacy Stout

4 boneless center cut pork chops (about 5 ounces each)
4 teaspoons Dijon mustard
½ cup plus 2 tablespoons yellow mustard seeds
2 tablespoons olive oil
½ cup dry red wine

■ Lightly pound the pork chops until about ½ inch thick.

■ Spread mustard lightly over chops.

■ Sprinkle with mustard seeds to coat. Repeat on other side.

■ Heat oil in a frying pan large enough to hold chops in a single layer.

■ Add pork chops. Cook over medium-high heat, turning once, until nicely browned outside with no trace of pink in the center, about 3 minutes each side.

■ Remove chops to a platter. Cover with foil to keep warm.

■ Pour wine in pan. Bring to a boil over medium-high heat. Scrape loose any browned bits from bottom of the pan and any mustard seeds that didn't cling to the meat. Boil, stirring, until sauce is slightly reduced, 1 to 2 minutes. Pour sauce over the chops and serve.

Serves 4

Orange Pork Tenderloins

Amy Kelly

Prepare ahead

- 1 cup orange juice
- ⅓ cup soy sauce
- ¼ cup olive oil
- 2 tablespoons chopped fresh rosemary, or 2 teaspoons dried rosemary
- 3 cloves garlic, pressed
- 2 12-ounce pork tenderloins
  pepper to taste

■ Combine first 5 ingredients in baking dish. Add pork and marinate in refrigerator at least 1 hour or overnight.

■ Preheat oven to 400°.

■ Drain pork, reserving marinade.

■ Place pork on baking sheet. Season generously with pepper. Roast until cooked through, about 30 minutes.

■ Bring reserved marinade to a boil in small saucepan.

■ Slice and serve, passing marinade separately, as sauce.

Serves 6

Nana's Rice Porkchops

Susan Nipper

- 1 cup rice
- 1 10.5 ounce can of consomme beef soup
- 6 porkchops
  salt to taste
  pepper to taste
- 1 small onion, sliced
- ½ medium green pepper, sliced

■ Preheat oven to 350°.

■ Place rice in 9x13-inch glass casserole.

■ Add soup.

■ Place porkchops on top of rice. Salt and pepper to taste.

■ Cover porkchops with onions and green peppers.

■ Bake at 350° for 45 minutes.

Serves 6

It's All Wrapped Up Chicken

Lori Anderson

1 17-ounce package
frozen puff pastry
sheets, thawed
1 4-ounce container garlic
and spice cream cheese
6 skinned and boned
chicken breast halves
½ teaspoon salt
¼ teaspoon pepper
1 egg, beaten
1 tablespoon water

■ Unfold pastry sheets, and roll each into a 14x12 rectangle on a lightly floured surface. Cut one sheet into four 7x6 rectangles. Cut second sheet into two 7x6 rectangles. Save remaining pastry sheet. Shape each rectangle into an oval by trimming the corners.

■ Spread each pastry with cheese.

■ Sprinkle each chicken breast with salt and pepper. Place in center of each oval.

■ Lightly moisten pastry edges with water and fold ends over chicken then fold sides over, press and seal.

■ Place each bundle seam side down, on lightly greased baking sheet.

■ Cut remaining pastry sheet into 12 long strips, braid two together and place crosswise over bundle, trim, and place remaining braid over bundle lengthwise. Tuck edges under bundle. Repeat with remaining bundles.

■ Cover and refrigerate for up to 2 hours, if desired. Combine egg and water; brush over bundles.

■ Bake at 400° on lower rack of oven for 25 minutes or until golden brown.

Serves 6

Makes a great appetizer by cutting pastry
sheet and chicken into smaller sections!

Crescent Chicken Squares

Marcia Otte

3 ounces cream cheese, softened
3 tablespoons melted margarine, divided use
2 cups cubed, cooked chicken
¼ teaspoon salt
⅛ teaspoon pepper
3 tablespoons milk
1 tablespoon chopped chives or onions
8 ounces quick crescent rolls
¾ cup crushed croutons

■ Preheat oven to 350°.

■ In medium bowl, blend cream cheese and 2 tablespoons melted margarine. Add chicken, salt, pepper, milk, and onions. Mix well.

■ Separate crescent rolls into four rectangles, firmly pressing perforations together.

■ Spoon ½ cup chicken mixture onto center of each rectangle. Pull 4 corners of dough together to top of mixture, making a bundle. Twist slightly to seal.

■ Brush tops with 1 tablespoon butter and sprinkle with crushed croutons.

■ Bake on ungreased cookie sheet for 20-25 minutes until golden brown.

Serves 4-6

Overstuffed Chicken

Lisa Johnson

2 10-ounce cans condensed golden mushroom soup
⅔ cup water
1 8-ounce package herb seasoned stuffing
¼ cup melted margarine
2 split broilers (2½ pounds each)
paprika
⅓ cup chopped onion
generous dash poultry seasoning
2 tablespoons margarine

■ Combine soup with water. In roasting pan, mix ⅔ cup soup mixture with stuffing and melted butter. Place broilers over stuffing; sprinkle with paprika.

■ Cover and bake at 400° for 1 hour. Uncover; bake 30 minutes longer or until tender.

■ In a saucepan, cook onion with seasoning in 2 tablespoons margarine until tender. Stir in remaining soup mixture. Heat; stirring occasionally.

■ Serve sauce over chicken and stuffing.

Serves 4

Herb-Stuffed Chicken with Sautéed Peppers and Mushrooms

Christine Power

1 cup herb stuffing mix
½ cup boiling water
3 tablespoons melted butter, divided use
4 chicken breasts, halved, skinned, deboned
3 ounces Monterey Jack cheese (block)
1 egg, slightly beaten
⅓ cup Italian-seasoned bread crumbs
butter flavored vegetable cooking spray
3 green onions, sliced diagonally
1 small sweet red pepper, cut into julienne strips
6 fresh sliced mushrooms
½ cup white wine Worcestershire sauce

■ Preheat oven to 375°.

■ Combine stuffing mix, boiling water and one tablespoon butter, set aside.

■ Place chicken breasts between wax paper. Flatten to ¼ inch thickness.

■ Cut cheese into four 2½ x 1 x ¼ inch strips.

■ Put cheese strip in center of each chicken breast. Spoon stuffing mixture evenly over cheese; fold sides of chicken breast over stuffing; roll up and secure with wooden pick.

■ Dip chicken in egg, roll in bread crumbs, place in a lightly greased 8-inch baking dish. Spray breasts with cooking spray. Bake at 375° for 35 minutes or until done. Remove from oven.

■ Sauté green onions and red peppers in 2 tablespoons butter until crisp-tender. Stir in mushrooms and white wine Worcestershire sauce; spoon vegetables over chicken and serve.

Serves 4

■ ■ ■ *"Handy-Andy" Tip: Mark purchase dates on containers of herbs and spices - if not used within one year, replace them. Store away from light and heat.*

🕐 Chicken Mushroom Risotto

Susan Andrews

¾ pound skinless boneless chicken breasts, cut into cubes
2 tablespoons butter
1 cup uncooked regular long-grain rice
1 medium carrot, finely chopped (about ⅓ cup)
1 small onion, finely chopped (about ¼ cup)
1 14½-ounce can clear chicken broth
1 10¾-ounce can cream of mushroom soup
⅛ teaspoon black pepper
½ cup frozen peas
1 6-ounce can sliced water chestnuts

■ Cook chicken until browned. Cube and set aside.

■ In saucepan, brown rice, carrot and onion in butter. When butter is browned, add chicken broth, soup, pepper and peas.

■ Cook until vegetables are tender and rice is cooked.

■ Add chicken cubes and water chestnuts.

Serves 4

🕐 Poulet d'Artichoke

Nancy Marston

2 14-ounce cans artichoke hearts, diced and drained
2¾ cups diced cooked chicken breasts
2 10½-ounce cans cream of chicken soup
1 cup mayonnaise
1 teaspoon lemon juice
½ teaspoon curry powder
1¼ cups grated Cheddar cheese
1¼ cups cracker crumbs
2 tablespoons melted butter

■ Preheat oven to 350°.

■ Arrange artichokes in a greased casserole dish. Put chicken on top of artichokes.

■ Combine soup, mayonnaise, juice and curry, pour over chicken.

■ Sprinkle with cheese. Toss crumbs with butter and place on top.

■ Bake at 350° for 25 minutes.

■ Serve over rice.

Serves 6-8

Chicken and Artichoke Buffet
Janny Strickland

2 cups carrots, cut in thin 1 inch strips
2 tablespoons butter
10 mushrooms, sliced
10 green onions, chopped
2 10-ounce cans cream of chicken soup
½ cup heavy cream
¼ cup sherry
¼ cup water
1 teaspoon salt
4 cups cooked chicken breasts, cubed
2 14-ounce cans artichoke hearts, drained and quartered
10 slices bacon, cooked and crumbled
3 cups grated mozzarella cheese
¾ cup white rice, cooked
¾ cup wild rice, cooked
Parmesan cheese

■ Preheat oven to 300°.

■ Blanch carrots for 5 minutes. Rinse and drain.

■ Sauté mushrooms and onions in butter. Add soup, cream, sherry, water and salt. Mix well.

■ Combine the rest of the ingredients except Parmesan.

■ Spread mixture in a 9x13 casserole dish sprayed with non-stick vegetable spray. Sprinkle with Parmesan.

■ Bake covered at 300° for 1 hour.

Serves 8-12

Hawaiian Chicken
Sherry McMenamy

Prepare ahead

6 chicken breasts
¼ cup margarine, melted
1 9-ounce can crushed pineapple
¼ cup brown sugar
2 tablespoons cornstarch
1 teaspoon salt
¼ cup vinegar
½ teaspoon Worcestershire sauce
1 teaspoon soy sauce
2 tablespoons chili sauce
⅓ cup ketchup

■ Mix all ingredients together and pour over chicken.

■ Marinate overnight in the refrigerator.

■ Bake chicken breasts in marinade at 300° for 1½ to 2 hours.

Serves 6

Chicken Divan
Julie Robins

2 10-ounce packages
  frozen broccoli spears
  or florets
4 cups sliced cooked
  chicken
¾ cup salad dressing
¼ cup mustard
  mayonnaise sauce (if
  omitted, use 1 cup salad
  dressing)
2 10-ounce cans cream of
  chicken soup
½ teaspoon curry powder
4 teaspoons lemon juice
½ cup grated Cheddar
  cheese
½ cup bread crumbs
1 tablespoon melted butter

■ Preheat oven to 350°.

■ Cook broccoli and drain.
Arrange stalks in greased 13x9
baking dish. Place chicken on
top of broccoli.

■ Combine salad dressing,
mustard mayonnaise sauce,
soup, curry and lemon juice. Pour
over chicken and sprinkle cheese
on top.

■ Combine bread crumbs and
butter. Sprinkle over all.

■ Bake at 350° for 25-30
minutes.

Serves 6-8

Chicken Rockefeller
Mary Pittman

1 tablespoon butter
1 tablespoon olive oil
4 chicken breasts, skinned
  and boned (can use split
  breasts with bone)
1 10-ounce package
  chopped spinach,
  cooked and well
  drained
1 10-ounce can cream of
  chicken soup
½ cup mayonnaise (lite or
  regular)
½ cup sour cream or plain
  yogurt
1 tablespoon lemon juice
¼ cup sherry
¾ cup grated yellow
  cheese
  paprika (optional)

■ Preheat oven to 350°.

■ Combine butter and oil in
skillet and brown chicken.

■ Place cooked spinach in
bottom of a 2 quart casserole,
top with chicken.

■ Mix remaining ingredients
together. Spoon sauce over
chicken. Sprinkle with paprika.

■ Bake at 350° for 30 minutes.
Can be assembled ahead of
baking, if refrigerated add 10
minutes to cooking time.

Serves 4

Can be easily doubled.

Thai Chicken with Peanut Garlic Sauce

Linda Gavigan

- 1 6.9-ounce package reduced salt chicken flavored rice vermicelli mix
- 1 tablespoon margarine
- 2 cloves garlic, minced
- 2¾ cups water
- 1 tablespoon honey
- 1 tablespoon peanut butter
- 1 tablespoon reduced sodium soy sauce
- ⅛-¼ teaspoon crushed red pepper flakes
- 2 cups skinless chicken breasts, cooked and chopped
- 3 medium carrots, cut into small thin strips
- 1 medium cucumber, peeled, seeded, halved lengthwise and sliced
- ¼ cup sliced green onions

■ In a large skillet, combine rice vermicelli mixture, margarine and garlic. Sauté over medium heat stirring frequently until vermicelli is golden brown.

■ Stir in water, contents of seasoning packet, honey, peanut butter, soy sauce and red pepper; bring to a boil. Cover, reduce heat to low and simmer 10 minutes.

■ Stir in cooked chicken, carrots, and cucumber. Cover; continue cooking 8-10 minutes or until liquid is absorbed and rice is tender.

■ Sprinkle with green onion before serving.

Serves 4

"Mother's Dream" Chicken

Gina Banister

- 4 chicken breasts
- 1 tablespoon butter
- 1 10-ounce can cream of mushroom soup
- 1 cup mild Cheddar cheese
- 2 ounces ground cashew nuts
- 1 tablespoon tarragon

■ Preheat oven to 350°.

■ Brown chicken in butter and remove to baking dish.

■ Combine other ingredients and spread over chicken.

■ Bake at 350° for 20 to 30 minutes, or until chicken is done.

Serves 4

Fish variation: Prepare the same way, but bake only until fish flakes easily.

"World's Prize" Chicken Breasts

Rene Tucei

¼ cup flour
2½ teaspoons salt
1 teaspoon paprika
6 chicken breasts, halved
   and skinned
¼ cup butter
¼ cup water
2 teaspoons cornstarch
1½ cups light cream or half-
   and-half, divided use
¼ cup cooking sherry
1 teaspoon lemon peel
1 tablespoon lemon juice
1 cup grated Swiss cheese
½ cup chopped parsley

■ Preheat oven to 350°.

■ Combine flour with salt and paprika on waxed paper. Coat chicken with flour mixture.

■ In large skillet, heat butter. Lightly brown chicken breasts on both sides. Add ¼ cup water and simmer, covered for 30 minutes or until chicken breasts are almost tender. Remove chicken from pan.

■ Mix cornstarch with ¼ cup half-and-half; stir into drippings in skillet. Cook, stirring. over low heat. Gradually stir in remaining half-and-half, sherry, lemon peel and lemon juice. Continue cooking and stirring until sauce is thickened; pour over chicken.

■ Bake chicken at 350°, covered, for 35 minutes or until sauce is bubbly hot. Remove cover, sprinkle with cheese and bake until cheese is melted - 1 to 2 minutes. Garnish with parsley.

Serves 12

Chicken Pot Pie

Kimberly Walters

1 refrigerated crust for
   2 crust pie
1 10-ounce can chunk
   white chicken, drained
1 13-ounce can mixed
   vegetables, drained
1 10-can cream of
   chicken soup
   poultry seasoning
   celery salt
   pepper

■ Preheat oven to 375°.

■ Place bottom crust in 8-inch pie pan.

■ Mix remaining ingredients together and pour into crust.

■ Add top crust. Bake at 375° for 30 minutes, or until crust is browned.

Serves 4-6

Neighborhood Chicken

Ann Baillargeon

Prepare ahead

> 4 4-ounce boneless,
>   skinless chicken breasts
> ¼ cup light Italian salad
>   dressing
> ½ cup Italian flavored
>   bread crumbs
> 1 tablespoon Parmesan
>   cheese
> 1½ teaspoons minced garlic

- Preheat oven to 350°.
- With meat mallet, pound chicken breasts to ¼ inch thick.
- Dip chicken in salad dressing and marinate for 2 hours.
- Mix bread crumbs, cheese and garlic in dish or baggy.
- Dredge chicken through bread crumbs.
- Place chicken in a 9x9 baking dish that has been sprayed with cooking spray.
- Bake at 350° for 20 minutes.

Serves 4

Time Saver Variation: For a quick dinner, dip chicken in salad dressing, dredge with bread crumbs and skip marinating.

Emma's Chicken

Gina Banister

> 1 3 pound fryer
>   olive oil
>   salt
>   pepper
>   oregano
>   garlic salt
> 2 large potatoes, cut in
>   eighths

- Preheat oven to 400°.
- Line shallow pan with foil. Wash fryer and dry inside and out. Rub outside with oil and season generously with salt, pepper, oregano and garlic salt.
- Place in pan, breast side down, surround with potatoes and bake uncovered at 400°. After 20 minutes, turn chicken breast side up. Cook another 40 minutes until chicken and potatoes are brown and crispy.

Serves 6

Dondo's Chicken & Dumplings

Carla Byars

2 cups flour
1 teaspoon salt
½ cup shortening
1 cup ice water
2 cups chicken broth
2 cups milk
   butter to taste
   salt and pepper
1 3-4 pound hen cooked
   and deboned or 6
   chicken breasts halves

■ Blend flour, salt, and shortening until it is crumbly. Slowly add water until it makes a dough. Roll dough on a floured board and cut into thin strips.

■ Combine together broth, milk, butter, salt and pepper. Bring to a boil.

■ Add dough strips one at a time to boiling mixture. Push down with fork.

■ Add chicken. Cook 10 minutes more.

Serves 4-6

For extra flavor add more butter!

Honey Dijon Chicken Nuggets

Marilyn Moore

1½ cups no-sugar apricot
   spread
½ cup Dijon mustard
¼ cup plus 2 tablespoons
   honey
1¼ teaspoons ground red
   pepper
¾ teaspoon garlic powder
6 chicken breasts,
   boneless, skinless, cut
   into 1 inch pieces
2 cups crushed pretzels
1 cup plus 2 tablespoons
   water, divided use
1 tablespoon plus 1
   teaspoon cornstarch

■ Preheat oven to 400°.

■ Combine first five ingredients in a medium bowl and stir well. Measure 1 cup apricot mixture and set aside.

■ Dip chicken pieces in remaining apricot mixture, dredge in crushed pretzels. Place on a large baking sheet. Bake at 400° for 15 minutes.

■ Combine reserved apricot mixture with 1 cup water in saucepan. Bring to a boil, reduce heat and simmer 3 minutes.

■ Combine cornstarch and 2 tablespoons water. Add to hot apricot mixture. Stir until thickened. Serve sauce with the nuggets.

Serves 6-8

Makes a great appetizer.

Fiesta Lasagna

Mary Pittman

6 chicken breast halves
2 10-ounce cans tomatoes
  with chilies
1 2¼-ounce can sliced
  black olives, drained
8 8-inch flour tortillas
2 large avocados, peeled
  and sliced
2 cups sour cream
1½ pounds grated Monterey
  Jack cheese

■ Preheat oven to 350°.

■ Cook chicken. Remove skin and bones. Shred chicken with fingers.

■ Combine tomatoes and olives, lightly crushing tomatoes with back of a spoon.

■ Spread one can of tomato mixture in the bottom of a 9x13 Pyrex dish, arrange flour tortillas over tomato mixture, overlapping to cover pan. Repeat.

■ Add layer of half the chicken, then half the avocado slices. Spread one cup of sour cream evenly over avocados. Sprinkle with half the cheese. Repeat using the balance of ingredients topping.

■ Bake uncovered at 350° for 35-45 minutes. Cut into squares to serve. Let stand for 10 minutes before cutting.

Serves 8-10

Recipe can be cut into half and baked in a 8x8 Pyrex dish.

Monterey Jack Chicken

Holly Sullivan

6 chicken breasts, cooked and cut up
1 10-ounce can cream of chicken soup
¾ cup milk
2 4 ounce cans green chili pepper, chopped
1 small package (6-8) corn tortillas torn into pieces
½ pint sour cream
8 ounces grated Monterey Jack cheese

■ Preheat oven to 350°.

■ Mix all ingredients together.

■ Bake at 350° for 30-40 minutes.

■ Add Monterey Jack cheese on top for last 15 minutes.

Serves 6

Arroz Con Pollo

Susan Scull

2 chicken breasts
2 cloves garlic, sliced
1½ teaspoons salt, divided use
2½ cups water
1 cup rice (long cooking)
2 tablespoons vegetable oil
⅓ cup picante sauce
½ teaspoon ground cumin
¼ teaspoon pepper
2 medium coarsely chopped tomatoes
3 green onions, sliced with tops

■ Simmer chicken , garlic, ½ teaspoon salt in water until chicken is cooked. Remove chicken, cube and reserve 2 cups stock.

■ Cook rice in oil over low heat until golden brown. Stir in 2 cups stock, chicken, picante sauce, cumin, pepper and remaining salt. Bring to a boil. Reduce heat and simmer 15 minutes.

■ Add tomatoes and green onions. Cover and continue to simmer until rice has absorbed most of liquid (about 5 minutes.)

Serves 4

Great served with cornbread!

Chicken Enchiladas

Nancy Marston

4 chicken breasts, deboned and baked or broiled
1 8-ounce package cream cheese
1 cup sour cream
1 4-ounce can chopped green chilies
1 diced medium onion, sautéed in butter
pinch of cayenne pepper
salt, to taste
hot pepper sauce, to taste
8-12 flour tortillas
1 pound mozzarella cheese, grated
½ cup whipping cream

■ Preheat oven to 350°.

■ Shred chicken and mix with cream cheese, sour cream, green chilies, onion, pepper, salt and hot pepper sauce.

■ Warm tortillas on low heat in ungreased frying pan. (Makes tortillas easier to roll.)

■ Fill tortillas with chicken mixture, roll and place in 9x13 inch baking pan. Cover with grated cheese. Pour whipping cream evenly over tortillas.

■ Bake at 350° for 30 minutes or until cheese is bubbly.

■ Serve with salsa.

Serves 4-6

Very easy and great variation from tomato-based Mexican food!

Chicken Enchilada Casserole

Kim Watson

1 medium onion, chopped
2-3 tablespoons butter
1 10-can cream of mushroom soup
1 4-ounce can chopped green chilies
1 pint sour cream
4 chicken breasts, cooked, deboned, cut into pieces
1 package corn tortillas (dipped in broth or water)
1 pound grated Cheddar cheese

■ Preheat oven to 350°.

■ Sauté onion in butter. Add soups, green chilies and sour cream.

■ Add chicken to mixture.

■ In a 9x12 baking dish layer tortillas, chicken sauce, and cheese. Repeat layers.

■ Bake at 350° for 30 minutes.

Serves 6-8

Time Saver Variation: Substitute 3 to 4 cans of white chicken for chicken breasts.

Sour Cream Enchiladas

Johnetta Davis

1 chicken fryer
10 soft flour tortillas
1 pint plus 8 ounces sour cream
   butter
1 large onion
   salt to taste
1 package frozen chopped spinach, thawed, drained, reserve liquid
2 4-ounce cans chopped green chilies
½ cup spinach water
¼ cup milk
1 pound grated Monterey Jack cheese

■ Boil chicken until tender; debone.

■ Preheat oven to 350°.

■ Combine together, sour cream, sautéed onions, salt, spinach water, spinach, green chilies, and milk.

■ Mix ½ sauce with chicken. Fill tortillas with meat mixture and roll.

■ Place seamed side down in a 13x9 casserole dish.

■ Layer enchiladas with grated cheese and then sour cream mixture. Repeat layers.

■ Bake uncovered 350° until hot (approximately 30 minutes).

Serves 6-8

Time Saver Variation: Prepare chicken a day ahead.

Have your organization make a quilt as a fundraising event. A great deal of camaraderie can be perpetuated by this kind of effort. When the quilt is completed, raffle tickets can be sold.

Much more goes on with this kind of project than just quilting. The bonding of an organization, the teamwork, the art, math, history, social studies and the act of sharing all come into play.

Chicken Tamale Pie

Tomi Morriss

1 package corn muffin mix
½ cup shredded Cheddar cheese
1 10-ounce can cream of chicken soup
1 teaspoon chili powder
1 clove garlic, minced
1 4-ounce can chopped green chilies
½ cup chopped green onions
1 13½-ounce can whole kernel corn (drained)
1½ cups shredded cooked chicken (4 breasts)
chopped green onions and cherry tomatoes, garnish

■ Preheat oven to 350°.

■ In a bowl, combine muffin mix and cheese. Prepare according to package directions.

■ In a saucepan, stir remaining ingredients until blended. Heat through.

■ Spoon muffin mixture into greased 2 quart casserole. Spoon soup mixture over muffin mixture, within ½ inches of the muffin mixture's edge. (Cornbread bakes around hot soup mixture.)

■ Bake at 350° for 25 minutes or until cornbread is golden. Garnish with additional cheese, green onions and cherry tomatoes.

Serves 4

Great served with salsa!

Turkey Sopa

Martha Welch

2 10-ounce cans cream of chicken soup
2-3 10-ounce cans of green enchilada sauce
1 pound cooked turkey or chicken
1 pound grated Monterey Jack cheese
12 shredded tortillas
1 4-ounce can chopped green chilies

■ Preheat oven to 350°.

■ Combine soups and enchilada sauce in a mixing bowl.

■ Shred or cut turkey.

■ Cover bottom of a 9x13 baking dish with a small amount of the sauce. Begin layering in the following order: sauce, tortillas, turkey, and cheese. Repeat layers until top baking dish is reached. Top with the green chilies.

■ Bake at 350° for about 1 hour or until mixture is bubbly.

Serves 4

Turkey Schnitzel

Martha Welch

Prepare ahead

4 turkey breast slices, cut
   about ½ inch thick
   (about ¾ pounds total)
2 tablespoons lemon juice
¼ cup olive oil or salad oil
⅛ teaspoon each salt and
   pepper
⅓ cup flour
⅓ cup Parmesan cheese
2-3 tablespoons margarine

■ Place meat between 2 sheets
of wax paper or plastic wrap
and pound to ¼ inch thick with
the smooth side of a mallet.

■ Mix together lemon juice, oil,
salt and pepper.

■ Place pounded turkey in a
shallow pan. Pour lemon juice
mixture over meat. Cover and
refrigerate at least 30 minutes or
as long as overnight.

■ Drain liquid from turkey. Mix
together flour and Parmesan
cheese; coat turkey generously
with mixture and shake off
excess.

■ Heat 2 tablespoons of margarine in wide frying pan over
medium heat. Quickly cook
turkey slices until browned on
both sides (3 to 5 minutes per
side), adding more margarine as
needed.

Serves 4

 Baked Shrimp   *Debbie Bradshaw*

1 cup melted butter
¼ cup dry white wine
¼ cup minced parsley
2 tablespoons fresh lemon juice
3 large cloves garlic, minced
2 teaspoons basil
1 teaspoon Worcestershire sauce
¾-1 teaspoon hot pepper sauce
½ teaspoon salt
2 pounds large shrimp, shelled and deveined (approximately 32)
½ cup dry unseasoned bread crumbs

■ Preheat oven to 450°.

■ Combine first nine ingredients in shallow 2 quart baking dish and mix well. Remove ¼ cup of mixture and set aside.

■ Add shrimp to dish and mix thoroughly.

■ Combine bread crumbs with reserved butter sauce and sprinkle over shrimp.

■ Bake at 450° for 10-15 minutes. Serve immediately over rice.

Serves 6-8

 Easy "Candlelight" Scampi   *Dana Bell*

¼ cup chopped onion
4 cloves garlic
4 sprigs fresh parsley, chopped
¾ cup melted butter
2 pounds fresh medium shrimp, peeled and deveined
¼ cup dry white wine
2 teaspoons lemon juice
salt and pepper

■ Sauté onion, garlic and parsley in butter until onion is tender. Reduce heat to low; add shrimp. Cook stirring frequently about 5 minutes.

■ Add remaining ingredients and simmer 2 minutes.

■ Serve over rice and garnish with extra chopped parsley.

Serves 6

166

Barbecue Shrimp

Renee Tucei

Prepare ahead

4 cloves garlic
½ cup parsley
¾ cup chopped green onions
2 cups tomato sauce
¼ cup Worcestershire sauce
1¼ cups honey
½ cup lime juice
¼ cup olive oil
¾ cup vegetable oil
4 bay leaves
1½ teaspoons thyme
2 teaspoons paprika
½ teaspoon red hot pepper sauce
1 to 2 teaspoons red pepper
2 teaspoons salt
1 teaspoon pepper
4 pounds (22-30 count) shrimp, peeled and deveined

■ Combine all ingredients. Marinate shrimp overnight.

■ Put on skewers and grill the next day.

Serves 6-8

 ## Shrimp Manale

Gina Banister

3 pounds raw shrimp (you can leave the shells on for a shrimp peel or take them off)
6 cloves crushed garlic
½ pound butter
½ cup Chablis wine

■ Combine all ingredients together in a skillet.

■ Sauté over medium heat until pink and done.

Serves 6-8

Serve with crusty French bread for dipping in the sauce.

167

Artichoke Shrimp Casserole

Pat Collins

1½ cups rice
1 can artichoke hearts
2 10-ounce cans cream of mushroom soup
4 tablespoons chopped onion
2 pounds fresh boiled shrimp, peeled, deveined
2½ cups shredded Cheddar cheese
1½ cloves garlic, chopped
2 tablespoons lemon juice
1 teaspoon cracked black pepper
4 tablespoons butter
3 teaspoons chopped parsley
green bell pepper rings (optional)

■ Preheat oven to 350°.

■ Cook rice according to package directions.

■ Line a greased Pyrex oblong casserole with canned artichoke hearts on the bottom.

■ Mix together the remaining ingredients, reserving ½ cup of cheese.

■ Pour mixture on arranged artichokes and top with reserved cheese. Arrange green pepper rings on top if desired.

■ Bake at 350° for 30 minutes, or until it bubbles and cheese is melted.

Serves 6-8

Hospitals using quilting as therapy is not a new idea. During the Civil War patients recovering from wounds used quilting to help pass the time.

Southwestern Shrimp Creole

Margaret Henry

2 cups chopped onion
2 tablespoons butter (for low fat cooking, use ¼ cup white wine)
1 4-ounce can chopped green chilies (for spicier recipe, use 8 ounces of chilies)
1 teaspoon dried parsley
½ cup dry white wine
4 14-ounce cans Italian style stewed tomatoes, drained
1 tablespoon minced garlic (fresh or jar)
2 tablespoons Worcestershire sauce
1 cup canned tomato sauce
½ teaspoon dried mint
salt to taste
hot sauce to taste
2 pounds raw, peeled shrimp, deveined

■ Sauté onions until clear.

■ Add all remaining ingredients except shrimp.

■ Cover and cook on medium heat until sauce comes to a boil. Lower heat, cover and simmer for at least an hour.

■ Add shrimp and continue to simmer for at least 30 minutes. Serve over rice.

Serves 8

Can be made in a crock pot!

Ray's Poblano Pepper Shrimp

Brenda Brandon

1 stick unsalted butter, divided use
2 cloves minced garlic
1 pound shrimp, peeled and deveined
1-2 tablespoons fresh chopped basil
1 diced onion
1-2 diced jalapeños, remove seeds
2 diced tomatoes
  salt and pepper to taste
1 can poblano peppers, cut into strips
½ bunch cilantro, chopped
½ lime

■ On medium heat melt ½ stick butter. Sauté garlic for 1½ minutes.

■ Add shrimp and sauté until they turn pink, then add basil. Continue stirring for 1-2 minutes.

■ Remove from heat. Transfer to a glass bowl with lid to keep warm.

■ Melt remaining ½ stick butter and sauté remaining ingredients, except cilantro and lime. Sauté until onions turn clear, about 3-5 minutes.

■ Return shrimp to skillet. Stir well. Squeeze lime juice into pan and add cilantro. Continue stirring for about 2 minutes. Serve warm.

Serves 3-4

Can be used as an appetizer!

Another story in the quiltmaking lore had to do with design at the corners. It was said that if a running design was used, it had to turn the corner without a break. A broken design forewarned that the quiltmaker's life would be cut short by disaster.

Camarones Enchilados (Shrimp Enchiladas)

Cuqui Levine

  2 pounds shrimp, peeled, deveined
½ cup olive oil
  1 onion, chopped
  1 bell pepper, chopped
  1 clove garlic, chopped
½ cup chopped parsley
  1 14-ounce can tomato sauce
½ cup ketchup
½ cup sauterne or white cooking wine
  1 teaspoon vinegar
  1 bay leaf
1½ teaspoons salt
1½ teaspoons pepper
  1 teaspoon Worcestershire sauce
  1 teaspoon hot pepper sauce

■ Heat oil and sauté shrimp until pink. Remove shrimp with slotted spoon.

■ Add onion, bell peppers, garlic and sauté 5 minutes or until onion starts browning.

■ Add remaining ingredients and slow cook for 25 minutes. Add shrimp last 5 minutes.

■ Serve over white rice or noodles.

Serves 6

Crawfish/Shrimp Etouffee

Anne Hobbs

  6 tablespoons butter
  2 cups chopped onion
  3 cloves garlic, minced
¼ cup chopped green pepper
¼ cup chopped celery
⅛ cup water
  1 pound shrimp, shelled, or crawfish tails
1¼ teaspoons salt
¼ teaspoon pepper
  2 tablespoons chopped green onion
  2 tablespoons minced parsley
  1 10-ounce can golden mushroom soup

■ Melt butter in heavy pot (Dutch oven). Sauté onion, green pepper, garlic and celery until onions are transparent. Add water; cover and simmer for 15 minutes.

■ Add shrimp/crawfish and seasonings; cook 15 minutes. Add green onions and parsley; simmer 5 minutes.

■ Mix in soup. Serve over rice.

Serves 4-6

Crawfish Casserole

Gene Liese

1 pound crawfish tails
1 10-ounce can French onion soup
1 10-ounce can cream of mushroom soup
1 10-ounce can tomatoes with chilies
1 cup uncooked converted rice
½ cup margarine (1 stick)
1 cup chopped green onion
⅛ cup chopped parsley
½ cup grated Monterey Jack cheese
salt and pepper to taste
1 cup grated Cheddar cheese

■ Preheat oven to 350°.

■ Mix all ingredients except Cheddar cheese.

■ Pour into a large greased casserole dish.

■ Bake covered at 350° for 45 minutes.

■ Uncover and top with cheddar cheese. Put in oven to melt.

Serves 6-8

Pescado Coronado

Martha Karren

4 teaspoons butter
2 large tomatoes, chopped
1 white onion, chopped
salt and pepper, to taste
cilantro, to taste
2 cups of water
¼ cup ketchup
½ cup Worcestershire sauce
2 tablespoons jalapeños packed in vinegar (more can be added)
4 orange roughy filets
fresh spinach leaves

■ Preheat oven to 350°.

■ In a large saucepan melt 4 teaspoons butter on medium heat. Add chopped tomatoes, onions, cilantro, salt and pepper, to taste. Sauté for 5 minutes.

■ Add water, ketchup, Worcestershire sauce and 1 tablespoon jalapeño. Bring to a boil.

■ Lower heat and add filets. Cook 5 minutes on each side.

■ Place in baking dish with sauce poured on top. Place spinach leaves over fish.

■ Bake at 350° for 10 minutes. Serve with white rice.

Serves 4

Can also use crabmeat, lobster or combo.

Grilled Texas Tequila Tuna

Cheryl Mokrzecky

Prepare ahead - Heat up outdoor grill!

¼ cup tequila
¼ cup red wine vinegar
2 tablespoons lime juice
1 tablespoon ground red chilies
2 cloves finely chopped garlic
1 finely chopped red bell pepper
2 pounds fresh tuna (4 steaks approximately ¾ inch thick)

■ Mix all ingredients together except tuna in a bowl. Place tuna in shallow dish. Pour marinade over. Refrigerate for 1 hour.

■ Remove tuna from marinade and reserve liquid.

■ Place tuna on grill over medium hot coals, turning once. Cook until done, approximately 6-7 minutes per side.

■ Heat marinade to boiling in saucepan. Cook until bell pepper is tender. Serve over tuna.

Serves 4

Alternative fish: swordfish and halibut.

■ ■ ■ *"Handy-Andy" Tip: To remove fish odor from hands, utensils and dish cloths, use one teaspoon baking soda to one quart of water mixture to soak or wash articles.*

Swiss Tuna Spaghetti Casserole

Renee Tucei

8 ounces of spaghetti
1 10-ounce can condensed cream of celery soup
¾ cup milk
½ cup sliced ripe olives
½ teaspoon seasoned salt
1 6½-ounce can tuna, drained and flaked
1 cup shredded Swiss cheese

■ Preheat oven to 350°.

■ Cook spaghetti according to package directions. Drain and set aside.

■ Blend soup, milk, olives and seasoned salt. Combine with spaghetti and tuna in a 2 quart casserole dish.

■ Top with cheese.

■ Bake at 350° for 20 minutes or until bubbling.

Serves 4-6

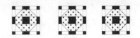

California Marinade for Steaks

Renee Tucei

Prepare Ahead

2 cloves crushed garlic
¼ cup olive oil
1 teaspoon crushed
  rosemary leaves
½ teaspoon dry mustard
2 teaspoons soy sauce
¼ cup red wine vinegar
¼ cup sherry

■ Cook garlic in oil.
■ Add rosemary, mustard and soy sauce.
■ Remove from heat and stir in vinegar and wine.
■ Pour marinade over steaks. Cover and refrigerate 12-24 hours before grilling.

Red's Barbecue Sauce

Kathy Mayfield

1 cup vegetable oil
1 teaspoon liquid smoke
½ cup Worcestershire
  sauce
1 teaspoon chili powder

■ Mix together on top of stove.
■ Bring to a slow boil.
■ Baste as meat cooks.

This sauce is great on any grilled meat.

Ty's Hot Sauce

Shannon Burton

Prepare Ahead

1 14-ounce can tomato
  sauce
1 cup water
1-2 chopped tomatoes
1-2 4 ounce cans chopped
  green chilies
½-1 chopped green pepper
½-1 chopped onions
  jalapeños chopped to
  taste
  garlic salt to taste
  pepper to taste

■ Mix all ingredients and chill. Thickens in refrigerator!

Cherry Sauce

Stephanie Nowacki

2 tablespoons cornstarch
¾ cup orange juice
2 teaspoons lemon juice
¾ cups sugar
1 16-ounce can cherries (packed in water); drained
1 teaspoon cinnamon
1 teaspoon whole cloves
    dash of salt
    red food coloring (optional)
2 tablespoons Grand Marnier liqueur

■ Mix cornstarch with orange juice and lemon juice.

■ Pour into saucepan with other ingredients, except Gran Marnier.

■ Simmer until it starts to boil (thick and clear).

■ Remove cloves and add Grand Marnier stir and serve warm.

Excellent for ham and poultry.

Skinny Shake Mix - For Oven Fried Foods

Lisa Matchett

4 cups (16 ounces) bread crumbs
½ cup salad oil
1 tablespoon salt
1 tablespoon celery salt
1 tablespoon paprika
1 teaspoon freshly ground pepper
    additional seasonings to taste

■ Put bread crumbs in a deep bowl. Stir in the oil with a fork or pastry blender.

■ Add salt, celery salt, paprika, pepper and any other desired seasonings- herbs, garlic or onion powder, etc.

■ Keep well covered in a moisture proof container with a tightly fitting lid. Use as needed.

■ Makes enough for about 20 cut-up chickens or 30 servings of fish.

Turkey Tenderloin Marinade
Amy Kelly

Prepare Ahead
- ¼ cup vegetable oil
- ¼ cup soy sauce
- ¼ teaspoon dried basil leaves
- ¼ teaspoon dried marjoram leaves
- ¼ teaspoon dried thyme leaves
- turkey breast tenderloin

■ Combine all ingredients in a glass dish or zip lock bag.

■ Add turkey breast tenderloin and refrigerate 2-4 hours.

■ Grill 20-30 minutes.

■ ■ ■ *"Handy-Andy" Tip:* **Herb bouquet or bouquet garnish** - *a blend of herbs wrapped in cheesecloth and bound at the top. This bag of spices is used during the cooking of some foods, much like a tea bag might be used in making tea. They are also used in the cooking of wonderful sauces, soups, stews, and vegetables.*

Classic bouquet - *2 sprigs of fresh parsley, 1 sprig of fresh thyme, ⅛ teaspoon of dried thyme and 1 bay leaf.*

Lamb Bouquet - *Comprised of rosemary, celery and parsley.*

Veal Bouquet - *Comprised of parsley, thyme and lemon rind.*

Beef Bouquet - *Consists of bay leaf, basil, clove and parsley.*

A little lady, a great-grandmother many times over, was overheard to remark that she still had 33 grandnieces and four more girls of the fourth generation to make quilts for...it begs the question, "How many lives might be saved from uselessness by learning to piece quilt tops?"

HARVEST SUN

From the Double Wedding Ring to the Rose of Sharon, old patchwork quilt patterns span a lifetime of experiences. While real quilt enthusiasts delight in this all-over pattern, the Double Wedding Ring is hardly the design for the novice to undertake. It is the ultimate challenge for the quiltmaker, as each segment of the arc is made of scrap pieces with the center and oval shapes carried out in the same color through the quilt.

The many superstitions concerning quilts indicate that they were not merely handcrafts, but objects of symbolic importance in the lives of the women and men who made them. Among the superstitions regarding the bridal quilt was the belief that if a young lady became too anxious about her future and started to make her bridal quilt before she was spoken for, terrible consequences might occur. It was also considered bad luck to use hearts as part of a patchwork or quilting design unless the quiltmaker was officially engaged. Pioneer brides made five or six quilts to set up housekeeping. Completion of a Wedding quilt proved the girl's readiness for the responsibilities of marriage.

One can almost imagine the happy young bride beginning to pack her belongings from her childhood; her shoes to be worn to church with her new husband and the quilt that told the world she was ready to become a wife. In the pictured quilt, the patches were done by Mildred Cool and then quilted by her mother Dollie Yenni in the early 1930's. We appreciate Sandra Gordon for loaning her family's heirloom to be a part of our TEXAS SAMPLER.

HARVEST SUN

From the Double Wedding Ring to the Rose of Sharon, old patchwork quilt patterns span a lifetime of experiences. While real quilt enthusiasts delight in this all-over pattern, the Double Wedding Ring is hardly the design for the novice to undertake. It is the ultimate challenge for the quiltmaker, as each segment of the arc is made of scrap pieces with the center and oval shapes carried out in the same color through the quilt.

The many superstitions concerning quilts indicate that they were not merely handcrafts, but objects of symbolic importance in the lives of the women and men who made them. Among the superstitions regarding the bridal quilt was the belief that if a young lady became too anxious about her future and started to make her bridal quilt before she was spoken for, terrible consequences might occur. It was also considered bad luck to use hearts as part of a patchwork or quilting design unless the quiltmaker was officially engaged. Pioneer brides made five or six quilts to set up housekeeping. Completion of a Wedding quilt proved the girl's readiness for the responsibilities of marriage.

One can almost imagine the happy young bride beginning to pack her belongings from her childhood; her shoes to be worn to church with her new husband and the quilt that told the world she was ready to become a wife. In the pictured quilt, the patches were done by Mildred Cool and then quilted by her mother Dollie Yenni in the early 1930's. We appreciate Sandra Gordon for loaning her family's heirloom to be a part of our TEXAS SAMPLER.

Artichoke Casserole

Susie Hatley

2 6-ounce jars marinated
  artichokes, reserve
  liquid from one jar
1 small onion
1 clove garlic, minced
2 tablespoons butter
4 eggs
¼ cup bread crumbs
  dash hot pepper sauce
¼ teaspoon oregano
  salt and pepper, to taste
2 cups shredded Cheddar
  cheese

■ Preheat oven to 325°.

■ Chop artichokes, reserving liquid from one jar, set aside.

■ Sauté onion and garlic in butter until tender.

■ Beat eggs. Add bread crumbs, seasonings, onions and cheese.

■ Stir in artichokes and mix well.

■ Bake in ungreased casserole for 30 minutes.

Serves 6-8

Braised Artichokes With Mint

Cheryl Mokrzecky

3 large or 4 small
  artichokes, quartered
½ cup water
3 tablespoons olive oil
2 tablespoons chopped
  fresh parsley
1 teaspoon minced garlic
½ teaspoon salt
¼ teaspoon dried mint
¼ cup chopped fresh mint
1 teaspoon minced lemon
  peel

■ Remove outer leaves and trim stems to 1-inch. Peel stems with small sharp knife. Slice off top of artichokes. Cut out "fuzzy chokes."

■ Arrange artichokes in a single layer in skillet. Drizzle with water and oil.

■ Combine parsley, garlic, salt and dried mint in a cup and sprinkle evenly over artichokes.

■ Bring to a boil; reduce heat, cover and simmer until tender, 20-25 minutes.

■ Continue to cook, uncovered until all but 2 tablespoons of liquid is evaporated.

■ Transfer to a serving dish. Combine fresh mint and lemon peel. Sprinkle on top.

Serves 4

Serve at room temperature.

Asparagus-Tomato Stir-Fry

Janie Trantham

¼ cup cooking oil
1 pound fresh asparagus, base snipped off and discarded
1 bunch green onions with tops
2 cups fresh sliced mushrooms
1 tablespoon cold water
1 teaspoon cornstarch
2 teaspoons soy sauce
1 teaspoon salt
2 small tomatoes, chopped
fresh ground black pepper, to taste

■ Cut asparagus and green onions on bias 1 to 1 ½-inches in length.

■ Preheat a wok or skillet over medium-high. Add cooking oil.

■ Place asparagus and onions into wok and stir fry for three minutes or until tender.

■ Add mushrooms and stir fry for one more minute.

■ Push vegetables up the side; combine water, cornstarch, soy sauce and salt. Pour mixture into center of pan and let it bubble slightly.

■ Stir in vegetables, add tomatoes and heat thoroughly.

■ Serve at once.

Serves 4-6

Broccoli can be substituted for asparagus.

Main Dish Variation: add thin strips of beef or chicken marinated in soy sauce.

■ ■ ■ *"Handy-Andy" Tip: On refrigerator clean-up day, wash and chop celery, carrots, cabbage, onions, lettuce, zucchini and all other vegetables. Sauté in butter for a quick stir-fry dish.*

Sweet and Sour Asparagus

Lori Anderson

Prepare ahead

    2 pounds fresh asparagus
    ⅔ cup white vinegar
    ½ cup sugar
    ½ cup water
    ½ teaspoon salt
    1 teaspoon whole cloves
    3 3-inch cinnamon sticks
    1½ teaspoons celery seed

■ Snap off tough ends of asparagus.

■ Steam asparagus 6 to 8 minutes until crisp tender. Set aside and drain. Place in baking dish.

■ Combine all other ingredients in a saucepan. Bring to a full boil.

■ Pour over asparagus, cover and chill 24 hours.

■ Drain and serve.

Serves 10 to 12

 ## Special Green Beans

Dawn Murphy

    2 10-ounce packages
      frozen French-style
      green beans
    2 tablespoons margarine
    1 small onion, minced
    1 tablespoon chopped
      fresh parsley
    1 teaspoon salt
    ¼ teaspoon white pepper
    1 tablespoon flour
    ¼ teaspoon freshly grated
      lemon rind
    1 cup sour cream
    1 tablespoon dry sherry
    1 cup sharp Cheddar
      cheese
    ½ cup bread crumbs,
      buttered

■ Preheat oven to 350°.

■ Cook beans according to package directions. Set aside.

■ In a saucepan, melt margarine and sauté onion and parsley for 5 minutes. Add salt pepper, flour lemon rind, sour cream and sherry and continue to cook another 3 minutes.

■ Add beans to mixture.

■ Pour into buttered 1½-quart casserole dish.

■ Sprinkle with cheese and bread crumbs.

■ Bake uncovered at 350° for 30 minutes.

Serves 6-8

Can be prepared a day ahead.

179

Beans 'n Chives Amandine

Sherry McMenamy

½ cup water
3 cups fresh green beans,
   cut diagonally into
   1-inch pieces or 1 16-
   ounce package of
   frozen cut green beans
2 tablespoons butter
⅓ cup slivered almonds
¼ cup chopped fresh
   chives

■ Bring water to a boil in medium saucepan.

■ Add beans. Cover, cook over
medium heat until beans are
crisp-tender, about 8-12 minutes.
Less if frozen.

■ Place in serving bowl and
keep warm.

■ In same saucepan, melt butter
over medium-hot heat. Add
almonds. Cook and stir 2 to 3
minutes or until lightly brown.

■ Stir in chives.

■ Pour mixture over beans; toss to
coat.

Serves 6

Variation: For a different flavor, substitute
chopped fresh dill for chives.

■ ■ ■ *"Handy-Andy" Tip: Freshen vegetables by adding a little vinegar to
the water when you wash them.*

Amalfi Green Beans

Cheryl Dowling

3 slices bacon, cut in half
2 cups sliced fresh
   mushrooms
½ cup chopped onion
1 clove garlic, minced
½ teaspoon basil leaves,
   crushed
1 10¾-ounce can
   condensed tomato soup
¼ cup water
2 9-ounce packages
   frozen Italian green
   beans, cooked and
   drained

■ Preheat oven to 350°.

■ In skillet, cook bacon until
crisp; remove.

■ Brown mushrooms, onion,
garlic and basil in drippings until
tender.

■ Add soup, water and beans.
Heat, stirring occasionally.

■ Pour into casserole dish.
Garnish top with bacon.

■ Bake in oven 350° for 20
minutes.

Serves 6-8 (4 cups)

Three Bean Bake

Susan Yarboro

1 16-ounce can pinto beans, undrained
1 16-ounce can chili beans, undrained
1 16-ounce can kidney beans, drained
½ cup ketchup
⅓ cup packed brown sugar
1 teaspoon salt
½ teaspoon ginger

■ In slow cooker, combine all ingredients; mix well; cover.
■ Cook on high for two hours.

Serves 10

Broccoli au Gratin

Patty Miller

2 10-ounce packages frozen chopped broccoli, cooked and drained
2 10-ounce cans cream of celery soup
1½ cups grated Cheddar cheese
½ cup mayonnaise
½ cup milk
  Ritz cracker crumbs
4 tablespoons butter, melted

■ Preheat oven to 350°.
■ Blend soup and cheese.
■ Blend mayonnaise with milk and stir into soup mixture.
■ Place broccoli in 13x9 baking dish and cover with sauce.
■ Cover top with cracker crumbs and drizzle with butter.
■ Bake at 350° for 45 minutes or until bubbly.

Serves 8-10

Can be prepared ahead.

Bacon Fried Carrots

Karen Washington

3-4 bacon slices
1 pound fresh or frozen
   carrots, peeled and
   sliced
1 medium onion, chopped
½ teaspoon salt
¼ teaspoon black pepper
   dash of sugar

■ In skillet, cook bacon slices until crisp. Remove and set aside.

■ Add carrots and onions to bacon fat.

■ Sprinkle with seasonings.

■ Cover and cook, slowly until just barely tender.

■ Uncover and cook, turning occasionally until carrots are slightly brown.

■ Crumble bacon and add to carrots.

■ Serve in a covered dish.

Serves 6 to 8

If using frozen carrots, reduce cooking time.

Honey Carrots

Lisa Johnson

10-12 small young carrots
2 tablespoons margarine
1 tablespoon brown sugar
1 tablespoon honey
2 tablespoons parsley or
   mint, finely chopped

■ Wash and trim carrots. Cook in a small amount of boiling salted water for 15 minutes, or until tender. Drain.

■ Melt margarine in a skillet or saucepan. Add sugar, honey and carrots.

■ Cook over low heat, turning carrots frequently until well-glazed.

■ Sprinkle with parsley or mint. Serve immediately.

Serves 4-6

Spicy Cream Corn

Holly Sullivan

4 3-ounce packages of cream cheese
½ cup milk
4 tablespoons butter
1 teaspoon garlic salt
2-3 cans chopped green chili peppers
4 12-ounce cans corn, drained

■ Preheat oven to 350°.
■ Place cheese, milk, butter, and garlic salt in saucepan. Cook over low heat until sauce-like.
■ Mix in chili peppers and corn.
■ Pour into dish.
■ Bake for 30 minutes at 350°.

Serves 8

Barron's Cheese Grits

Ann Hobbs

3½ cups water
¾ cup old fashioned grits, uncooked
½ roll jalapeño cheese
1 roll garlic cheese
2 tablespoons butter
1 egg, beaten

■ Preheat oven to 350°.
■ Stir grits into boiling water. Reduce heat to low, cover and continue cooking 15 to 20 minutes or until thickened, stirring occasionally.
■ Add cheeses, butter, egg and let melt thoroughly into grits. Continue stirring occasionally.
■ Pour into greased 1½-quart casserole dish.
■ Bake for 45 minutes or until top is set.

Serves 4

Elegant and Easy Eggplant Casserole   *Dinah Miller*

1 large eggplant, peeled
  and cubed
2 tablespoons butter
2 tablespoons flour
1 cup milk
1½ cups grated American
  cheese
1½ cups soft bread crumbs
1 small onion, finely
  chopped
1 tablespoon grated onion
1 tablespoon ketchup
2 eggs, separated, whites
  beaten
  salt and pepper, to taste

■ Preheat oven to 350°.

■ Cook eggplant in small amount of water until tender. Mash and drain. Set aside.

■ In large skillet, melt butter. Blend in flour.

■ Add milk gradually and cook, stirring constantly until thickened.

■ Add eggplant, cheese, bread crumbs, onion, ketchup, and egg yolks. Season.

■ Fold in beaten egg whites.

■ Pour into casserole dish and bake at 350° for one hour and fifteen minutes.

Serves 6-8

■ ■ ■ *"Handy-Andy" Tip: A general rule of thumb for cooking vegetables is if they are grown underground, cook covered; grown above ground, cook uncovered.*

Mushroom Casserole   *Kathy Tuthill*

1 pound fresh mushrooms,
  coarsely chopped
3 tablespoons butter
2 small onions, chopped
2 eggs
⅔ cup bread crumbs
¾ cup milk
¾ cup cream
2 teaspoons seasoned salt
½ teaspoon pepper
1 tablespoon parsley

■ Preheat oven to 350°.

■ Sauté onions and mushrooms in butter.

■ Beat eggs. Add crumbs, milk, cream, salt and pepper, and parsley.

■ Fold in mushrooms and onions.

■ Bake at 350° for 1-1¼ hours or until golden and set.

Serves 6-8

Sautéed Mushrooms Spectacular

Nancy Marston

3 green onions with tops,
   chopped
¼ cup butter or margarine,
   melted
1 pound fresh mushrooms,
   sliced
¼ cup dry white wine
¼ teaspoon salt
¼ teaspoon pepper
⅛ teaspoon garlic powder
2 teaspoons
   Worcestershire sauce

■ Sauté green onions in butter until tender.

■ Stir in remaining ingredients. Cook uncovered , over low heat 30 to 35 minutes or until mushrooms are tender.

Serves 4

Au Gratin Potatoes

Amy Kelly

4 pounds red potatoes
1 teaspoon salt
2 cups grated sharp
   Cheddar cheese,
   divided
½ cup chopped onion
¼ cup butter, cut into small
   pieces
¼ teaspoon white pepper
½ teaspoon seasoned salt
2 10-ounce cans
   mushroom soup
½ cup milk

■ Preheat oven to 350°.

■ Peel and cook potatoes in boiling salted water for 5 minutes. Drain immediately.

■ In a large bowl, cut potatoes in bite-sized pieces.

■ Mix potatoes with 1¾ cups cheese, onion, butter, pepper, seasoned salt and soup mixed with milk.

■ Pour mixture into buttered 3-quart casserole. Top with remaining cheese.

■ Bake 45 minutes to 1 hour, or until potatoes are cooked but still firm.

Serves 10 to 12

Buffet Potatoes

2 pounds frozen hash
brown potatoes
½ cup melted butter
¼ cup minced onion
1 pint sour cream
1 10-ounce can cream of
mushroom soup
10 ounces grated Cheddar
cheese

■ Preheat oven to 350°.

■ Mix all ingredients and put in
13x9 casserole.

■ Bake for one hour at 350°.

Serves 8

■ ■ ■ *"Handy-Andy" Tip: Give mashed potatoes a beautiful whipped cream
look by adding hot milk to them before you start mashing.*

Potato Mounds   *Stephanie Zimmermann*

2 pounds baking potatoes
2 tablespoons flour
½ teaspoon salt
¼ teaspoon pepper
2 tablespoons minced
parsley
1 clove garlic, crushed
2 eggs
¼ cup melted butter
paprika, to garnish

■ Preheat oven to 375°.

■ Peel and quarter potatoes. Boil
in salted water until done. Drain
and mash.

■ Beat in flour, salt, pepper,
garlic, parsley and eggs.

■ When smooth, form into 12
balls and place in buttered,
shallow baking dish.

■ Brush lightly with butter and
sprinkle with paprika.

■ Bake at 375° for 25 minutes
or until puffed and lightly
browned.

Serves 4-6

Refrigerator Mashed Potatoes

Dawn Murphy

5 pounds potatoes, pared
   and quartered (9 large)
2 3-ounce packages
   cream cheese
1 cup sour cream
2 teaspoons onion salt
1 teaspoon salt
¼ teaspoon pepper
2 tablespoons butter or
   margarine
   grated Cheddar cheese,
   to garnish

■ Cook potatoes in boiling salted water until tender. Drain well. Mash until smooth.

■ Add cream cheese, sour cream, onion salt, salt, pepper and butter.

■ Beat until smooth and fluffy.

■ Place in refrigerator container. Cover.

■ To serve: Place desired amount of potatoes in a greased casserole dish. Dot with butter and or top with grated cheese. Bake at 350° for 30 minutes or until heated thoroughly.

Recommended storage time: 2 weeks.

 # Sweet Potato Casserole

Reba Pennington

Potatos
1 ½ cups mashed and
   cooked sweet potatoes
½ stick oleo
½ cup sugar
1 egg
½ can coconut
⅓ cup cream or milk
1 tablespoon vanilla
Topping
½ cup brown sugar
½ cup flour
½ cup pecans (finely
   chopped)
½ cup melted oleo

■ Preheat oven to 350°.

■ Combine all potato ingredients. Mix well. Pour into a buttered casserole dish.

■ In a separate bowl, mix topping ingredients. Spread crumb mixture over top of potato casserole.

■ Bake at 350° for 20-30 minutes.

Serves 6

Freezes well.

Roasted Potatoes

Brenda Brandon

3 pounds baby new
   potatoes
2 teaspoons olive oil
   salt and pepper, to taste
3 unpeeled cloves garlic
4 sprigs thyme or
   rosemary

■ Preheat oven to 400°.

■ Rub potatoes with oil and
sprinkle with salt and pepper.

■ Arrange potatoes in a baking
pan and scatter garlic cloves and
herb sprigs around them.

■ Roast 25 to 40 minutes,
shaking pan from time to time
until potatoes are tender.

Serves 8

Grilled Potato Salad

Lisa Matchett

Heat up the grill

  ½ pound bacon, diced
  ¾ cup onion, chopped
  ⅓ cup green pepper,
     chopped
  6 cups cooked potatoes,
     cubed
  ¾ cup mayonnaise
  ⅓ cup pimento, chopped
  ¼ cup prepared mustard
  1 teaspoon salt
  ¼ cup sugar
  ⅛ teaspoon pepper

■ Cook onion and pepper with
partially cooked bacon until
bacon is crisp.

■ Add remaining ingredients and
toss lightly.

■ Wrap and cover securely.

■ Heat on grill 30-40 minutes.

Serves 6-8

**Can also be heated in a 325° oven for 30-40
minutes or as desired.**

■ ■ ■ *"Handy-Andy" Tip: To prevent peeled potatoes from turning brown,
keep in cold water during preparation.*

Warm Potatoes Vinaigrette

Brenda Brandon

2 pounds tiny new
potatoes
8 teaspoons olive oil
6 tablespoons tarragon
vinegar
8 scallions
fresh ground black
pepper

■ Scrub potatoes with skins on.

■ Boil until tender, approximately
20 minutes.

■ Beat oil with vinegar.

■ Slice scallions into rings and
stir into dressing. Season with
pepper.

■ When potatoes are cooked,
drain and cut in halves or quarters. Stir with dressing.

Serves 6

Baked Onions

Debbie Longanecker

12 medium onions, sliced
1 3-ounce bag of potato
chips, crushed
½ pound American
cheese, sliced
2 10-ounce cans cream of
mushroom soup
½ cup milk
1 teaspoon pepper

■ Preheat oven to 350°.

■ Butter a 2-quart baking dish.

■ Layer sliced onions, potato
chips and cheese. End with layer
of cheese.

■ Mix soup, milk, and pepper.
Pour over onions.

■ Bake 1 ½ hours.

Serves 8

French Onion Rice

Kathleen Stephen

1 cup rice (not instant)
1 can French onion soup
1 can broth (beef, chicken
or vegetable)
1 4-ounce can
mushrooms, drained
1 tablespoon butter
(optional)

■ Preheat oven to 350°.

■ Mix in 1-quart casserole.

■ Bake at 350° about 50
minutes or until liquid is absorbed. Fluff with fork before
serving.

Southwestern Risotto

Pat Lawler

½ cup chopped onion
2 cloves garlic, crushed
2 tablespoons butter or
   margarine, melted
1 cup medium-grain rice,
   uncooked
½ cup dry white wine
6 cups chicken broth,
   divided
½ cup whipping cream
2 medium tomatoes,
   seeded and chopped
1 jalapeño pepper,
   seeded and minced
½ cup sliced green onions
½ cup grated Parmesan
   cheese
3 tablespoons minced
   cilantro
   fresh cilantro sprigs,
   cubed tomatoes, garnish

■ Cook onion and garlic in butter in a large skillet or saucepan over medium heat, stirring constantly, until tender.

■ Add rice; cook 2 to 3 minutes, stirring frequently with a wooden spoon.

■ Add wine and cook, uncovered, until liquid is absorbed.

■ Add one cup broth; cook, stirring constantly, over medium-high heat 5 minutes or until broth is absorbed. Add remaining broth, 1 cup at a time, cooking and stirring constantly until each cup is absorbed, about 25 to 30 minutes. (Rice will be tender and have a creamy consistency).

■ Stir in whipping cream and next five ingredients. Cook 2 minutes.

■ Garnish, if desired, and serve immediately.

Serves 6

Can be served as a main meal, with a nice green salad.

"Star patterns abound in the history of quiltmaking. Their point of light created through clever use of triangles, diamonds and other geometric shapes. Quilters of the past, their feet planted on the ground, stitched heavenly beauties to warm their families on cold prairie nights."

Quilts from America's Heartland

Southwestern Rice

Brenda Brandon

1 teaspoon salt
1½ cups white rice
2 cups frozen vegetables
1 4-ounce can diced green chilies
1 tablespoon margarine

■ In a large pot of boiling water, add salt and rice. Bring back to a medium boil and cook uncovered, for approximately 12 minutes. Stir in vegetables halfway through cooking.

■ Drain mixture through strainer. Return to pan and add chilies and margarine. Stir.

■ Season to taste.

Serves 4

■ ■ ■ *"Handy-Andy" Tip: Rice is cooked if it is soft when squeezed between the fingers.*

Snow Peas Canton

Amy Kelly

1 tablespoon peanut oil
4-5 cloves of fresh garlic, minced
½ pound Chinese pea pods, end trimmed and strings removed
1 5-ounce can sliced bamboo shoots, drained
1 8-ounce can water chestnuts, drained and sliced
¼ cup canned or fresh chicken broth
2 teaspoons soy sauce
1 teaspoon cornstarch
2 teaspoons water

■ Heat oil in a large skillet or wok.

■ Sauté garlic until light brown.

■ Add snow peas, bamboo shoots and water chestnuts. Stir fry one minute.

■ Add chicken broth and soy sauce. Cover and cook another minute.

■ Combine cornstarch and water. Stir into skillet.

■ Cook over high heat until sauce thickens and appears glossy, about one minute.

Serves 4

Squash and Peppers on the Grill

Lori Anderson

Heat up the grill.

¼ cup margarine or butter, melted
1 tablespoon chopped fresh oregano or 1 teaspoon dried oregano
1 clove garlic, crushed
½ teaspoon salt
¼ teaspoon pepper
6 small pattypan squash or 3 medium zucchini or 3 yellow squash
1 large red or green bell pepper, cut into sixths, seeded
1 large onion, cut into sixths

■ In a small bowl combine margarine, oregano, garlic, salt and pepper; mix well.

■ Cut vegetables in half lengthwise.

■ Place vegetables in wire grill basket or directly on grill 4 to 6 inches above medium coals.

■ Brush vegetables with margarine mixture.

■ Cook 8 minutes; turn grill basket or using tongs turn vegetables.

■ Brush with margarine mixture. Cook 4 to 6 minutes or until vegetables are crisp-tender.

■ Garnish with fresh oregano.

Serves 6

Variation: May be prepared under the broiler.

Stories of bravery abound in Texas quilts. When Polly McCright made her Octagon Star quilt in 1890, she stitched into it the memories of holding off an Indian attack in a one-room cabin sheltering thirty-eight terrified settlers.

Summer Vegetables Italiano
Lori Anderson

Crouton Crumbs
(directions below)
2 tablespoons margarine
or butter
1½ teaspoons instant
chicken bouillon (dry)
¾ teaspoon snipped fresh
or ¼ teaspoon dried
basil
1 medium onion, chopped
2 medium zucchini, thinly
sliced
8 ounces mushrooms,
sliced
2 large tomatoes, each cut
into 10-12 wedges

■ Prepare Crouton Crumbs.

■ Place margarine, bouillon, basil and onion in 3-quart micro-wave safe casserole.

■ Cover tightly and microwave on high for 3 minutes.

■ Stir in zucchini and mushrooms

■ Cover and microwave until zucchini is crisp-tender, approximately 3-4 minutes.

■ Stir in tomatoes. Cover and microwave until tomatoes are hot, approximately 2 to 3 minutes.

■ Sprinkle each serving with Crouton Crumbs.

Crouton Crumbs

1 cup baking mix
½ cup coarsely chopped
walnuts
3 tablespoons margarine
or butter, softened
3 tablespoons boiling
water
⅛ teaspoon garlic powder

■ Mix all ingredients thoroughly with fork in microwave safe pie plate (9x11-inches). Spread evenly.

■ Microwave on high 2 minutes; break up with a fork and stir.

■ Rotate plate ½ turn.

■ Microwave until puffed and dry, 1½ to 2½ minutes longer.

■ Break into about ¼-inch pieces.

Serves 5 to 6

Can be prepared ahead and stored in an air tight container.

Zucchini and Cheese Casserole

Amy Kelly

3 medium zucchini
1 teaspoon salt
2 tablespoons olive oil
½ cup chopped onions
1 clove garlic, minced
1 16-ounce can tomatoes, undrained
½ teaspoon dried basil leaves, crushed
½ teaspoon dried oregano, crushed
¼ teaspoon pepper
1 cup grated Parmesan cheese
2 cups shredded mozzarella cheese

■ Preheat oven to 350°.

■ Cut unpeeled zucchini into ½-inch thick slices; sprinkle with salt and spread on wax paper. Let stand 15 minutes and rinse.

■ Heat olive oil in a large skillet. Sauté onion and garlic until tender. Add tomatoes and seasonings. Cover and simmer.

■ Place ½ of zucchini in a single layer in a buttered 10x7-inch baking dish.

■ Cover with ½ of the tomato mixture, ½ of Parmesan and ½ of mozzarella.

■ Repeat layers.

■ Bake uncovered at 350° for 45 to 60 minutes.

Serves 6 to 8

Best Ever Squash Casserole

Julie Robinson

1½ pounds sliced, cooked and drained yellow squash
1 can cream of chicken soup
1 cup sour cream
2 medium onions, chopped
1 stick margarine
1 can chopped water chestnuts
1 sleeve Ritz crackers, plus a few extra for topping
1 medium carrot, sliced
salt and pepper, to taste

■ Preheat oven to 350°.

■ Crush half of crackers. Spread in bottom of 9x13 casserole dish.

■ Dot with half of margarine and then half of: squash, onions, water chestnuts, carrots, salt and pepper.

■ Mix soup and sour cream together. Spread half of mixture over the other layers. Repeat. End with soup mixture.

■ Crush a few extra crackers and sprinkle over the top.

■ Bake at 350° for 45 minutes.

Serves 6-8

Spinach Pudding

Renee Tucei

2 10-ounce packages
frozen chopped
spinach, cooked,
drained well
1 egg
1 pound cottage cheese
¾ cup Italian bread
crumbs
¾ cup grated Parmesan
cheese
salt and pepper to taste
¼ teaspoon dried dill

■ Preheat oven to 350°.

■ Mix spinach with all other
ingredients. If dry, add 2 tablespoons milk.

■ Pour spinach mixture in a
greased 8x8 inch casserole.

■ Bake at 350° for 25 minutes
or until heated through.

Serves 6-8

Baked Tomatoes with Corn Soufflé

Brenda Brandon

4 medium tomatoes
Dijon mustard
1-2 strips bacon, fried and
crumbled
1 package corn soufflé,
thawed

■ Preheat oven to 300°.

■ Cut off top of tomatoes.
Remove pulp.

■ Turn tomatoes upside down.
Drain on paper towels.

■ Spread a small amount of
mustard on the inside of the
tomatoes.

■ Sprinkle crumbled bacon in the
tomatoes.

■ Fill tomatoes with corn soufflé.

■ Bake uncovered at 300° for
20 minutes.

Serves 4

Easy dish for entertaining.

May substitute spinach soufflé.

Be careful not to overbake the tomatoes or
they will fall apart.

Baked Tomatoes with Mushrooms

Dorin Harrison

1 garlic clove, pressed
1 teaspoon minced fresh
  basil
3 tablespoons peanut oil,
  divided use
1 tablespoon butter
½ pound fresh mushrooms,
  chopped
  salt, to taste
  pepper, to taste
4 large tomatoes, halved
2 teaspoons sugar
½ cup dry bread crumbs

■ Preheat oven to 425°.

■ In frying pan, sauté garlic with basil in one tablespoon hot oil until brown.

■ Add butter and heat.

■ When hot, add mushrooms and stir over high heat for 2 minutes.

■ Remove from heat, stir in salt and pepper and keep warm.

■ Sprinkle each tomato with ¼ teaspoon sugar and additional pepper. Set aside.

■ Mix bread crumbs with 2 tablespoons oil.

■ Spread on tomatoes, place in 11x7-inch baking dish and bake at 425° for 20 minutes.

■ Top with mushroom mixture.

Serves 8

 ## Oyster Dressing

Pam Polsky

1 pint oysters, drained
  (reserve liquid)
⅓ cup cream
¼ cup melted butter
4 cups large bread
  crumbs
¼ teaspoon pepper
2 tablespoons sherry
1 teaspoon
  Worcestershire sauce

■ Preheat oven to 425°.

■ Mix cream with reserved oyster liquid and set aside.

■ Mix butter and bread crumbs. Add cream sauce and remaining ingredients. Mix well.

■ Butter the bottom of a shallow baking dish and pour in the bread crumb mixture.

■ Bake at 425° for 15 minutes.

Serves 10

Mom's Thanksgiving Dressing

Anne Hobbs

Prepare ahead

2 small packages of cornbread mix
3 pieces toasted bread
2 large onions, finely chopped
5 stalks of celery, finely chopped
1 bunch parsley, finely chopped
1 bunch green onions, finely chopped
1 stick butter
3 eggs, well beaten
1/16 teaspoon poultry seasoning
1-3 14½-ounce cans chicken broth (as needed for moisture) salt, red pepper, black pepper to taste

■ Prepare cornbread mix according to directions. Toast bread. Let cornbread and toast sit out overnight.

■ Preheat oven to 350°.

■ Sauté vegetables in butter.

■ Crumble cornbread and toast together. Add vegetables.

■ Mix together with chicken broth, eggs and seasonings.

■ Bake at 350° for 45 minutes.

Serves 6-8

THE SMELL OF THANKSGIVING
Salty
Sour
Spicy
Sweet
Buttery
Toasty
Crispy
Roasty
Gingery
Tary
Peppery
Sharp
Candied
Sugary
Fresh
Mmmmmm Good!

197

Sage Dressing

Lisa Johnson

2 cans biscuits
1 small package of
   cornbread mix
10 eggs (raw or boiled)
2 14½-ounce cans
   chicken broth
1 onion, chopped
1 bunch celery, chopped
   sage and thyme to taste

■ Preheat oven to 375°.

■ Cook biscuits and cornbread according to box directions. and crumble into a large bowl.

■ Add eggs (raw or boiled). If boiled, shell, and grind up all eggs. Add to bowl.

■ Add chicken broth. If turkey is cooked, add 2 cups of broth from roasting pan.

■ Sauté in skillet: onions and celery until soft. Add to mixture. Stir completely and season to taste.

■ Put into an aluminum or glass baking dish coated with non-stick vegetable spray.

■ Bake at 375° for 45 minutes to 1 hour if raw eggs, 30-45 minutes if boiled eggs.

Serves 6

When a five year old boy was diagnosed with cancer, all he wanted to take to the hospital beside his teddy was the quilt his mom had made him. Recognizing the comfort her small son drew from his quilt, she realized that many a "small visitor" to the hospital could benefit from the same. She engaged the quilting community by requesting squares of fabric to be turned into simplistic quilts. The response was so tremendous, that a quilting guild has now taken the project over and has produced dozens of quilts for the pediatric wing of the local hospital to provide the warmth and comfort that only a quilt and a mother's love can give.

Turkey Tracks Dressing

Toni Anderson

1 package of cornbread mix
3 or 4 pieces white bread
1 onion, chopped
1 celery stalk, chopped
1 stick butter
½ cup milk
8 eggs (4 raw, 4 hard boiled)
broth from cooking neck and gizzards
sage, salt and pepper, and poultry seasoning to taste

■ Preheat oven to 375°.

■ Crumble white bread with corn bread.

■ Prepare cornbread mix according to package directions.

■ Melt stick of butter and sauté onions and celery until transparent.

■ Add 4 raw eggs and milk to bread. Add sliced, peeled hard boiled eggs.

■ Add broth until soupy.

■ Season with sage, poultry seasoning, salt and pepper to taste.

■ Put mixture in a 13x9-inch Pyrex dish coated with non-stick vegetable spray.

■ Bake at 375° for 1 hour.

Serves 6-8

■ ■ ■ *"Handy-Andy" Tip: Allow about ¾ cup stuffing for each pound of poultry you are roasting. For turkeys over 14 pounds, allow ½ cup stuffing for each pound.*

A superstitious woman would never allow a young boy to be covered by a pattern named Wandering Foot. It was thought to cause him to grow up discontented, unstable and of a roving nature. The name was later changed to Turkey Tracks, thus breaking the curse and clearing the way for future generations

Hot Alabama Fruit

Mary Pierson

1 stick butter, divided use
¼ cup flour
1 large can pear halves
1 large can pineapple chunks
1 large can apricot halves
1 large can peach halves
1 small jar maraschino cherries
1 cup brown sugar
¼ teaspoon curry powder
½ teaspoon cinnamon
½ teaspoon nutmeg

■ Preheat oven to 325°.

■ Melt half stick butter, work in flour to make a paste.

■ Spread paste on bottom of greased baking dish.

■ Drain fruit. Add fruit on top of paste, adding cherries last.

■ Combine brown sugar, curry powder, cinnamon and nutmeg, and sprinkle on top of fruit evenly.

■ Pour remaining melted butter over fruit.

■ Bake for one hour.

Great with ham!

Serves 8

Another quilt carries a story of unrequited love in its Oak Leaf and Acorn design. Made by a Texas girl for the man she hoped to marry, instead it was given to him as a wedding gift when he married someone else. The quilt was never used because his wife refused to sleep under it!

SUGAR BOWL

All the romanticism of an old-fashioned suitor presenting his girl with a bouquet of flowers is captured in the Nosegay quilt. Pink, blue, orchid, yellow and green are combined in the patches treatment. The Nosegay design was inspired by bouquets of small colorful flowers wrapped in green paper. Parisian men traditionally gave these bouquets to women whose hearts they wanted to win. Having fallen by the wayside, along with the gesture of giving flowers, the simple pleasures of smelling an apple pie cooling in a window, the softness and warmth of a kitten on one's lap, even reading to your child at bedtime by the light of a fire is only a memory. It is this wish to "turn back the clock" that precipitated the feeling recreated in the charm of the Nosegay quilt and the cabinet of covers in this picture.

During the Depression, feed sack materials utilized for the necessary purposes of making clothing then found their way into the scrap bags of quilters. It is no longer as easy to date a quilt utilizing these material prints, as Barbara Kauffman's quilt testifies. She utilized reproductions of 1930's patterns that can now be obtained in cloth stores. She and five friends made this festive quilt while belonging to a friendship group they nicknamed the "Make It On Monday" group. Barbara named her quilt Posies of Friendship and received a third place ribbon in the 1995 Dallas Quilt show.

The TEXAS SAMPLER appreciates Barbara Kauffman helping us return to a slower pace (even just for a moment) as well as thanking the following ladies for providing the quilts displayed in the antique chest: Bowtie - Janie Trantham, Single Wedding Ring - Betty Cox, Star and Double Wedding Ring - Charlotte Fowler, Log Cabin and Tennessee Waltz - Barbara Kauffman.

Imagine the delight of a guest when offered the selection of these prized quilts! It would indeed be like stepping back in time when easygoing hospitality for your family and friends was an expression of love and a sense of heritage!

Bill and Rita Clements' Apple Cake

Sarah Bishop, Executive Chef at the Texas Governor's Mansion

- 1 cup cooking oil
- 2 cups sugar
- 3 eggs
- 2½ cups flour
- 2 teaspoons baking powder
- 1 teaspoon baking soda
- 1 teaspoon salt
- 1 teaspoon ground cinnamon
- 1 teaspoon ground nutmeg
- 1 teaspoon vanilla
- 4 cups peeled and chopped Granny Smith apples
- 1 cup chopped pecans

■ Preheat oven to 350°.

■ Combine oil and sugar.

■ Beat each egg in one at a time.

■ Sift together dry ingredients and stir into egg mixture.

■ Fold in vanilla, apples, and pecans.

■ Pour into an 8½x11 pan that has been sprayed with cooking oil.

■ Bake for 55 to 60 minutes, or until a knife inserted in the center comes out clean.

Orange Glazed Carrot Cake

Charlotte Sullivan

Cake

- 4 eggs, beaten
- 2 cups sugar
- 1¼ cups oil
- 1 teaspoon vanilla extract
- 2 cups flour
- 2 teaspoons baking soda
- 2 teaspoons baking powder
- 1 teaspoon salt
- 1 teaspoon cinnamon
- ¼ cup buttermilk
- 3 tablespoons grated orange peel
- 1 cup pecans, chopped
- 1 pound carrots, shredded

Glaze

- 8 ounces cream cheese, softened
- 1 pound powdered sugar
  orange juice

■ Preheat oven to 350°.

■ Beat eggs with sugar, oil and vanilla.

■ Sift next five dry ingredients. Mix with egg mixture. Stir in buttermilk. Fold in orange peel, pecans and carrots.

■ Pour into greased and floured 10-inch tube pan. Bake for approximately 30 minutes or until done. Allow cake to cool.

■ Glaze: with mixer, blend cream cheese and sugar. Gradually stir in orange juice until glaze reaches desired consistency. Glaze cake once cooled.

Serves 12

Italian Cream Cake

Charlotte Fowler

Cake

- 1 stick margarine, softened
- ½ cup shortening
- 2 cups sugar
- 5 egg yolks
- 2 cups flour
- 1 teaspoon baking soda
- 1 cup buttermilk
- 1 teaspoon vanilla
- 1 can coconut, flaked
- 1 cup chopped nuts
- 5 egg whites, stiffly beaten

Cream Cheese Frosting

- 8 ounces cream cheese, softened
- 1 stick margarine, softened
- 1 teaspoon vanilla
- 16 ounces powdered sugar
  chopped pecans for garnish

■ Preheat oven to 350°.

■ Cream margarine and shortening. Add sugar and beat until smooth. Add egg yolks and beat.

■ Combine flour and baking soda, alternately with buttermilk. Stir in vanilla. Add coconuts and nuts. Fold in egg whites.

■ Pour into 3 greased and floured 8-inch cake pans. Bake for 25 minutes. Cool and frost.

■ For frosting, cream margarine and cream cheese. Add vanilla and powdered sugar. Spread frosting between layers and outside of cake.

■ Sprinkle top with pecans.

Serves 10 to 12

The same generation that knew the language of flowers devised the language of quilts. Pineapples denoted hospitality and were considered lucky and able to bring friends closer. The dove symbolized femininity and a happy marriage. A group of young women was called a "dove party"...far more flattering than our today term of "hen party".

Golden Carrot Cake

Ann Baillargeon

Cake

3 eggs
2 cups sugar
1½ cups vegetable oil
2 teaspoons vanilla
2 cups flour
2 teaspoons baking soda
2 teaspoons cinnamon
1 teaspoon salt
2 large carrots, coarsely grated
1⅓ cups pineapple, unsweetened, chopped, drained
3½ ounces flaked coconut, optional
1 cup chopped pecans

Cream Cheese Frosting

4 ounces cream cheese, softened
1 stick butter, softened
3 cups powdered sugar
1 tablespoon vanilla

■ Preheat oven to 350°.

■ Beat eggs, add sugar and oil. Add vanilla.

■ In small bowl, sift flour, baking soda, cinnamon, and salt. Combine flour mixture with egg mixture.

■ Add carrots, pineapple, coconut and pecans, in order. Beat until mixed thoroughly.

■ Pour into greased 9x13 inch pan. Bake for 50 minutes. Allow to cool.

■ Beat cream cheese, butter, powdered sugar, and 1 teaspoon vanilla until creamy. Spread on carrot cake.

Serves 10 to 12

■ ■ ■ *"Handy-Andy" Tip: Layer cakes frost easier if frozen 30 minutes prior to frosting.*

The Swastika, for thousands of years until World War II, was considered by many races of men a sign of good fortune and fertility.

Lemonade Cake

Lori Anderson

1 package lemon cake mix
1 small package lemon instant pudding
⅔ cup oil
1½ cups water
4 eggs
1 small can frozen lemonade, thawed
2 cups powdered sugar

■ Preheat oven to 350°.

■ Mix together cake mix, pudding, oil and water. Add eggs and beat for 2 minutes at medium speed.

■ Pour into greased 9x13 inch pan. Bake for 40 minutes.

■ While cake is baking, mix together lemonade and powdered sugar.

■ When cake is done, poke holes all over top of cake with a cake tester. Pour lemonade mixture over top. Bake 5 more minutes.

■ Cool.

Serves 10 to 12

■ ■ ■ *"Handy-Andy" Tip: Soak lemon in hot water for five minutes, and roll on the countertop before squeezing to yield more juice.*

 ## "Garden of Eden" Cake

Barbara Cicchillo

3 cups flour
2½ cups plus 5 tablespoons sugar, divided use
1 cup oil
4 eggs
½ teaspoon salt
⅓ cup orange juice
3 teaspoons baking powder
4 large apples, cored and diced
1 teaspoon cinnamon

■ Preheat oven to 350°.

■ Combine flour, 2½ cups sugar, oil, eggs, salt, orange juice and baking powder. Beat until smooth.

■ Mix together apples, cinnamon and remaining sugar.

■ Layer batter and apple mixture in a greased 9x3 inch tube pan. End layering with apple mixture.

■ Bake for 1 hour 45 minutes.

Serves 10 to 12

Freezes great!

"Topsy Turvy" Cake

Julie Robinson

- ¼ cup butter or margarine
- 1 cup brown sugar
- 1 large can pineapple, chunks or rings, drained
- ⅓ cup maraschino cherries, halved
- ¾ cup sugar
- ¼ cup oil
- 1 egg
- 1¼ cups flour, sifted
- 2 teaspoons baking powder
- ½ cup milk
- 1 teaspoon vanilla

■ Preheat oven to 350°.

■ Melt butter or margarine in saucepan. Add brown sugar. Stir and warm until sugar begins to dissolve. Pour into round or square cake pan.

■ Arrange pineapple and cherries over butter/sugar mixture.

■ Mix together remaining ingredients. Pour over fruit.

■ Bake 25 to 30 minutes.

■ Cool five minutes and invert onto serving dish.

■ When cool, carefully lift cake pan off.

Serves 12

This makes a nice size cake for a family.

Cream Cheese Banana Cake

Karen Washington

Cake
- 3 cups sugar
- 1 cup shortening
- 4 eggs
- ½ cup sour milk (milk with approximately 1 tablespoon vinegar)
- 3 cups flour
- 2 teaspoons vanilla
- 2 teaspoons baking soda
- 2 cups pecans, optional
- 2 cups bananas, mashed

Frosting
- 4 ounces cream cheese, softened
- 2 cups powdered sugar
- 2-3 tablespoons milk

■ Preheat oven to 325°.

■ Cream sugar, shortening and eggs. Alternate adding sour milk and flour. Add remaining ingredients.

■ Pour into a greased and floured pan.

■ Bake for 1 hour. Allow to cool.

■ Cream together cream cheese, powdered sugar and milk. Frost cake.

Serves 10 to 12

Grandma's Hint of Mint Chocolate Cake   *Carol Gockel*

Cake
>   2 cups flour
>   2 cups sugar
>   ¼ cup cocoa
>   1 teaspoon cinnamon
>   1 cup butter
>   1 cup water
>   1 teaspoon baking soda
>   1 egg
>   ½ cup buttermilk
>   1 teaspoon vanilla
>   1 14-ounce package
>   miniature chocolate-
>   covered soft
>   peppermints,
>   unwrapped

Chocolate Frosting
>   ½ cup butter
>   ⅓ cup milk
>   16 ounces powdered
>   sugar, sifted
>   ¼ cup cocoa
>   1 teaspoon vanilla

- Combine flour, sugar, cocoa, and cinnamon and set aside.
- Combine butter and water in a saucepan and bring to a boil. Remove from heat. Stir in baking soda.
- Add flour mixture and stir well. Stir in egg, buttermilk, and vanilla.
- Pour batter into a greased and floured 9x13 inch pan. Bake for 30 minutes.
- Top with chocolate-covered soft peppermints and bake for 2 additional minutes. Gently spread melted candy over top.
- Combine butter and milk in a saucepan; bring to a boil. Remove from heat. Combine sifted powdered sugar and cocoa; add to butter mixture. Add vanilla, stir until smooth.
- Allow cake to cool and frost.

Serves 10 to 12

Poppy Seed Pound Cake   *Anne Hobbs*

>   1 box butter yellow cake
>   mix
>   8 ounces sour cream
>   ½ cup sugar
>   4 eggs
>   ¾ cup oil
>   2 tablespoons poppy
>   seeds

- Preheat oven to 350°.
- Beat together butter yellow cake mix, sour cream, sugar, eggs and oil for 3 to 4 minutes.
- Mix in poppy seeds.
- Grease 10x3½ inch bundt pan and coat with sugar.
- Pour batter in bundt pan. Bake for 1 hour.

Serves 10 to 12

Freezes well.

Chocolate Chip Pound Cake

Stella Daniel

1 package yellow cake mix
1 3.9-ounce package instant chocolate pudding
½ cup sugar
¾ cup oil
¾ cup water
4 eggs
1 small package tiny chocolate chips
8 ounces sour cream
1 teaspoon vanilla

■ Preheat oven to 350°.

■ Grease and flour a 9x3 inch bundt pan.

■ Combine all ingredients in order. Mix thoroughly. Pour into bundt pan.

■ Bake for approximately 45 minutes, or until cake tester, when inserted in cake, comes out clean.

Serves 10 to 12

■ ■ ■ *"Handy-Andy" Tip: When making chocolate cake, use cocoa instead of flour to prepare the pan.*

Mary's Buttermilk Pound Cake

Missy Griffy

2 sticks butter, softened
3 cups sugar
4 eggs
1 teaspoon vanilla
3 cups flour
¼ teaspoon baking soda
1 cup buttermilk
dash of salt

■ Preheat oven to 350°.

■ Cream together butter and sugar. Add unbeaten eggs, one at a time. Add vanilla.

■ Mix in flour and baking soda, alternately with buttermilk. Add a dash of salt.

■ Pour batter into greased and floured 9x3 inch tube pan. Bake for one hour and 10 minutes.

■ Cool for 15 minutes and remove from pan.

Serves 10 to 12

Texas Mud Cake

Stephanie Nowacki

Cake
- 4 eggs
- 2 cups sugar
- 2 sticks margarine, softened
- 1¼ cups flour, sifted
- 4 tablespoons cocoa
- 1⅓ cups pecans, coarsely chopped
- 2 teaspoons vanilla
  miniature marshmallows

Frosting
- 1 stick margarine
- 16 ounces powdered sugar
- 4 tablespoons cocoa
- 5 tablespoons milk

■ Preheat oven to 350°

■ Slightly beat eggs in large bowl, add sugar. Stir well. Do not beat. Stir in margarine. Mix well.

■ Add flour, cocoa, and pecans. Stir well, do not beat. Add vanilla. Stir until smooth.

■ Pour batter into well greased and floured 9x13 inch pan. Bake for 40 minutes or until done.

■ Immediately after removing cake from oven, cover top of cake with miniature marshmallows. Turn off oven. Return cake to oven for one minute to slightly melt marshmallows.

■ Combine margarine, powdered sugar, cocoa, and milk to make frosting. Frost cake carefully while it is still hot.

Serves 10 to 12

Many women found the pioneer experience a desperately lonely life. The social and aesthetic values of quilt making offered solace to them as they dealt with isolation, cold and oftentimes colorless homes. The quilting bee established itself as one of the main social events in the sparsely populated areas of early Texas.

"Hosannah" Chocolate Cake

Cindy Hartley

Cake
- 1 stick margarine
- ½ cup vegetable oil
- 3 tablespoons (heaping) cocoa
- 1 cup water
- 2 cups flour
- 2 cups sugar
- 2 eggs
- ½ cup buttermilk
- 1 teaspoon baking soda
- 1 teaspoon vanilla

Frosting
- 1 stick margarine
- 3 tablespoons (heaping) cocoa
- 6 tablespoons milk
- 1 pound powdered sugar
- 1 teaspoon vanilla
- 1 cup pecans, chopped

■ Preheat oven to 400°.

■ Combine in a saucepan 1 stick margarine, oil, 3 tablespoons cocoa and water and bring to a boil.

■ Combine flour and sugar. Make well in dry ingredients. Add contents of saucepan.

■ Beat at medium speed. Add eggs, buttermilk, baking soda and vanilla. Mix well.

■ Pour into two greased and floured 8 or 9-inch round cake pans, or in 9x13 inch cake pan. Bake for 20 minutes.

■ Frosting: Combine margarine, cocoa and milk in a saucepan. Bring to a boil. Add powdered sugar and vanilla. Beat until smooth and thick. Stir in pecans.

■ Allow cake to cool before frosting.

Serves 10 to 12

■ ■ ■ *"Handy-Andy" Tip: The recipe that is not shared with others will be soon forgotten, but when it is shared it will be enjoyed by future generations.*

Chocolate Chip Bundt Cake

Kathy Whipple

¾ cup unsalted butter
¾ cup sugar
1 cup light brown sugar, firmly packed
3 eggs
1½ teaspoons vanilla
1½ cups semisweet chocolate chips
1½ teaspoons baking soda
1½ cups sour cream
3 cups cake flour, sifted powdered sugar, optional

■ Preheat oven to 350°.

■ Grease and lightly flour 10x3½ inch bundt pan.

■ Cream butter with both sugars until light and fluffy. Add eggs, one at a time. Beating thoroughly after each addition. Add vanilla and chocolate chips. Beat just until blended.

■ Dissolve baking soda into sour cream and add, alternately, with flour, beginning and ending with flour.

■ Pour into prepared pan. Bake one hour. When done, cake should be golden brown, dry on top, and shrink from sides of pan.

■ Cool on wire rack 30 minutes. Invert to finish cooling. Sprinkle generously with powdered sugar, if desired.

Serves 10 to 12

In the olden days, flowers used on a quilt had the same meaning as a bouquet. Red roses meant "love", lilies "purity", and daisies "innocence".

Deutche-Schokolade Pfund Kuchen (German Chocolate Pound Cake)

Jill Oborny

4 sticks margarine
3 cups sugar
6 eggs
3 cups flour
½ teaspoon salt
½ teaspoon baking
   powder
1 cup chocolate syrup
1 teaspoon vanilla
1½ cups milk

■ Preheat oven to 350°.

■ Cream margarine and sugar together in a large bowl. Add eggs and blend well. Add remaining ingredients and blend well.

■ Bake in greased 10x3½-inch bundt pan for one hour and twenty-five minutes.

■ Cool thoroughly before removing from pan.

Serves 12

Start with your first child's Christmas outfit and continue with all your children's Christmas outfits. Make patches each year until they all turn 17 or graduate from High School. Quilt the patches when your last child has left home. The result will be not only a festive quilt, but one that will keep you and your heart warm in more ways than one!

Add the following Sugar Bowl recipes and you are sure to never be alone during this wonderful holiday:

Tic-Tac-Toe in One Cookie Mix
Old Homestead Pecan Pie
Forbidden Fruit Cobbler
Deutche-Schokolade Pfund Kuchen
Raspberry Walnut Shortbread Bars
Love-Laughter-Friends-Family
Merry Christmas!

Cappuccino Angel Food Cake
Brenda Brandon

Lowfat

- 1 ¼ cups plus 2 tablespoons sugar, divided use
- 1 cup flour
- 1 teaspoon ground cinnamon
- 1 ½ cups egg whites (from 10 to 12 large eggs)
- 1 ½ teaspoons cream of tartar
- 1 tablespoon instant coffee, powder or granules, preferably espresso

■ Check that rack is in middle of oven. Preheat oven to 325°.

■ Lightly butter bottom of 10-inch tube pan. Line bottom of pan with lightly buttered wax paper or parchment paper, cut to fit. Measure all ingredients and have them ready for mixing.

■ Thoroughly mix ¼ cup of sugar with flour.

■ Mix 2 tablespoons of sugar with cinnamon.

■ Beat egg whites in large bowl on medium speed for approximately 2 minutes, or until frothy and well broken up. Add cream of tartar. Increase speed to medium-high. Beat until whites lose their yellow cast, greatly increase in volume and start to turn white.

■ With mixer running, slowly sprinkle in remaining sugar over egg whites. After 3 to 4 tablespoons of sugar, add the coffee powder.

■ Beat until egg whites become very thick, very glossy, pale beige in color and beaters leave a deep trail. Reduce speed to the lowest possible setting.

■ Quickly sprinkle flour-sugar mixture over egg whites. As soon as it is all added, but not completely mixed in, stop beating and remove beaters.

■ With a rubber spatula, complete mixing in flour by folding or gently stirring.

(Continued on next page)

(Cappuccino Angel Food Cake, continued)

■ Scrape approximately half of batter into prepared pan and spread evenly. Sprinkle cinnamon sugar mixture evenly over surface of the batter.

■ Drop spoonfuls of remaining batter over cinnamon. Spread evenly. Using a spatula, inscribe a circle deep in batter to release any large air bubbles.

■ Bake 50 minutes, or until a cake tester inserted in the center comes out clean.

■ Turn pan upside down on wire rack. Let cool completely. Loosen outside edge and around tube with a knife. Turn out cake and peel off paper.

■ Store wrapped airtight.

Serves 16

While the pioneer women truly believed that "idol hands are the devil's workshop", they were possibly wise ahead of their time. Does anything work more magic than sewing, mending, crocheting (or having something in our hands that looks like work), for catching a few minutes of peace from our loved ones? Perhaps this small ploy was what enabled our ancestors to rear nine children and still smile when their day was done!

Chocolate Angel Food Cake with Chocolate-Yogurt Mousse and Raspberry Sauce

Brenda Brandon

Lowfat
Prepare ahead

- 1 ¼ cups plain nonfat yogurt
- 1 ⅓ cups flour
- ½ cup plus 1 tablespoon unsweetened cocoa powder (divided use)
- 1 teaspoon baking powder
- 12 eggs whites
- 1 ¾ cups plus 3 tablespoons powdered sugar, sifted (divided use)
- 1 teaspoon cream of tartar
- 2 teaspoons vanilla extract
- 2 ounces semisweet chocolate, chopped
- 1 10 ounce package frozen raspberries in light syrup, defrosted

■ Drain yogurt by lining colander with piece of cheesecloth. Place yogurt in colander, set in large bowl and drain overnight in refrigerator.

■ Preheat oven to 325°.

■ Lightly butter bottom of 10-inch tube pan. Line bottom with lightly buttered wax or parchment paper cut to fit.

■ Combine flour, ½ cup cocoa powder and baking powder. Sift twice. Set aside.

■ Place egg whites in mixing bowl. Beat with an electric mixer until frothy. Continue beating and gradually add 1 ¾ cups powdered sugar and cream of tartar to egg whites. Beat until medium peaks begin to form.

■ Using rubber spatula, fold sifted dry ingredients into beaten egg whites until batter is blended evenly. Fold in vanilla.

■ Pour batter into prepared pan. Bake for 30 minutes or until cake tests clean.

■ Invert pan onto cooling rack and let cake cool in pan upside down. When cool, remove from pan; remove wax paper. The cake can be wrapped and set aside for 24 hours.

(Continued on next page)

(Chocolate Angel Food Cake with Chocolate-Yogurt Mousse and Raspberry Sauce, continued)

■ Remove drained yogurt from refrigerator 1 hour before finishing mousse.

■ Melt chocolate, cool slightly and whisk in yogurt. If chocolate does not blend into yogurt smoothly, put mixture into microwave for approximately 30 seconds on medium power. Whisk until blended.

■ Sift together remaining powdered sugar and cocoa powder. Whisk into chocolate yogurt.

■ With knife, cut cake into two layers. Spread bottom layer with mousse. Put top layer back.

■ Place on cake platter. Cover loosely. Refrigerate until ready to serve.

■ Sauce: puree raspberries with their syrup. Strain and refrigerate.

■ Sift powdered sugar over cake. Serve slice with raspberry sauce.

Serves 12

■ ■ ■ *"Handy-Andy" Tip: When melting chocolate, small amounts of water may cause it to "seize" or become thick, lumpy and grainy. Chocolate can sometimes be returned to melting consistency by adding 1 teaspoon of solid shortening for every 2 ounces of chocolate and reheating it.*

 Death By Chocolate   *Dawn Murphy*

Prepare ahead

  1 package chocolate cake
    mix
  1 cup coffee-flavored
    liqueur
  4 boxes chocolate mousse
    mix
  2 containers frozen
    whipped topping
  3 chocolate-toffee candy
    bars, crumbled

■ Prepare and bake cake according to package directions, using a 9x13 inch pan. Poke holes in cake and pour coffee-flavored liqueur over entire cake. Leave overnight.

■ Crumble ½ the cake into large bowl as bottom layer.

■ Prepare chocolate mousse according to package directions.

■ Spread approximately half the chocolate mousse over crumbled half of cake. Continue layering with one container of frozen whipped topping. Top with candy bar. Repeat sequence beginning with cake.

■ Chill until ready to serve.

Serves 12

Makes an attractive dessert when layered in glass bowl or trifle dish.

An especially creative friend of mine had a coffee she named "Hats to You". She requested all the participants to come sporting their finest hats and gloves (she allowed no one to enter without). As the partygoer entered, she snapped their photo with an instant camera to allow the moment to be carried home and shared. She reports all had great fun either wearing their fashion statement of the moment or a cherished hat from their grandmothers, mothers, etc. She used the following menu for her smash success:

Cloved Caffe Frappe	**Ben's Guilty Pleasures**
Almond Iced Espresso	**Texas Mud Cake**
Iced Caffe Latte	**Lemonade Cake**
Iced Cappuccino	**Death by Chocolate**

Banana Spice Bars

Creamy Cheesecake

Anne Koval

Prepare ahead

Cake

    1 prepared graham
      cracker crust
  16 ounces cream cheese,
      softened
    1 cup sugar
    2 eggs, beaten
    1 teaspoon vanilla

Topping

    1 pint sour cream
    2 tablespoons sugar
  ½ teaspoon vanilla

■ Prepare graham cracker crust according to package directions.

■ Preheat oven to 350°.

■ Combine cream cheese, sugar and eggs. Mix until creamy. Add vanilla. Pour into pie crust.

■ Bake for 25 minutes. Let cool.

■ Raise oven temperature to 410°.

■ Mix together sour cream, sugar and vanilla. Pour on top of cooled pie.

■ Bake pie at 410° for 5 minutes.

■ Cool and chill at least 2 hours.

■ ■ ■ *"Handy-Andy" Tip: Desserts with a soft creamy filling and/or layers can be cut easily with an electric knife. No pressure is required when cutting, so the filling is not pressed out between the layers.*

Torrejas Especiales (Sweet Breads Specialty)

Cuqui Levine

Prepare ahead

- 8 ounces oil, or enough to fill 3 inches in pan
- 3 egg yolks
- 8 ounces evaporated milk, or regular milk
- 1 cup sugar
- ¼ cup white wine
- 1 teaspoon vanilla
- 1 teaspoon cinnamon
- 1 loaf of bread, sliced (French or regular), may be cut into shapes

Syrup

- 1 cup sugar
- 1 cup water
- 1 lemon peeled, cut into small pieces
- ½ teaspoon vanilla
- 1 cinnamon stick

■ Heat oil in frying pan to medium heat.

■ Whip egg yolks with milk, sugar, wine, vanilla and cinnamon.

■ Dip bread slices in egg yolk mixture.

■ Gently drop bread slices into heated oil. Fry until golden brown. Set aside.

■ Syrup: combine sugar, water, lemon peel, vanilla and cinnamon stick in a saucepan. Heat until sugar dissolves and is texture of honey. Allow to cool.

■ Serve torrejas and syrup cold. May also be served with powdered sugar.

In a part of New England during the last half of the 19th Century, any young man who traveled to the West carried along a quilt made and signed by his mother and other female relatives and friends. It was believed that their visible names and good wishes kept the young gentlemen safe from evil influences. Who among us can say it did not?

Amaretto Flavored Bread Pudding

Pam Polsky

Prepare ahead

- 1 loaf French bread
- 1 quart half and half
- 2 tablespoons unsalted butter, room temperature
- 3 eggs
- 1½ cups sugar
- 2 tablespoons almond extract
- ¾ cup raisins
- ¾ cup almonds, sliced Whiskey Sauce, page 250 (optional)

■ Preheat oven to 325°.

■ Break up bread into small pieces. Place in a bowl and cover with half and half. Cover and let stand for 1 hour.

■ Grease a 9-inch by 9-inch or 12-inch by 12-inch pan with butter.

■ Beat together eggs, sugar and almond extract. If serving with a whiskey sauce, omit almond extract.

■ Stir into bread mixture. Fold raisins and almonds into mixture.

■ Spread evenly in buttered dish and bake for 50 minutes, until golden.

■ Remove and cool.

■ Ladle Whiskey Sauce over bread pudding if desired.

Serves 10

"Old Homestead" Pecan Pie

Lynne Dildy

- 3 eggs, slightly beaten
- ¾ cup sugar
- 1 stick butter, softened
- 1 cup dark corn syrup
- 2 cups pecans
- 1 deep dish prepared pie crust

■ Preheat oven to 400°.

■ Blend eggs and sugar. Add butter, and cream ingredients. Add syrup and pecans.

■ Pour into crust.

■ Bake for 10 minutes. Lower oven temperature to 300°. Continue baking until done for approximately 45 minutes.

Serves 8

Peaches and Cream Pie

Jill Oborny

1 3.9-ounce box vanilla pudding (not instant)
¾ cup flour
1 teaspoon baking powder
½ teaspoon salt
3 tablespoons butter, softened
1 egg
½ cup milk
1 16 ounce can sliced peaches
8 ounces cream cheese, softened
½ cup plus 1 teaspoon sugar, divided use
½ teaspoon cinnamon

■ Preheat oven to 350°.

■ Grease and flour a 9-inch pie plate.

■ Mix together first seven ingredients. Pour into pie plate.

■ Drain peaches, reserve juice. Spread peaches on top of batter.

■ Cream together cream cheese, ½ cup sugar and 3 tablespoons of reserved peach juice. Spread over peaches.

■ Mix 1 teaspoon sugar and cinnamon and sprinkle on top.

■ Bake 30 to 35 minutes.

Serves 8

To Die For Chocolate Chip Pie

Connie Baird

2 eggs
½ cup margarine, melted
1 cup sugar
½ cup flour
1½ teaspoons vanilla
1 cup semi-sweet chocolate chips
1 cup pecan pieces
1 10-inch prepared pie shell

■ Preheat oven to 350°.

■ Mix together first five ingredients.

■ Let mixture cool so chocolate chips will not melt. Stir in chocolate chips and pecan pieces.

■ Pour into pie crust. Bake for 55 minutes to 1 hour.

Serve with whipped topping or vanilla ice cream.

Serves 10

Mud Pie

Sydney Cox

Prepare ahead

- 21 chocolate sandwich cookies
- 6 tablespoons butter, melted
- 1 quart chocolate ice cream
- 2 tablespoons ground coffee granules (optional)
- 2 tablespoons instant decaffeinated coffee
- ½ pint whipping cream, whipped
- 2 tablespoons brandy
- 2 tablespoons coffee-flavored liqueur
- 12 ounces fudge topping

■ Crush cookies very fine and mix with butter.

■ Press into a 9-inch pie pan. Freeze.

■ Whip together ice cream, coffees, 4 tablespoons whipped cream, brandy and coffee-flavored liqueur. Pour into frozen pie shell.

■ Freeze until very hard. Making pie a day in advance allows plenty of time for pie to freeze.

■ Spread fudge over pie with a knife dipped into hot water.

■ Return to freezer.

■ Serve with remaining whipped cream.

Serves 8

 ## Chocolate Toffee Pie

Gina Banister

Prepare ahead

- 2 chocolate-covered toffee candy bars, crushed
- 2 small boxes instant chocolate pudding
- 1½ cups milk
- 1 quart vanilla ice cream
- 1 large graham cracker crust, prepared frozen whipped topping

■ In a large mixing bowl, stir together crushed candy bars, pudding, milk and vanilla ice cream until well mixed.

■ Pour into pie shell. Top with whipped topping.

■ Sprinkle with toffee crumbs.

■ Freeze. Defrost to serve.

Serves 8

 # Peanut Butter Fudge Pie

Amy Kelly

Prepare ahead

- ¼ cup plus 6 tablespoons corn syrup, divided use
- 2 tablespoons brown sugar
- 3 tablespoons butter or margarine
- 2½ cups crispy rice cereal
- ½ cup creamy peanut butter
- 1½ cups fudge sauce, divided use
- 1 to 2 quarts vanilla or vanilla fudge swirl ice cream
- ½ cup peanuts, chopped

■ Crust: place ¼ cup corn syrup, brown sugar and butter in a medium saucepan. Heat until mixture boils. Remove saucepan from heat. Add cereal to syrup mixture. Gently stir until thoroughly mixed.

■ Press into buttered 10-inch pie plate, bottom and sides, to form crust. Allow to cool.

■ Pie filling: in a medium saucepan, combine the peanut butter, ½ cup fudge sauce and remaining corn syrup. Heat and stir mixture over low heat until smooth.

■ Spread mixture on top of cooled cereal crust. Place crust in freezer for 2 to 3 hours.

■ Scoop ice cream into pie crust. Freeze crust for 4 hours or overnight until firm.

■ Sprinkle top evenly with peanuts. Spread remaining 1 cup fudge sauce over chopped peanuts.

■ Store pie in freezer. Before serving, allow to soften slightly at room temperature.

Serves 8

■ ■ ■ *"Handy-Andy" Tip: Sprinkle pie crust with powdered sugar to keep crust from becoming soggy.*

To prevent meringue from shrinking, make sure it touches the crust of the pie on all sides. Mix 1 tablespoon of cornstarch with sugar to prevent meringue for pie from weeping.

Gram's Old Fashioned Apple Pie   *Lori Anderson*

Pie Filling

    5-6 large cooking apples
    ¾ cups plus 1 tablespoon
       sugar, divided use
    2 tablespoons flour,
       divided use
  1½ teaspoons ground
       cinnamon
    1 tablespoon butter or
       margarine

- Preheat oven to 400°.
- Slice enough apples to fill pie pan. (Skins can be left on if you like.)
- In large bowl, mix apples with ¾ cup sugar, 1 tablespoon flour, and cinnamon.
- Sprinkle 1 tablespoon each of sugar and flour in bottom of pie crust.
- Put apples in pie crust. Dot with butter.

Crust

    2 cups flour
    1 teaspoon salt
    ⅔ cup shortening
    6 tablespoons cold water
    1 teaspoon sugar

- Sift flour and salt together.
- Cut in shortening with pastry blender until mixture resembles small peas.
- Sprinkle water over mixture while tossing lightly with fork until particles stick together.
- Form into two balls. Roll one ball into circle one inch larger than pie plate. Lift onto plate, pat out air.
- Roll out remaining dough to fit top of pie.
- Wet edges of bottom crust. Put top on pie and crimp edges.
- Sprinkle with sugar.
- Bake at 400° for 40 minutes.

Crumb Crusts

Janet May

Graham Cracker

- 1 ½ cups fine graham cracker crumbs (approx. 24 squares)
- ⅓ cup butter or margarine, melted
- ¼ cup sugar

■ Preheat oven to 350°.

■ In a bowl combine all ingredients.

■ Press mixture firmly over bottom and up sides of a 9-inch pie pan.

■ Bake 10 minutes at 350°.

One pie shell

Chocolate Wafer Crusts

- 1 ½ cups fine chocolate wafer crumbs (approx. 27 cookies)
- ⅓ cup butter or margarine, melted

■ Follow directions for graham cracker crust.

Gingersnap Crust

- 1 ½ cups fine gingersnap crumbs (approx. 27 cookies)
- ⅓ cup butter or margarine, melted

■ Follow directions for graham cracker crust.

Vanilla Wafers Crust

- 1 ½ cups fine vanilla wafer crumbs (approx. 36 cookies)
- ⅓ cup butter or margarine, melted

■ Follow directions for graham cracker crust.

Winning Meringue

Karla Baldelli

- 1 cup egg whites, at room temperature
- ½ teaspoon cream of tartar
- ¼ teaspoon salt
- 1 teaspoon vanilla extract
- 2 cups extra fine sugar

■ Preheat oven to 250°.

■ Beat egg whites until frothy.

■ Add cream of tartar, salt and vanilla. Beat until soft peaks form.

■ Add sugar a tablespoon at a time. Beat until stiff peaks form.

■ Bake at 250° for 1 to 1 ½ hours.

"Forbidden Fruit" Cobbler

Janie Trantham

5-6 apples, peeled, cored and sliced
1 can sweetened condensed milk
1 teaspoon cinnamon
½ cup plus 2 tablespoons butter, divided use
1½ cups biscuit baking mix, divided use
½ cup brown sugar
½ cup chopped nuts

■ Preheat oven to 375°.

■ Mix apples, sweetened condensed milk and cinnamon in a large bowl.

■ Mix ½ cup butter into 1 cup biscuit baking mix; mix until crumbly.

■ Stir in apple mixture. Pour into a greased 9x13 inch baking dish.

■ In a small bowl, mix brown sugar, nuts and remaining butter and biscuit baking mix. Sprinkle over apples and cook for 1 hour.

Serves 12

Quickie Peach Cobbler

Kathleen Denny

1 cup flour
1 cup sugar
1 teaspoon baking powder
1 stick margarine
1 8-ounce can evaporated milk
1 can (32 ounces) peaches, drained
1-2 cans peach nectar
sugar
cinnamon

■ Preheat oven to 350°.

■ Combine flour, sugar, baking powder, margarine and milk. Less milk may be used for desired consistency of crust.

■ Cut peaches into halves or thirds.

■ Put crust into 8x8-inch baking pan.

■ Pour on to crust.

■ Pour 1 to 2 cans of peach nectar on top of peaches. Two cans of nectar provide a juicy cobbler.

■ Bake approximately one hour or until golden brown.

■ Sprinkle sugar and cinnamon over crust.

Serves 8

Moore Peach Cobbler

Mary Moore

2 cups peaches, peeled
and sliced
1¾ cups sugar, divided use
1 stick butter, melted
1¼ cups flour
2 teaspoons baking
powder
¾ cup milk
pinch salt

■ Preheat oven to 350°.

■ Mix peaches with 1 cup sugar, set aside.

■ Melt butter in 9x13 inch pan.

■ Mix together ¾ cup sugar, flour, baking powder, milk and salt.

■ Pour batter evenly over melted butter. DO NOT STIR.

■ Spoon fruit evenly over batter. DO NOT STIR.

■ Bake for one hour.

Serves 8

"Blue Skies" Cobbler

Nancy Marston

2 cups plus 2 tablespoons
sugar, divided use
2 teaspoons grated lemon
peel
2 cups flour, divided use
8 cups blueberries
2 tablespoons baking
powder
½ teaspoon salt
8 tablespoons unsalted
butter
1 egg, lightly beaten
1 egg yolk, lightly beaten

■ Preheat oven to 375°.

■ Combine 1½ cups sugar, grated lemon peel, ¼ cup flour and blueberries. Pour into 3 quart buttered dish.

■ Mix together remaining sugar and flour, baking powder, salt and butter until the texture of cornmeal.

■ Add eggs and blend. Sprinkle over berries. Sprinkle 2 tablespoons sugar over all.

■ Bake for 35 minutes.

Serves 8

Peaches in Beaujolais

Brenda Brandon

1 bottle red Beaujolais wine
3 cups water
1 ½ cups sugar
   juice of 1 lemon
1 cinnamon stick, 3 inches in length
8 peaches, unblemished and underripe

■ Bring all ingredients to a boil, except peaches.

■ Reduce to a simmer. Add peaches. Simmer 10 to 15 minutes.

■ Remove peaches from wine; cool and slip off skins.

■ Strain wine into a large bowl. Add peaches.

■ To serve, place peaches into individual compote dishes. Ladle ¼ to ½ cup of wine over each portion of fruit.

Serves 8

No cholesterol, 1 gram of fat and only 184 calories!

Fruit Pizza

Kim Hext

1 roll sugar cookie dough
8 ounces cream cheese, softened
⅓ cup powdered sugar
1 ½ teaspoons vanilla
1 pint strawberries, sliced
2 kiwi, sliced
2 bananas, sliced

■ Preheat oven to 350°.

■ Roll cookie dough out to fit pizza pan.

■ Bake cookie dough approximately 15 minutes, or until golden brown. Allow crust to cool.

■ Blend cream cheese, powdered sugar and vanilla together until smooth. Spread on top of cookie crust.

■ Arrange sliced fruit on top of filling.

■ Slice and serve.

Serves 10

Clafouti

Brenda Brandon

1¼ cups milk
⅔ cup sugar (divided use)
3 eggs
1 tablespoon vanilla
⅛ teaspoon salt
⅔ cup flour, sifted
3 cups black cherries, pitted
powdered sugar

■ Preheat oven to 350°.

■ Place milk, ⅓ cup sugar, eggs, vanilla, salt, and flour in a blender at top speed for 1 minute.

■ Pour ¼-inch layer of batter in lightly buttered 9 inch pie plate.

■ Set over moderate heat for 1 to 2 minutes until batter has set slightly.

■ Spread cherries over batter. Sprinkle on remaining sugar. Pour on remaining batter and smooth surface.

■ Place in middle of oven. Bake for approximately one hour.

■ Clafouti is done when it is puffed and browned or a tooth-pick or knife comes out clean.

■ Sprinkle top with powdered sugar. Serve warm.

Serves 6 to 8

How to Preserve a Husband - Be careful in your selection. Do not choose too young and take only such as have been reared in a good and moral atmosphere. Some insist on keeping them in a pickle, while others keep them in hot water. This only makes them sour, hard and sometimes bitter. Even poor varieties may be made sweet, tender and good by garnishing them with patience, well sweetened with smiles and flavored with kisses. Then wrap them in a mantle of love. Keep them warm with a steady fire of domestic devotion and serve with peaches and cream. When thus prepared, they will keep for years.

Barbara Davis

Russian Cream

Lori Anderson

Prepare ahead

Cream

   1½ cups sugar
     2 envelopes unflavored
       gelatin
     1 cup cold water
     2 cups whipping cream
   24 ounces sour cream
     2 teaspoons vanilla

Raspberry Sauce

     1 10-ounce package
       frozen raspberries,
       thawed
     2 tablespoons sugar
     1 tablespoon raspberry-
       flavored liqueur
       cheese cloth

■ To prepare cream, combine sugar and gelatin in a saucepan; add water. Stir well. Let sit 1 minute.

■ Cook over medium heat, stirring constantly, until gelatin dissolves. Stir in whipping cream. Set aside.

■ Combine sour cream and vanilla in a large bowl. Gradually whisk in whipping cream mixture until blended.

■ Cover and chill at least 8 hours.

■ Stir and spoon into individual dessert dishes.

■ Raspberry sauce: combine all ingredients in electric blender; process until smooth. Strain through 2 layers of cheese cloth. Discard seeds.

■ Spoon raspberry sauce over each serving.

■ ■ ■ *"Handy-Andy" Tip: If sweet cream is just starting to sour, restore the sweetness with a pinch of baking soda.*

Strawberry Delight

Meg Jones

Prepare ahead

Meringue

> 6 egg whites
> ¼ teaspoon cream of tartar
> 1 teaspoon vanilla
> 1 ½ cups sugar

Filling

> 6 ounces cream cheese,
> softened
> 1 cup sugar
> 2 cups whipped cream
> 2 cups miniature
> marshmallows

Topping

> 1 can cherry pie filling
> 1 teaspoon lemon juice
> 2 cups fresh strawberries,
> sliced

■ Preheat oven to 275°.

■ Meringue: beat egg whites, cream of tartar and vanilla until frothy. Slowly add sugar. Beat until stiff and glossy.

■ Spread in greased 9x13-inch dish. Bake for 1 hour. Turn off oven and leave in for 12 hours.

■ Filling: blend cream cheese with sugar and fold in whipped cream and marshmallows.

■ Spread on meringue and refrigerate 12 hours. (The filling may be refrigerated for 12 hours simultaneously with baking of the meringue.)

■ Topping: mix together cherry pie filling, lemon juice and strawberries. Spread over top of filling.

Serves 10 to 12

■ ■ ■ *"Handy-Andy" Tip: Egg whites achieve their greatest volume and achieve stiffness better when whipped at room temperature with warm beaters.*

Lime Fool

Nancy Marston

2 cups whipping cream, divided use
½ cup fresh lime juice
2 teaspoons grated lime peel
12 ounces white chocolate, chopped
6 tablespoons sugar
4 kiwi, sliced
4 cups strawberries, sliced
2 limes, sliced for garnish

■ Combine in saucepan, ½ cup whipping cream, lime juice and lime peel. Bring to a boil.

■ Reduce heat to low and add white chocolate. Stir until melted.

■ Refrigerate 25 minutes, do not let it set.

■ Beat remaining whipping cream and sugar until stiff. Fold into chocolate mixture.

■ Layer in parfait glasses with fruit.

■ Top with lime slice and strawberry.

Serves 6 to 8

■ ■ ■ *"Handy-Andy" Tip: An easy way to peel kiwi fruit is to cut off both ends. Use soup spoon and slide the spoon under the skin and gently turn the fruit until the spoon goes all the way around. Remove spoon and the fruit will slide out with a little push. This is easy and you don't get knife marks.*

"Four Stars" Fruit Ice Cream

Karen Washington

Prepare ahead

2 10-ounce packages frozen strawberries
3 bananas, mashed
juice of 3 lemons
juice of 3 oranges
2 cups sugar
½ pint whipping cream
1 pint half-and-half
2 cups milk
4 eggs

■ Mix all ingredients together.

■ Pour into ice cream freezer container. Freeze until desired consistency.

Makes 4 quarts

Tipsy Coffee Ice Cream

Lisa Matchett

Prepare ahead

- 1 ½ teaspoons unflavored gelatin
- 1 cup milk
- 2 eggs, separated
- 1 teaspoon vanilla
- ½ cup coffee-flavored liqueur
- ¼ teaspoon salt
- 2 tablespoons sugar
- 1 cup whipping cream

■ Sprinkle gelatin over milk in a small saucepan and let stand a few minutes. Beat egg yolks and add to milk. Cook over low heat, stirring constantly, until gelatin dissolves and mixture thickens slightly.

■ Remove from heat and cool. Stir in vanilla and coffee-flavored liqueur. Chill until mixture begins to thicken and jell.

■ Beat egg whites with salt to soft peaks. Gradually beat in sugar. With same beater, beat cream to soft peaks. Fold cream and meringue into gelatin mixture.

■ Turn into loaf pan (8½x4½). Place in freezer until firm, about 4 to 6 hours.

Makes 2½ pints ice cream

■ ■ ■ *"Handy-Andy" Tip: Cream will whip faster and stiffer if the cream is cold and the bowl and beaters have also been chilled prior to beating.*

Sweet Cream Ice Cream

Kathy Whipple

Prepare ahead

- 2 eggs
- ¾ cup sugar
- 2 cups heavy whipping cream
- 1 cup whole milk

■ Whisk eggs. Gradually add sugar, whisking constantly until lemon yellow.

■ Whisk in cream and milk.

■ Pour into ice cream maker and follow manufacturer's directions.

Makes 1 quart

 # Raspberry-Walnut Shortbread Bars　　*Beth Adler*

Shortbread Base
- 1 ¼ cups flour
- ½ cup sugar
- ½ cup butter

Topping
- ⅓ cup raspberry jam
- 2 eggs
- ½ cup brown sugar, packed
- 1 teaspoon vanilla
- 2 tablespoons flour
- ¼ teaspoon salt
- ⅛ teaspoon baking soda
- 1 cup walnuts, chopped

■ Preheat oven to 350°.

■ To prepare shortbread base, combine flour and sugar. Cut in butter until mixture is like fine meal.

■ Press shortbread base evenly into bottom of lightly greased 9-inch square baking pan. Bake for 20 minutes or until edges become lightly golden.

■ Remove from oven. Spread raspberry jam over shortbread.

■ Beat eggs with brown sugar and vanilla until well blended. Stir in flour mixed with salt and baking soda. Add walnuts.

■ Spoon over jam. Spread lightly to corners of pan.

■ Return to oven. Bake 20 to 25 minutes longer or until top is set.

■ Cool in pan. Cut into bars.

Makes 24 bars

Freezes well!

Banana Spice Bars

Julie Robinson

Bars

- 1 small ripe banana, mashed
- ¼ cup shortening
- 1 egg
- 1 cup flour
- ¾ cup sugar
- ½ teaspoon baking powder
- ¼ teaspoon baking soda
- ½ teaspoon salt
- ¾ teaspoon cinnamon
- ¼ teaspoon allspice
- ⅛ teaspoon ground cloves
- ¼ cup milk
- ⅓ cup pecans, chopped

Lemon Frosting

- 1 cup powdered sugar, sifted
- 2 tablespoons butter or margarine
- 1 tablespoon water
- 2 tablespoons lemon juice

- ■ Preheat oven to 350°.
- ■ Combine banana and shortening. Beat two minutes at high speed. Add egg; beat for one minute.
- ■ Sift together dry ingredients. Add to banana mixture. Stir well. Stir in milk and pecans.
- ■ Pour batter into a greased 9x13 pan. Bake for 20 to 25 minutes.
- ■ Lemon frosting: combine powdered sugar, butter, water and lemon juice; beat until smooth.
- ■ While bars are still warm, spread with lemon frosting.
- ■ Allow to cool. Cut into 2x1½ inch bars.

Makes 30 to 36 bars

Congo Squares

Daisy Batman

- 1 pound light brown sugar
- 3 eggs
- ⅔ cup oil
- 2¾ cups flour
- 2½ teaspoons baking powder
- ½ teaspoon salt
- 1 cup pecans or walnuts, broken
- 6 ounces chocolate chips

- ■ Preheat oven to 350°.
- ■ Combine sugar, eggs and oil. Mix thoroughly. Sift together flour, baking powder and salt. Add to sugar/eggs/oil mixture. Mix thoroughly. Mixture will be very thick and sticky. Stir in chips and nuts.
- ■ Pour into 9x13 inch greased pan. Bake for 25 to 35 minutes.
- ■ Cool in pan. Cut into squares.

Makes 24 bars

Freezes well!

Choco-Cola Brownies

Mary Pittman

Brownie

2 cups flour
2 cups sugar
1 cup butter or margarine
3 tablespoons cocoa
1 cup cola-flavored
  carbonated drink
½ cup buttermilk
2 eggs, beaten
1 teaspoon baking soda
1 teaspoon vanilla
1 ½ cups miniature
  marshmallows

Frosting

1 cup margarine
3 tablespoons cocoa
6 tablespoons cola-
  flavored carbonated
  drink
16 ounces powdered
  sugar, sifted
1 cup pecans or walnuts,
  chopped
1 teaspoon vanilla

■ Preheat oven to 350°. Grease 9x13 inch pan.

■ Brownies: sift together flour and sugar. Heat butter, cocoa and cola-flavored carbonated drink to boiling point; pour over flour/sugar mixture. Mix buttermilk, eggs, baking soda and vanilla. Add to mixture. Mix well. Batter will be thin.

■ Pour half of the batter into prepared pan. Sprinkle marshmallows on top. Add remaining batter. Bake for 35 minutes.

■ Frosting: combine margarine, cocoa and cola-flavored carbonated drink. Heat to boiling point. Pour over powdered sugar. Blend with mixer until smooth. Add nuts and vanilla.

■ Pour over brownies while still warm and frosting is hot.

■ Cool. Cut into squares.

Makes 2 dozen brownies

■ ■ ■ *"Handy-Andy" Tip: To cut cookies easily, line the pans with foil. When bars are cool, lift bars out with the foil and cut.*

Caramel Chocolate Squares

Patty Miller

14 ounces caramel squares
5 ounces evaporated milk (divided use)
1 package super moist German chocolate cake mix
⅔ cup margarine, melted
12 ounces semi-sweet chocolate chips

■ Preheat oven to 350°.

■ Heat caramels and ¼ cup of evaporated milk in saucepan over medium heat, stirring constantly. Keep mixture over low heat, stirring occasionally.

■ Combine cake mix with melted margarine and remaining evaporated milk.

■ Spray 9x13 inch pan with non-stick vegetable spray.

■ Spread half of the dough into pan. Bake six minutes. Remove from oven.

■ Sprinkle chocolate chips over hot dough. Drizzle caramel over chocolate chips. Drop remaining dough onto caramel layer. Spread evenly to cover top.

■ Bake until slightly dry, approximately 15 to 20 minutes.

■ Cool completely. Cut into squares.

Makes 24 squares

Freezes well!

Black Bottom Goodies
Dana Bell

1½ cups flour
1 teaspoon baking soda
½ teaspoon + ⅛ teaspoon
  salt, divided use
1½ cups sugar, divided use
¼ cup cocoa
1 cup water
⅓ cup oil
1 tablespoon vinegar
1 tablespoon vanilla
8 ounces cream cheese,
  softened
1 egg
6 ounces semi-sweet
  chocolate mini-morsels

■ Preheat oven to 350°.

■ Combine first five ingredients using ½ teaspoon salt, 1 cup sugar in large bowl. Make a well in center of mixture. Combine water, oil, vinegar and vanilla. Add to dry ingredients, stirring well.

■ Spoon batter into paper lined muffin pans, filling two-thirds full.

■ Combine cream cheese, eggs, and remaining sugar and salt, stir well. Stir in chocolate mini-morsels.

■ Spoon approximately 2 tablespoons of cream cheese mixture over chocolate batter.

■ Bake for 20 minutes.

Makes 2 dozen

Butterscotch Bars
Martha Welch

½ cup butter
2 cups brown sugar
2 eggs
1 teaspoon vanilla
2 cups flour, sifted
2 teaspoons baking
  powder
¼ teaspoon salt
1 cup coconut, shredded
1 cup walnuts, chopped
  (optional)

■ Preheat oven to 350°.

■ In a 2-quart saucepan, melt butter over low heat.

■ Remove from heat. Stir in brown sugar. Add eggs, one at a time, beating well, after each addition. Stir in vanilla.

■ Sift together flour, baking powder and salt; add coconut and nuts. Add to brown sugar mixture. Mix thoroughly.

■ Spread in a greased 9x13 inch pan. Bake for approximately 25 minutes.

■ Cut into bars while still warm. Remove from pan before completely cool.

Makes 30 bars

 Brownie Cupcakes

Lisa Matchett

1 cup flour
1½ cups sugar
    dash salt
2 sticks margarine
4 squares semi-sweet
    chocolate
4 eggs, beaten
1 teaspoon vanilla

■ Preheat oven to 325°.

■ Sift flour with sugar and salt.

■ Melt margarine and chocolate in double boiler. Stir to mix. Combine flour mixture, eggs and vanilla.

■ Put cupcake liners in muffin tins. Fill half full with batter.

■ Bake for 20 minutes. Do not over cook, leave tender.

■ Allow to cool.

Makes 1½ dozen

 Brownie Chip Cookies

April Minton

1 21½-ounce package
    brownie mix
2 eggs
½ cup oil
6 ounces chocolate chips

■ Preheat oven to 350°.

■ Combine brownie mix, eggs and oil. Stir until moistened. Stir in chocolate chips.

■ Drop by teaspoon onto greased cookie sheet.

■ Bake for 10 to 12 minutes.

Makes 4 dozen cookies

■ ■ ■ *"Handy-Andy" Tip: Cookie dough can be stored in a tightly covered container in refrigerator for up to one week or in the freezer for up to 6 months.*

Pecan Pie Brownies

Lori Anderson

Brownies

    1 21½-ounce package of
       brownie mix
    ½ cup water
    ¼ cup oil
    1 egg

■ Preheat oven to 350°.

■ Grease bottom only of 13x9-inch pan.

■ In large bowl, combine all brownie ingredients; beat 50 strokes with spoon.

■ Spread in prepared pan.

Topping

    ¼ cup margarine
    2 tablespoons flour
    ¾ cup firmly packed
       brown sugar
    2 eggs
    1½ cups chopped pecans

■ Melt margarine in medium saucepan. Stir in flour until smooth

■ Add brown sugar and eggs; mix well. Cook over medium to low heat for 5 minutes, stirring constantly.

■ Remove from heat. Stir in pecans.

■ Spoon topping over brownies.

■ Bake at 350° for 30-35 minutes or until set. DO NOT OVERBAKE.

■ Cool completely. Cut into bars.

Makes 24 bars

Lemon Crisps

Alberta Armstrong

Prepare ahead

Cookie

- ½ cup margarine, room temperature
- 1 cup sugar
- 1 egg, beaten
- 2 teaspoons grated lemon zest
- 2 tablespoons lemon juice
- 1 teaspoon lemon extract
- 2 cups flour
- 3 tablespoons powdered sugar
- 2 tablespoons cornstarch
- ½ teaspoon baking soda

■ In large bowl, beat together margarine and sugar until well blended.

■ Add egg, lemon zest, juice and extract. Beat well.

■ In separate bowl, combine flour, sugar, cornstarch and soda and sift over margarine mixture. Mix well.

■ Divide dough into 4 equal portions. Shape each portion on waxed paper, into logs about 2 inches thick. Wrap well.

■ Place in plastic bag and freeze 45 minutes, or until needed.

■ Preheat oven to 350°. Lightly grease baking sheets.

■ With knife, cut ¼-inch thick slices and set 1½ inches apart on prepared baking sheets.

■ Bake 10 minutes at 350°. Cool on wire rack.

Glaze

- ⅔ cup powdered sugar
- 1 teaspoon grated lemon zest
- 1½ tablespoons lemon juice

■ While cookies are baking, make glaze by stirring together all ingredients.

■ With pastry brush, coat hot cookies with glaze.

Makes 4 dozen cookies

 ## "Tic-Tac-Toe" in One Cookie Mix   *Lisa Matchett*

Oatmeal Mix
>   7 cups flour
>   3½ cups sugar
>   2 tablespoons salt
>   ¼ cup baking powder
>   2¼ cups shortening
>   1 box (1 pound 2 ounces)
>   quick cooking oats

Spicy Drop Cookies
>   3 cups Oatmeal Mix
>   1½ teaspoons cinnamon
>   ½ teaspoon nutmeg
>   ½ teaspoon allspice
>   ½ cup nuts, chopped
>   1 egg, beaten
>   ¼ cup butter or margarine,
>   melted
>   ½ cup milk

Chocolate Chip Cookies
>   3 cups Oatmeal Mix
>   ⅓ cup brown sugar
>   6 ounces semi-sweet
>   chocolate pieces
>   1 egg, beaten
>   1 teaspoon vanilla
>   ¼ cup milk

Hermits
>   3 cups Oatmeal Mix
>   1 teaspoon cinnamon
>   ½ teaspoon cloves
>   ¼ cup brown sugar
>   ¼ cup mixture of chopped
>   nuts, raisins and dates
>   1 egg, beaten
>   ⅓ cup milk

■ For oatmeal mix, sift together three times: flour, sugar, salt and baking powder.

■ With pastry blender or two knives, cut in shortening until consistency of cornmeal. Add oats and mix well.

■ Store in a tight, covered container at room temperature.

■ To measure mix for using, pile lightly into measuring cup and level off with spatula.

■ Preheat oven to 350° for all of the three drop cookies.

■ Combine oatmeal mix with all dry ingredients of desired cookie variation.

■ Combine beaten egg with all liquid ingredients of desired cookie variation.

■ Add liquid mixture to dry mixture and stir until all ingredients are well blended.

■ Drop by teaspoon onto a greased cookie sheet. Bake for 15 minutes.

Oatmeal mix makes 22 cups.
Each cookie recipe makes
2 dozen cookies.

Total Yield: 14 dozen cookies

■ ■ ■ *"Handy-Andy" Tip: Freeze cookie dough drops on cookie sheet. Bag and keep in freezer. Remove from freezer as needed. Thaw on cookie sheet and bake for a quick treat.*

Special Request Sugar Cookies

Lori Anderson

Prepare ahead

> 1½ cups powdered sugar, sifted
> 1 cup butter or margarine
> 1 egg
> 1 teaspoon vanilla
> ½ teaspoon almond flavoring
> 2½ cups flour
> 1 teaspoon baking soda
> 1 teaspoon cream of tartar

■ Preheat oven to 375°.

■ Cream sugar and butter. Add egg, vanilla and almond flavoring, mix well. Stir dry ingredients together. Blend well with sugar mixture.

■ Refrigerate dough 2 to 3 hours.

■ Divide dough in half and roll ³⁄₁₆ inch thick on lightly floured pastry cloth. Cut with cookie cutter; sprinkle with sugar.

■ Place on lightly greased baking sheet. Bake 7 to 8 minutes, or until delicately golden.

*Makes 5 dozen
2 to 2½ inch cookies*

These are great frosted! They can also be frozen!

■ ■ ■ *"Handy-Andy" Tip: Frosted cookies can be easily frozen. Lay in single layer on a cookie sheet, when frozen layer between freezer paper in an air-tight container. Can be frozen up to 3 months.*

When rolling cookie dough, sprinkle board with powdered sugar instead of flour. Too much flour makes the dough heavy.

Cajun Cowboy Cookies

Terry Landry

2 cups sugar
2 cups brown sugar
1 pound margarine
3 teaspoons vanilla
4 large eggs
4 cups flour
2 teaspoons baking soda
1 teaspoon salt
2 teaspoons baking
   powder
4 cups oats
18 ounces chocolate chips
4 cups nuts, chopped

■ Preheat oven to 350°.

■ Combine sugar, brown sugar, margarine, vanilla, and eggs. Beat until fluffy.

■ Sift and blend flour, baking soda, salt, and baking powder. Combine into first mixture.

■ Stir in oats and chocolate chips.

■ Form dough into 1 inch balls and roll in nuts.

■ Bake for 18 minutes. Watch closely, these burn easily.

Makes 6 dozen

■ ■ ■ *"Handy-Andy" Tip: To moisten dry brown sugar, place a slice of apple or an apple core in the box. Sugar will be moist in about 2 days.*

Surprise Snowballs

Lisa Matchett

Prepare ahead

1 cup margarine
½ cup sugar
1½ teaspoons vanilla
2 cups flour
1 cup pecans, finely
   chopped
42 Hershey Kisses
   powdered sugar

■ Cream together margarine, sugar, and vanilla. Add flour and pecans. Mix well.

■ Let dough chill for 2 hours.

■ Preheat oven to 375°.

■ Shape dough into balls around kisses and place on greased cookie sheet. Bake for 12 minutes.

■ Remove from cookie sheet and roll in powdered sugar while warm.

Makes 3½ dozen

Caramel-Filled Chocolate Cookies

Rene Tucei

2½ cups flour
¾ cup unsweetened cocoa
1 teaspoon baking soda
1 cup plus 1 tablespoon
   sugar (divided use)
1 cup brown sugar
1 cup butter, softened
2 teaspoons vanilla
2 eggs
1 cup pecans, chopped
   (divided use)
1 9-ounce package
   chocolate-covered
   caramel candy
4 ounces vanilla flavored
   candy coating

■ Preheat oven to 375°.

■ Combine flour, cocoa and baking soda. Set aside.

■ In a large bowl, beat 1 cup sugar, brown sugar and butter until fluffy. Add vanilla and eggs, beat well. Add flour mixture, blend well. Stir in ½ cup of pecans.

■ For each cookie, flour hands, shape about 1 tablespoon of dough around 1 chocolate-covered caramel candy, covering completely.

■ In a small bowl, combine remaining pecans and sugar. Press one side of each cookie ball into pecan mixture. Place nut side up on greased cookie sheet.

■ Bake for 7 to 10 minutes until slightly cracked.

■ Cool for 2 minutes, remove from cookie sheet. Cool completely on wire rack.

■ Melt candy coating in microwave, and drizzle over each cookie.

Makes 4 dozen

■ ■ ■ *"Handy-Andy" Tip: Cookies stay moist if a slice of bread is placed in the jar or bag with them.*

Ben's Guilty Pleasures

Lynne Dildy

1½ cups butter flavored shortening
3 eggs
½ teaspoon vanilla
¾ cup sugar
1½ cups brown sugar
½ teaspoon baking soda
½ teaspoon salt
3 cups plus 3 tablespoons flour
24 ounces white chocolate chips
1 7-ounce jar macadamia nuts, slightly crushed

■ Preheat oven to 375°.

■ Cream together shortening, sugars, eggs and vanilla. Sift salt, baking soda and flour.

■ Blend flour mixture into creamed mixture. Gently mix in chocolate and nuts.

■ Form cookies and place on greased cookie sheet.

■ Bake for 8 minutes or until delicately golden.

Makes 24 4-inch cookies

Freedom quilts were made by mothers for their sons' twenty-first birthdays. They were full of exhortations and moral truths. Men often gave their freedom quilts to their brides as gifts - a symbolic gesture, to be sure!

Homemade Peanut Butter Cups

Charlotte Sullivan

½ cup margarine
2 cups peanut butter (smooth or crunchy)
2¾ cups powdered sugar
¾ cup brown sugar
1 teaspoon vanilla
12 ounces chocolate chips
2 tablespoons margarine

■ Melt ½ cup margarine, remove from heat.

■ Add peanut butter, powdered sugar, brown sugar and vanilla. Mix well. Pour into an ungreased 9 by 13 inch pan.

■ Melt chocolate chips with 2 tablespoons margarine and spread on top of peanut butter layer.

■ While still warm cut into 1-inch squares.

Make 8 dozen 1-inch squares

245

 Caramel Dip For Apples

Mary Pittman

   8 ounces cream cheese,
        softened
   ½ cup sugar
   ¾ cup brown sugar
   1 teaspoon vanilla
   1 cup walnuts or pecans,
        coarsely chopped

- Beat together cream cheese and sugar until well blended.
- Add brown sugar, beat again until well blended.
- Add vanilla and nuts.
- Serve with sliced juicy fruit or grapes.

Refrigerated will keep for a while.

 Baked Caramel Corn

Lisa Matchett

   2 sticks butter
   2 cups brown sugar
   1 teaspoon salt
   ½ cup light corn syrup
   ½ teaspoon baking soda
   1 teaspoon vanilla
   6 quarts popped popcorn

- Preheat oven to 250°.
- Melt butter. Stir in brown sugar, salt and syrup.
- Bring to a boil, stirring constantly.
- Boil without stirring for 5 minutes. Remove from heat.
- Stir in soda and vanilla.
- Gradually pour over popped corn, mixing well and fast while hot.
- Turn in 2 large, shallow buttered pans.
- Bake for one hour, stirring every 15 minutes.
- Remove from oven and cool completely. Break apart and store in airtight container.

Makes 6 quarts

Pecan Sho Wung

Gina Banister

3 tablespoons butter or margarine
2 teaspoons salt
1 pound shelled pecans
3 tablespoons Worcestershire sauce
½ teaspoon cinnamon
¼ teaspoon cayenne pepper
dash of Tabasco sauce

■ Preheat oven to 300°.

■ Melt butter in baking dish. Stir in salt.

■ Add nuts and toss until thoroughly mixed.

■ Add remaining ingredients to mixture and toss again.

■ Place on cookie sheet and bake for approximately 30 minutes, until nuts are slightly brown and crisp. Stir several times while baking.

 ## White Chocolate Crunch

Cindy Hartley

2 pounds white chocolate, coarsely chopped
2 tablespoons shortening
3 cups Captain Crunch cereal
1½ cups miniature marshmallows
1 cup pecans, chopped

■ Melt chocolate and shortening on top of double boiler.

■ Combine with other ingredients.

■ Drop by spoonfuls onto waxed paper. Let cool completely.

Makes 5 dozen

Use Holiday Captain Crunch at Christmas.

Peanut Clusters

Kathy Mayfield

12 ounces peanut butter
   bits
12 ounces almond bark
 1 12-ounce can toasted
   Spanish peanuts
 1 teaspoon vanilla

■ In a glass bowl, melt peanut butter bits and almond bark in microwave.

■ Add peanuts and vanilla. Mix well.

■ Drop on to wax paper by spoonful.

For variation, use dark almonds and/or roasted pecans.

Hot Fudge Sauce

Kathy Whipple

½ cup butter
 4 1-ounce unsweetened
   chocolate
   pinch of salt
 3 cups sugar
1⅔ cups evaporated milk

■ Melt butter and chocolate in microwave oven.

■ Pour chocolate mixture into saucepan.

■ Add salt, sugar and milk alternately over medium-low heat.

■ Heat until mixture starts to bubble.

Makes 1 quart

 # German Chocolate Sauce

Patty Braud

1 stick butter
1 bar German sweet chocolate
1 8-ounce can evaporated milk
pinch of salt
1 ½ cups sugar
1 teaspoon vanilla

- Melt butter and chocolate.
- Add milk. Stir until blended. Add pinch of salt.
- Stir in sugar and vanilla.
- Bring mixture to boil. Continue to boil for 7 minutes, stirring constantly.

Makes 1 quart

Great on ice cream or pound cake! Makes a terrific gift!

 # Wendy's Romanoff Sauce

Lynne Dildy

2 8-ounce packages cream cheese, softened
⅙ cup milk
8 ounces powdered sugar
½ teaspoon vanilla
1 cup heavy cream
cinnamon or nutmeg

- Blend together cream cheese and milk.
- Add sugar and vanilla.
- Add cream. Whisk.
- Sprinkle cinnamon or nutmeg for garnish.

Excellent on strawberries.

Warm Cinnamon Berry Sauce

Brenda Brandon

2 pints mixed berries
  (raspberries,
  blackberries,
  blueberries)
5 tablespoons sugar
1 tablespoon lemon juice
1½ teaspoons cinnamon

■ Combine berries, sugar, lemon juice and cinnamon in a saucepan. Set aside 5 minutes to allow juices of berries to start to form.

■ Warm berries over medium heat. Stir gently until berries have heated through and have given off some of their juices, about 5 minutes.

■ Remove the berries with a slotted spoon.

■ Bring the liquid to a boil and continue boiling until slightly thickened, about 1 minute.

■ Pour over the berries.

■ Serve over vanilla ice cream or frozen yogurt

Makes 8 servings

Whiskey Sauce

Janie Trantham

8 ounces butter
2 cups powdered sugar
2 eggs
2 ounces whiskey

■ Melt butter.
■ Whip in powdered sugar.
■ Fold in eggs
■ Add whiskey
■ Serve warm over bread pudding.

Serves 10-12

CHILDREN'S DELIGHT

Life is like a patchwork quilt
Little squares of every hue
Some of silk and calico
Some of pink and gold and blue.

But each piece will do its part
Help to make the pattern fine
And when at last
The quilt is spread
Lovely is its whole design.

-Author unknown-

This poem so poignantly expresses the effect, on our children, of each and every experience on the pattern of their lives. Pioneer children, by design and from necessity, were an ever-present part of their families' lives, both in social and routine situations. With the advent of easily obtained caretakers, portable phones, blended families and friendly neighbors, children spend more time alone than ever. This section endeavors to provide the reader with ideas and opportunities for creating memories.

Included in this section are projects such as bubble wands, chase the pepper, edible glues and paints, clay playdough, gingerbread houses and the ever popular "green-haired spud folks". Food delights, such as chocolate banana pops, porcupines, old fashioned pull taffy, puppy chow mix for kids, eat your words cookies and the walking salad also abound.

TEXAS SAMPLER hopes you take the time to create and design your own special patchwork block for inclusion in your children's, grandchildren's, nieces', nephews', or young friends' quilt of life!!!

Kids' Talk

APPETIZING: Anything as advertised on TV with enough preservatives to retain present age indefinitely.

BOIL: The point a parent reaches upon hearing the automatic "yuk".

CASSEROLE: Combination of favorite foods that go uneaten because the dish is quick and easy to make.

COOKIE: An item that must be eaten in front of a sibling who is being punished.

CRUST: The part of a sandwich children save for the starving children in China, India, Africa or Europe.

DESSERTS: The reason for the entire meal.

EVAPORATE: Magic performed when it comes time to help prepare the meal or clear the table and wash the dishes.

FAT: Microscopic substance detected visually by children on pieces of meat they do not care for.

FORK: Eating utensil made obsolete by fingers.

FROZEN: Condition of children's jaws when spinach is offered.

FRUIT: A sweet which is not to be confused with dessert.

GERMS: Something shared freely by all children.

GOURMET: Any food fried.

KITCHEN: The only room in the house where children don't want to eat.

LEFTOVERS: Commonly referred to as "gross".

LOLLIPOP: A snack provided by people who don't have to pay the dental bills, all dental providers, and loan institutions.

MEASURING CUP: A kitchen utensil stored in the sandbox, dog's water dish, commode, etc.

NAPKINS: Cloth objects, such as pants and shirt sleeves.

PLATE: A breakable Frisbee.

REFRIGERATOR: An expensive and rather ineffective room air conditioner.

SALIVA: A liquid used for blowing bubbles.

SODA POP: An euphemism for "shake 'n spray".

TABLE: A place for storing gum until after the meal.

TABLE LEG: A percussion instrument.

THIRSTY: A feeling your child gets after the final "good night" has been said and the lights are out.

VEGETABLE: The only known substance that satisfies your children's hunger by sight.

WATER: Beverage utilized only in underdeveloped countries.

Candy House - Christmas Delight!

6 squares graham crackers, for each house milk cartons, ½ pint size, washed and dried - staple the tops shut small candies multicolored marshmallows dry cereal in assorted shapes ice cream sugar cone, sturdy paper plate for each house

Frosting:

1 pound confectioners' sugar
3 egg whites at room temperature
½ teaspoon of cream of tartar

■ To prepare frosting: Mix all ingredients in a large bowl with an electric mixer at low speed. Increase speed and beat for about seven minutes, or until the frosting stands in stiff peaks when a knife is pulled through. This will make about 2 cups of frosting. Each house will need about 1 cup of frosting.

■ Dab a tablespoon of frosting on bottom of milk carton, and stick it firmly in the middle of the plate. The icing acts like glue and keeps the house from sliding on the plate.

■ Dab a tablespoon of frosting on back of four square graham crackers. Press in place, against the sides of the carton.

■ To form roof: dab 2 table-spoons of frosting on the backs of two graham crackers. Gently position into place on top of carton. Hold in place for a few minutes, until the frosting dries slightly. If frosting is too thin, add more powdered sugar to stiffen.

■ Add frosting to eaves of house to cover milk carton, or use two triangular shaped graham crackers.

■ Spread roof with frosting and place marshmallows, cereal or candy in rows.

■ Create doors, windows, chimney and a path by pressing back side of candies into frosting.

(Continued on next page)

(Candy House - Christmas Delight!, continued)

■ To create a tree, invert sugar cone on plate, and cover with frosting. Stick seeds, beans, peas or candies all over.

■ Add gummy bears to front of the house by dabbing frosting onto their bases.

These houses make yummy treats! If you want to save them wrap them up very tightly.

Keep frosting covered at all times because it dries quickly.

■ ■ ■ *"Handy-Andy" Tip: To make brown frosting, combine equal amounts of red, yellow and blue food coloring in white frosting. To make black frosting, mix 1½ teaspoons of green food coloring, 1½ teaspoons of red food coloring and 5 drops of blue food coloring with white frosting.*

Add food coloring - one drop - to aerosol shave cream for foamy creative fun on top of a washable surface.

It's For the Birds

Jay Sartin

Peanut Butter Bird Feeder

1 pine cone
peanut butter
bird seed
yarn

■ Spread peanut butter on each "leaf" of a pine cone.

■ Roll pine cone in bird seed.

■ Tie yarn on pine cone and hang from a tree.

Citrus Buckets

grapefruit, halved, pulp scooped out
bird seed
pipe cleaner

■ Punch two holes on either side at top of halved grapefruit.

■ Hook each end of pipe cleaner through hole to make handle

■ Fill grapefruit with bird seed. Hang from tree

Bird Seed Nectar

1 cup bird seed
1 cup oatmeal
1 cup cornmeal
1 cup shortening
1 cup peanut butter

■ Mix nectar ingredients together.

■ Hollow out holes in dead tree branch (about 2-inches in diameter). Fill with mixture.

■ Hang in tree and watch the birds enjoy!

Other ways to feed birds:

Melt shortening. Before it hardens, add corn and nuts. Hang in an open mesh net.

String green peas or thread popcorn and cranberries on cord. Hang in tree.

Hang lettuce leaves from lower branches.

Whole corn cobs are nice treats.

Stick watermelon and pumpkin seeds into a stale doughnut. Loop yarn through doughnut hole and hang in tree.

Cookie cut pieces of stale bread. Make a variety of shapes. Coat with shortening or peanut butter. Press in seeds, nuts or grains.

No-Cook Play Dough

1 cup salt
1 cup flour
1 tablespoon salad oil
  food coloring, if desired
  water

■ Mix dry ingredients; add oil.

■ Add food coloring to water. Slowly add water until desired consistency is reached.

■ Store in an airtight container or plastic bag

Creative Clay

1 pound package baking
  soda
1 cup cornstarch
1¼ cups cold water
  food coloring (optional)

■ Mix soda and cornstarch together; add water. Cook and stir over medium heat until consistency of mashed potatoes. Remove from heat. Cover with damp cloth until cool.

■ Clay can be colored with food coloring added to the water or painted with tempera paints when dry.

■ Leave finished products out to dry overnight.

■ Use shellac or clear nail polish to seal.

■ Store in plastic bags to keep clay from drying out.

Use clay for jewelry shaping or roll it out to make ornamental cookie decorations.

To hang cookies on a tree or make as a necklace, use a plastic straw and push it into a hot cookie removed from the oven and twist out a hole at the top. The punched holes can be used as a decoration.

Decorative Bread Dough

1 cup salt
4 cups flour
1-1 ¼ cups water

■ Mix ingredients and knead about 20 minutes, or until desired consistency.

■ To make ornaments, roll dough and use cookie cutters. Prick to prevent air bubbles. Dampen to make pieces stick together.

■ Bake at 300° until golden brown. Paint with acrylic paint, if desired. Varnish and dry.

Clay for Keeps

1 cup salt
½ cup water
2 tablespoon vegetable oil
2 cups flour

■ Mix together salt, water and vegetable oil

■ Add flour. Stir well.

■ Creations can be baked at 250° for several hours.

Soap Bubbles

2 cups warm water
2 tablespoons liquid detergent
1 tablespoon sugar
1 tablespoon glycerin (optional)

■ Combine ingredients. Glycerin make the bubbles iridescent.

■ Blow bubbles through wire loops or spools.

■ ■ ■ *"Handy-Andy" Tip: Bubble wands can be made from rubber bands, paper clips bent into various shapes, plastic drinking straws with the ends split, plastic six-pack holders, and cans with both ends cut out. For giant bubble wands, use coat hangers, embroidery hoops or old foil pans with the centers cut out.*

Use food coloring to make the different colors of bubbles.

Soap Crayons

2 tablespoons water
Ivory Flakes
food coloring

■ Pour water into a 1 cup measuring cup. Finish filling cup with Ivory Flakes.

■ Mix with a spoon the water and soap flakes together until mixture becomes a thick soapy paste without any big lumps.

■ Add about 30 or 40 drops of food coloring to the soap mixture. Stir well until soap has color.

■ Spoon some of the mixture in a cube space of ice cube tray. Press soap paste down into the cube until filled. Continue filling the tray until all soap mixture is used.

■ Dry cubes in a warm dry place for 1-2 days until soap paste gets hard. Soap crayons will pop out of tray.

Great bath fun!

Instant Kitchen Paste

½ cup flour
water
pinch of salt

■ Mix flour with water to achieve a nice gooey consistency

■ Add salt.

■ Store in air tight container.

Will also work as a papier mache paste.

■ ■ ■ *"Handy-Andy" Tip: Egg white glue is strong and almost weightless. It works great when making paper kites.*

Library Paste

1 cup flour
1 cup sugar
1 teaspoon alum
3-4 cups water
30 drops oil of cloves

■ In a saucepan, combine flour, sugar, alum and water. Cook until mixture thickens and is clear.

■ Add drops of clove.

■ Store in an airtight container.

Make Your Own Stickers

¼ cup white glue
⅛ cup white vinegar
paper, crayons, markers, glitter, scissors, etc.

■ Mix glue and vinegar.

■ Draw and/or design on paper. Cut out design.

■ Brush back of each sticker with glue mixture.

■ Allow to dry 15 minutes. Lick and stick!!

Finger Paint

dry tempera colors
liquid detergent or
liquid starch

■ Mix together dry tempera colors with either liquid detergent or liquid starch and use as finger paint.

More Finger Paint

3 tablespoons sugar
½ cup cornstarch
2 cups cold water
food coloring
pinch of detergent

■ Mix sugar and cornstarch. Add water.

■ Cook over low heat. Stir constantly until well-blended.

■ Fill four or five containers with mixture. Add food coloring and pinch of detergent to each container.

Garden of Magic

¼ cup salt
¼ cup liquid bluing
¼ cup water
1 tablespoon ammonia
    charcoal briquettes
    food color

■ Mix together first four ingredients.

■ Place charcoal in pie tin. Pour mixture over charcoals.

■ If desired, add a few drops of food color over charcoal.

■ Garden will begin to grow in a few hours.

Green-Haired Spud Folks

1 large potato
    dirt
    grass seeds

■ Slice off bottom so it will stand upright. Scoop hollow in top of a big potato.

■ Fill hollow about ¾ full with dirt. Sprinkle grass seed into the hollow. Cover with dirt and pack lightly.

■ Keep watered and place in a sunny location.

■ The spud will grow green hair in a few days.

Give your spud a face. Anything that you can stick into the potato will be great.

Kitchen Silly Putty

½ cup white glue
¼ cup liquid starch

■ Mix ingredients well.

■ Allow to dry a little. Add more glue or starch if necessary to achieve the correct consistency.

■ Store in an airtight container.

Use with care around carpet or clothes.

The Shades of Pasta

Rubbing Alcohol
Pasta of all shapes &
sizes
Food coloring

■ Mix alcohol and food coloring. Store in separate containers. Mix.

■ Place pasta shapes in the different colored solutions. Allow to soak several hours.

■ Spoon pasta out of the solutions. Drain and dry pasta on paper.

String pasta and make jewelry or glue on paper for some great Kitchen Art!

■ ■ ■ *"Handy-Andy" Tip: Popcorn for stringing should be allowed to stand until it loses its crispness. Dye popcorn by dipping in cranberry juice, etc.*

Chase the Pepper: Fill a pie plate with water. Shake pepper on the water. Take a piece of wet soap and dip it in the water. The pepper will run away from the soap. What happens when sugar is shaken in the clear area?

Stained Glass Colors

Broken crayon pieces,
paper removed

■ Preheat oven to 400°.

■ Place broken crayons of all colors in well greased muffin tins.

■ Bake at 400° for a few minutes - until melted.

■ Remove from oven and allow to cool before using.

Eggshell Mosaic

24 eggshells, rinsed and dried

Dye

few drops food coloring
1 teaspoon vinegar
½ cup hot water

Art Supplies

glue
cotton swabs
construction paper

■ Crush and store eggshells in container while saving.

■ Put dye ingredients in jar. Mix well.

■ Place crushed shells in water and allow to soak a few minutes.

■ Spoon shells out and dry on cookie sheet. Shells can be baked in 200° oven.

■ Paint with glue and sprinkle eggshells on design. Shake off the excess.

Egg-strodinare designs!

■ ■ ■ *"Handy-Andy" Tip: Make an egg-shaped cookie cutter by bending and shaping the open end of a 6-ounce juice can.*

Make a snack tree with conical Styrofoam covered with green paper. Use toothpicks with various edibles to decorate. Serve with a dip.

Starfish

cornmeal
glue
posterboard
yellow construction paper
scissors

■ Cut identical star out of posterboard and construction paper. Glue together.

■ Spread glue on star.

■ Sprinkle cornmeal on wet glue. Shake off excess when dried.

Foamy Plastic Paint

6 tablespoons plastic
   starch
1 cup dry detergent
   water
   powdered colors

■ Mix starch and detergent with water.

■ With whisk, whip to consistency of marshmallow cream.

Beads of Salt

½ cup salt
1 cup all-purpose flour
   water
   food coloring
   toothpicks

■ Mix salt, flour and water until dough-like.

■ Add coloring (optional).

■ Tear off small pieces and form into beads.

■ Pierce each with toothpick. Allow to dry. String.

Colorful Sugar

1 cup granulated sugar
   liquid food coloring

■ Place sugar in a glass jar.

■ Add desired number of food coloring drops (number of drops determines color intensity.

■ Put lid on jar. Shake to distribute color evenly.

Different colors of sugar can be carefully layered in a glass jar for a thoughtful gift.

■ ■ ■ *"Handy-Andy" Tip: To decorate cookies with icing, cut a small hole on the top of a plastic baggy. Add icing and squeeze onto cookies like a professional.*

Shiny Cookie Glaze

¼ cup warm water
1 tablespoon corn syrup
3 cups powdered sugar, sifted
¾ teaspoon glycerin
¼ teaspoon flavoring
food coloring

■ To warm water, add corn syrup and stir until dissolved.

■ Add remaining ingredients.

■ Spread on cookies.

Gingerbread Men Cookies

1 cup shortening
1 cup sugar
½ teaspoon salt
1 egg
1 cup molasses
2 tablespoons vinegar
5 cups all-purpose flour
1½ teaspoons baking soda
1 tablespoon ground ginger
1 teaspoon cinnamon
1 teaspoon ground clove

■ Preheat oven to 375°. Lightly grease baking sheet.

■ Cream shortening, sugar and salt.

■ Add eggs, molasses and vinegar. Mix well.

■ Add dry ingredients.

■ Roll out on a lightly floured surface. Cut with floured cookie cutter.

■ Place on prepared baking sheet. Bake until lightly browned.

25 Gingerbread Men

Graham Cracker Brownies

2 cups graham cracker crumbs
1 can sweetened condensed milk
1 cup chocolate chips
1 cup chopped walnuts
pinch of salt
1 teaspoon vanilla

■ Preheat oven to 350°. Grease 8½x8½-inch pan.

■ Mix graham cracker crumbs, milk, chocolate chips, walnuts, salt and vanilla in bowl.

■ Press mixture in prepared pan.

■ Bake at 350° for about 25 minutes.

Play Dough To Eat!

Lisa Matchett

18 ounces peanut butter
6 tablespoons honey
   non-fat dry milk or milk
   plus flour to the right
   consistency
   cocoa for chocolate
   flavor (optional)

■ Mix all ingredients together. Create and eat.

■ Store in an airtight container.

Cut the top off of an orange, scoop out the inside and fill with orange sherbet. Freeze until ready to eat for a different ice cream treat.

Porcupines

1 orange or apple, halved
   cold meat, cheese, cold
   cuts, vegetables or
   cherry tomatoes
   toothpicks

■ Put fruit half on plate, cut side down.

■ Put meats, cheeses, vegetables on toothpicks.

■ Stick toothpicks in fruit. Let each child make their own creation. Eat and enjoy!

Serves 2

Supervise carefully when children are using toothpicks.

Walking Salad

1 cabbage leaf
peanut butter

■ Wash cabbage leaf.

■ Spread peanut butter on leaf.
Roll lengthwise.

■ Walk and eat!

Serves 1

■ ■ ■ *"Handy-Andy" Tip: Kids and cookie cutters go together. They make all food tastier, are great for art projects, can be used with play dough and mud pies and even make pretty cookies!!!*

Easy Pretzels

1 16-ounce loaf of frozen
bread dough
1 beaten egg
sesame seeds

■ Preheat oven to 350°.

■ Thaw frozen bread dough.

■ Roll out dough on a floured board into a 12x6-inch rectangle. Cut into 6x1-inch strips.

■ Roll strips and shape. Brush beaten egg on pretzels.

■ Sprinkle with sesame seeds. Bake on a cookie sheet at 350° for 15-20 minutes.

The kitchen printing press can turn out great art! Just cut potato, carrot or turnip in half, carve a raised design and spread paint on design or use ink pad. Stamp on paper. Citrus fruits, apples, celery and onions can make great prints, too. Don't forget about printing with cut sponges and kitchen utensils also.

Roasted Pumpkin Seeds

2 cups pumpkin seeds, cleaned
1½ teaspoons Worcestershire sauce
1½ tablespoons butter
1¼ teaspoons seasoning salt

■ Preheat oven to 250°.

■ Mix remaining ingredients. Pour over the pumpkin seeds and toss gently.

■ Spread seeds evenly on cookie sheet.

■ Bake at 250° for one hour.

Variation: Seeds can be fried after cleaning in 1 tablespoon of oil. Salt after golden brown.

Stick Toasties

day old bread, cut in strips
butter, melted
brown sugar
powdered sugar
cinnamon

■ Preheat oven to 350°.

■ Dip strips of bread in butter.

■ Mix brown sugar, powdered sugar and cinnamon in bowl. Roll strips of buttered bread in cinnamon and sugar mixture.

■ Place on ungreased cookie sheet in hot oven for five minutes or until toasted.

Each quilt is a creation. You wouldn't have a child without naming it. Naming a quilt is the natural outgrowth of the love and creative process that goes into making them. I want my pieces to continue to live on, so of course, they all have names.

Syble Sartin

Cinnamon Sugar Butter

½ cup softened butter
2 cups sugar
2 teaspoons cinnamon

■ Beat until thoroughly blended. Mixture will be crumbly. Store in jar in refrigerator.

Makes 2½ cups butter

Take the sexism out of quilting! Use quilting as an art project for any grade level. Be sure to take the age level into consideration when procuring volunteers. Nothing is more frustrating for a child than having to wait endlessly for help. Let's pass along the joys of fine handcrafting to our children!

Eat Your Words

1 roll of packaged sugar cookie dough
frosting tubes

■ Preheat oven as directed.

■ Slice cookies. Place on cookie sheet. With knife, cut each cookie in thirds. Bake as directed.

■ Cool cookies. Print one letter per cookie slice.

■ Spell and eat some three-letter words.

■ ■ ■ *"Handy-Andy" Tip: Edible paint for sugar cookies can be made by blending ¼ teaspoon of food color with one egg yolk. Divide the mixture in several small containers. Put a different food color in each bowl and paint on cookies before baking.*

Thumbprint Cookies

1 cup flour
1 teaspoon salt
⅓ cup plus 1 tablespoon
shortening
2 tablespoons water
jam, jelly or peanut
butter for filling
powdered sugar

■ Preheat oven to 350°.

■ Mix all ingredients together.

■ Roll dough into small balls.
Place balls on cookie sheet.
Mash each ball down with
thumb. Leave a print.

■ Bake at 350° for about 10
minutes. Remove from oven and
cool.

■ Put jam, jelly or peanut butter in
thumbprint. Sprinkle with powdered sugar.

Surprise a parent or grandparent with a quilt. Either take the necessary quilting supplies to a family reunion, or mail paper and fabric crayons to family members for them to design the blocks; favorite events, pets, houses or vacations are some subject ideas.

Puppy Chow Mix for Kids

Martha Park

1 stick butter
1 cup of peanut butter
1 cup chocolate chips
1 regular box of chex rice
cereal
2½ cups of powdered sugar
1 large brown paper bag

■ Melt in microwave the following: butter, peanut butter and
chocolate chips.

■ In large bowl, put cereal and
pour mixture over.

■ Put coated cereal in large
paper bag filled with powdered
sugar and shake!!

Friendship Message Cookies

4 egg whites
½ cup rice flour
¾ cup sugar
  pinch of salt
½ cup melted butter
2 tablespoons water

■ Preheat oven to 350°.

■ Beat egg whites until they stand up in peaks. Stir in dry ingredients.

■ Add melted butter and water. Beat mixture until it is like thin cream.

■ Pour batter from a spoon onto a greased cookie sheet. Bake at 350° for 8 minutes.

■ Write messages on strips of paper while cookies are cooking.

■ While cookies are warm, place message on each one, fold in thirds, bend gently in center.

■ Store in an airtight container.

■ ■ ■ *"Handy-Andy" Tip: Sponge icing cookies: Cover cookies with white icing made of a normal consistency. Make the remaining icing thinner by adding water and food coloring. Sponge onto cookies with a sponge.*

Cup Cake In The Cone

1 cake mix, any flavor,
  batter ready to bake
30 flat-bottomed waffle ice
  cream cones
  frosting
  cake decorations

■ Preheat oven as specified on cake mix.

■ Pour batter in ice cream cone to fill ½ full.

■ Set on baking sheet or in muffin tins.

■ Bake 15-18 minutes at temperature specified on cake mix.

■ Cool. Frost and decorate.

Makes 24 to 30 cone cakes

■ ■ ■ *"Handy-Andy" Tip: A pumpkin-shaped cake can be made by baking the batter in a greased and floured metal mixing bowl.*

The children and grandchildren soon spend the money grandpa leaves, but they hold onto the quilts grandma makes and hands down to them.

Claude Callan

Old-Fashioned Pull Taffy

2 cups sugar
½ cup light corn syrup
½ cup water
¼ teaspoon cream of tartar
food coloring
flavoring desired

■ Combine sugar, corn syrup, water and cream of tartar. Place over heat. Stir until sugar dissolves.

■ Cook, without stirring, to 265° F on candy thermometer. Remove from heat; add coloring and flavoring if desired.

■ Pour on greased platter or pie pan. Cool until easily handled. Pull into ropes until chalky and porous. Break or cut into bite-size pieces with scissors.

This makes a mess but is a lot of fun! Greased hands make pulling easier.

A friend of mine, not even a quilter, had a birthday party for her first grader. She so loved the idea of creating a memory incorporating the past that she handwrote each invitation on reproduced parchment paper. She asked that each child come dressed as they would in pioneer days. She was fortunate that she had an uncle who lived out of town and a friend who had access to a pony. Each young friend arrived not knowing what to expect. Were they in for a treat! Along with the expected cake, ice cream and punch; they had a good ole' fashioned taffy pull. When all hands had been appropriately washed, she brought out individual blocks of material for each child to design with drawings, handprints, even footprints. Each child signed their square with the last one reserved for the birthday girl's name, date and handprint. She used bright party-type fabric in the lattice and sashing and made it into a lovely wallhanging.

When the time came for the pony ride (five times around the ring each) my friend stood by with camera in hand. To the delight of each friend, as well as their parents, a 3 x 5-inch photograph arrived one week later, capturing a "memory from the past". It's twelve years later and my son's memory still hangs in our family hall of fame.

Yogurt-Banana Shake

1 ripe banana
⅓ cup plain yogurt
1 tablespoon honey
1 cup milk

- Blend ingredients well.
- Pour in glass.

Serves 2

For extra coolness, serve over ice or blend ice in shake.

 ## Yogurt Popsicles

Lisa Matchett

Prepare ahead

8 ounces plain yogurt
6 ounces concentrated unsweetened fruit juice dash of vanilla and/or honey (optional)

- Mix well and freeze in molds. Three ounce paper cups work well as molds.
- For handles insert wooden sticks or spoons when mixture is partially frozen.

 ## Penny's Drip-less Popsicles

Lori Anderson

Prepare ahead

1 small package gelatin (any flavor)
1 package fruit-flavored drink mix (any flavor)
1 cup sugar
2 cups hot water
2 cups cold water

- In large container mix the gelatin, fruit-flavored drink mix, sugar, and hot water until all are dissolved.
- Add cold water and stir well.
- Pour into molds and freeze.

Makes 18 popsicles

If you use sugar free fruit-flavored drink mix, omit sugar.

These are terrific for small children and babies.

 ## Chocolate Banana Pops

Sherri Hancock

Prepare ahead

- 3 medium bananas, firm and ripe
- 6 flat wooden sticks, 4-inches in length
- ½ cup semi-sweet chocolate chips
- 2 tablespoons shortening optional toppings; sprinkles, nuts, granola or coconut

■ Line a baking sheet with waxed paper.

■ Peel bananas, cut each in half crosswise. Insert a stick into the cut end of each banana half. Place on baking sheet.

■ In a 2-cup glass measuring cup, microwave chocolate and shortening on high for 1 ½ - 2 minutes until almost melted, stirring halfway through cooking. Stir until smooth.

■ Dip bananas into chocolate, using a spoon to completely coat.

■ Sprinkle each banana with toppings, if desired.

■ On prepared baking sheet, freeze bananas for 15 to 30 minutes, until chocolate is set.

■ Serve immediately or wrap in wax paper and place in zipper top plastic bag. Store in freezer.

Makes 6 pops

Without toppings; 160 calories, 9 grams fat, 0 mg cholesterol, 5 mg sodium.

To use up the leftover chocolate, add raisins, nuts, coconut, etc. and drop by teaspoonful on a cookie sheet. Cool in refrigerator. great candy.

Cream Pops

2 ounces of juice
1 teaspoon vanilla ice
cream, melted

■ In 3-ounce paper cup, mix
juice with ice cream.

■ Freeze, adding handle when
partially frozen.

Serves 1

Snowman Ice Cream Dish

Prepare ahead
3 scoops vanilla ice cream
decorations

■ Put three balls of ice cream in
row in order of size. Small
(head), medium (body) and large
(base).

■ Decorate to make face, but-
tons, etc.

Serves 1

Variation: You can also make a bunny ice
cream or try orange sherbet (one scoop) for
a pumpkin.

Jam'n Shake

2 tablespoons jam (any
flavor)
1 cup cold milk

■ Place ingredients in blender.

■ Blend for 10 seconds. Serve.

Serves 1

*Make gelatin trees by pouring lime gelatin in pointed paper cups. Cut cup
away when firm.*

Fudgesicles

Prepare ahead

1 14-ounce package of
chocolate pudding
3 cups milk

■ Mix pudding and milk.

■ Pour into paper cups or popsicle molds.

■ Put stick in each cup when partially frozen.

■ Freeze overnight.

■ ■ ■ *"Handy-Andy" Tip: Edible glue for decorating cookies can be made by painting honey on baked cookie and sprinkling cookie decorations on top.*

Clown Cones

Prepare ahead

1 scoop of ice cream
1 sugar cone
decorations
canned whipping cream

■ Place scoop of ice cream on plate. Top scoop with cone for a hat.

■ Decorate face. Spray whipping cream for "hair".

■ Freeze to harden.

Serves 1

Do It Yourself-Sundae Party - Children help themselves to their favorite toppings on a scoop of ice cream. Topping ideas: whipped cream, coconut, fudge, honey, maple syrup, strawberry jam, nuts, crushed pineapple, candies.

PARENT/CHILD BASEBALL PARTY

AGE: Appropriate for a variety of ages

SEX: Boys and Girls

INVITATION: Purchase sports theme invitations or...
Write information on hollow plastic baseball and deliver to houses

DRESS: Baseball uniforms

ACTIVITIES: Introduce players just like at real games
Parents vs. Children
Parents play in some different way. Some ideas are:
Hop to bases
Run all bases twice
Bat with tiny plastic bat and foam ball
Do a "wave"
Have a seventh inning stretch
Pass out "awards" following game

FAVORS: Use a paper bucket (available at party good stores) for holder
Give baseball cards, sport shaped erasers, note pads, pencils, bendable baseball players
Fill with popcorn and wrap with colored cellophane

FOOD: "Ballgame food"
　　　Hot Dogs
　　　Chips
　　　Sodas
　　　Cake in shape of Baseball - white frosting with stitching in color of your choice. Write name on cake. or...
　　　Sheet cake. Decorate with frosting in shape of Ball Diamond.

VARIATIONS: Same idea can be done with Basketball, Soccer, Football, etc.

COWBOY PARTY

AGE: 8 - 10 years

SEX: Boys or girls

INVITATION: Cut paper out in shape of cowboy hat or....
Purchase cowboy theme invitations

DRESS: Cowboys and Cowgirls

ACTIVITIES: Line dancing to country tunes
Fake calf roping
Cactus ring toss
Stick horse obstacle course
Jail and sheriff (kids are the sheriff, parents the outlaws)

FAVORS: Take Polaroid pictures in a western backdrop
Present favors tied in a bandanna
Western pencil holder filled with candies

FOOD: Have a "chuck wagon". Circle "the wagons around"
"Cowboy food" - baked beans with hot dogs, Johnny cakes
Serve the beans in a cleaned tin can
Cake: Shape of cactus or...
Sheet cake with boots, rope, cowboy hat decorations

TREASURE HUNT PARTY

AGE: 7 - 9 years

SEX: Boys or girls

DRESS: Pirates

INVITATIONS: Hand deliver notes sticking out of bottles (use small plastic soda bottles) or...
Purchase treasure/pirate theme invitations

ACTIVITIES: While children are arriving have children decorate treasure chests.   Using square paper gift boxes, have children decorate with glue, glitter, markers and stamps and stamp pads.
Have a "treasure hunt" Be prepared to do it again!!
Divide groups into teams and 2 or 3 separate sets of clues
Treasures should be at end
Pirate ship race relays
In small plastic swimming pool have children in two groups. In turn, each child will blow a plastic boat across the "sea". Decorate one as the "pirate ship" and the other as the "good guys". Keep track of the good guys vs. the pirates to see who wins.

FAVORS: Fill each treasure chest made by the children with gold coin candies, pirate eye patches, plastic boat

FOOD: Treasure Island Cake or Treasure Chest Cake
Golden Chicken Nuggets and French Fries
Golden Punch

VARIATION: For older children and even teenagers adjust the party and have a scavenger hunt. Dress could be in the style of their favorite pirate.

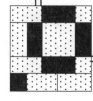
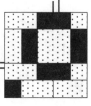

DRESS UP PARTY

AGE: 5 - 8 years

SEX: Girls

INVITATION: White card with red lips "kissed" on card
or...purchase themed invitation

ACTIVITIES: As girls arrive, have them string a beaded necklace
Rent a trunk full of clothes
Put lots of mirrors around the room for admiring!!
Fix hair, paint fingernails and do makeup (the girls will
really enjoy doing their own) Ask a special friend to
help with pampering the girls
Style Show
"Kiss" a Poster - each girl can "kiss" poster for a
keepsake for the birthday girl
Dress up Relay - girls put on men's clothes (too large)
and run to end-take off clothes and carry to next child
in line

FAVORS: Polaroid picture from the style show
Beaded necklace made by each girl
Place favors in paper bucket filled with netting of
various colors
Include small items such as: stick-on earrings,
"cosmetics", small mirror

FOOD: Cake in shape of hat or...Shape of red lips or...
Sheet cake decorated with netting and flowers.
Punch

HINT: Have girls remove rented clothing before eating!

SAFARI PARTY

AGE: 4 - 6 years

SEX: Boys and/or girls

INVITATION: Paper cut in shape of animal footprint or...
Purchase animal themed invitations

ACTIVITIES: Make toilet paper binoculars as children arrive
Go on safari to find hidden animals (stuffed). Bring a wagon to carry captured animals
Musical animal footprints. Played like musical chairs. Make large footprints out of poster board
Play animal charades. Show child picture of animal and have them act out.
Pin the tail on the tiger
Make animal masks

FAVORS: Hats with animal "skin" band
Animal Crackers
Small plastic jungle animals
Before the party, have your child decorate the party bags by drawing stripes, spots, etc. on paper bags
Animal masks

FOOD: Tiger cake
Monkey Juice
Fresh fruit

CIRCUS PARTY

AGE: 4 - 6 years

SEX: Boys or girls

INVITATION: Box of animal crackers with information taped on box

ACTIVITIES: Make clown/party hats. Have table set up with all kinds of things to decorate with
Hire a clown to do magic tricks
Face painting
Have animal noses and ears for children to wear and do animal tricks
Have some circus acts set up for children to do

FAVORS: Party hat
Clown noses
Balloons
Put all favors in popcorn bag
Assorted candies

FOOD: Sugar cookies cut in shape of animals
Ice Cream Clowns
Circus Punch

VARIATION: Hire a magician to do the magic tricks. Give magic tricks, card deck for favors. Cake could resemble a top hat with magic potion punch. Children could take turns to do magic of their own.

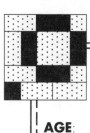

TEDDY BEAR TEA PARTY

AGE: 4 - 7 years

SEX: Girls

DRESS: Dress Up

INVITATION: Invitation in shape of teddy bear or
Purchase teddy bear theme invitations

ACTIVITIES: Everyone brings their favorite teddy
Read a teddy bear story
Have a tea party and use party manners
Have a teddy bear parade
Put all the teddy bears in a pile. Divide the group in teams and have a relay to retrieve their teddy bear.
Have a teddy bear hunt. One bear disappears and clues are given to find it. (Choose a bear whose owner will not be upset)

FAVORS: Teddy bear stickers
Pretty ribbons for the teddy bears
Tea cup and saucer or tiny tea set

FOOD: Little tea sandwiches cut in bear shapes
Bear cookies
Lemonade
Ice cream with gummy bears

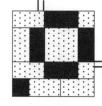

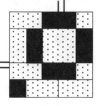

OLYMPICS

AGE: Appropriate for a variety of ages

SEX: Boys or girls

INVITATION: Resembles an Olympic torch or...
purchase American themed invitations

ACTIVITIES: Opening ceremonies - Honored host symbolically
"lights" the eternal flame
Food and Nose Relay - Divide in teams - each runner
holds his nose with one hand and his foot with the
other.
"Javelin-straw" Throw - children line up behind line
and see who can throw the straw the farthest
"Discus-Plate" Toss - each child throws paper plate
Water Relay - Two teams, each player holds a full
glass of water and hops to goal and back. Winning
team has the most water at the end.
Sock Put - Using a knotted sock, children throw to see
whose goes the farthest
Closing ceremonies: Each participant and/or team
receives the respective awards.

FAVORS: Olympic ribbons
Picture during the medal ceremony
Sweatbands
American items: such as a small flag

FOOD: Sheet cake with five Olympic rings and small flags
from world-wide countries
Olympic lemonade

HAWAIIAN LUAU

AGE: 6 - 8 Years

SEX: Girls

INVITATION: Lei with information attached

ACTIVITIES: Upon arrival give each girl a lei
Make grass skirt with crepe paper. Attach paper to ribbon and tie around waist
Have children string flowers and cut up straws and hollow colored pastas with elastic threads to make wrist and ankle bracelets.
Make star fish art
Play Find the Penny Under the Shell (three shells, children guess which shell has the penny under it)
Dance the hula with Hawaiian music
Hula Hoop contest
Limbo contest
Play: Hop the Island

FAVORS: Each girl keeps her lei, "grass" skirt, ankle and wrist bracelets and starfish art
Glue flowers on colored paper bags and put in tropical candies: lifesavers, gummy shapes, flavored fruit candies, etc.

FOOD: Tropical punch (cherry juice, orange juice and pineapple juice)
Pineapple sherbet served in clear container-pineapple and maraschino cherry garnish
Sheet cake - green frosting on sides with coconut (dyed green), silk flowers along plate, and blue frosting on top
Eat on beach towels

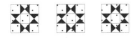
TABLE OF MEASUREMENTS AND EQUIVALENTS

Dash or Pinch	Less than ⅛ teaspoon
1 teaspoon	60 drops
1 tablespoon	3 teaspoons
8 tablespoons	½ cup
10 tablespoons	⅝ cup
12 tablespoons	¾ cup
14 tablespoons	⅞ cup
16 tablespoons	1 cup or 8 ounces
1 cup	½ pint
2 cups	1 pint
4 cups	1 quart
16 cups	1 gallon
2 pints	1 quart
2 quarts	½ gallon
4 quarts	1 gallon
1 fluid ounce	2 tablespoons
2 fluid ounces	¼ cup
4 fluid ounces	½ cup
6 fluid ounces	¾ cup
8 fluid ounces	1 cup
16 fluid ounces	1 pint
32 fluid ounces	1 quart
48 fluid ounces	6 cups
128 fluid ounces	1 gallon

FOOD EQUIVALENTS AND SUBSTITUTIONS

Apples	3 medium (1 pound)	3 cups, sliced
	1 medium	1 cup, chopped
Bacon	4 slices, cooked	¼ cup, crumbled
Baking Powder	1 teaspoon	¼ teaspoon baking soda + ¼ teaspoon cream of tartar
	1 teaspoon	2 egg whites
Bananas	3-4 medium	1¾ cups mashed
Barbecue Sauce	1 cup	1 cup ketchup + 2 tablespoons Worcestershire sauce
Beans		
Dried	1 pound	6 cups, cooked
Green	1 pound	2½ cups, cut
Bell Pepper	1 large	1 cup, diced
Biscuit Mix	1 cup	1 cup flour + 1 ½ teaspoons baking powder and 2 tablespoons shortening
Butter or Margarine	1 stick	½ cup
	1 pound	2 cups
	1 cup	1 cup margarine
	1 cup	⅞ cup corn oil + pinch of salt
	1 cup	⅞ cup solid shortening + ½ teaspoon salt
	1 cup	1 ¼ cups whipping cream
Cabbage	1 head (1 pound)	4½ cups shredded
Carrots	1 medium	½ cup, sliced
	1 pound	3 cups, shredded
Cauliflower	½ pound	½ cup flowerettes
Celery	2 medium stalks	1 cup, sliced
Cheese		
Cheddar	4 ounces	1 cup, grated
Cream	3 ounces	6 tablespoons
Chicken	3½ pound fryer, cooked	4 cups, chopped
Chocolate		
Cocoa Powder	¼ cup	1 envelope (1 ounce) soft baking chocolate
Semi-Sweet	3 squares (3 ounces)	½ cup semi-sweet morsels
Unsweetened	1 square (1 ounce)	3 tablespoons cocoa + 1 tablespoon oil
	1 square (1 ounce)	1 envelope (1 ounce) soft baking chocolate
Coconut	3½ ounce can, flaked	1⅓ cups
	1 pound	5 cups shredded
Corn	1 medium ear	½ cup kernel

FOOD EQUIVALENTS AND SUBSTITUTIONS

Crumbs		
Bread	1 slice white bread	¼ cup fine
Chocolate	10 cookies	½ cup crushed
Graham Cracker	16 squares	1 ¼ cups crushed
Saltines	14 crackers	½ cup fine
Vanilla	11 cookies	½ cup fine
Flour		
All-Purpose	1 cup	1 cup + 2 tablespoons cake flour
Cake, Sifted	1 cup	1 cup sifted all-purpose less 2 tablespoons
Self-Rising, Sifted	1 cup	1 cup sifted all-purpose + 1 teaspoon baking powder and ½ teaspoon salt
Lemon	1 medium	2-3 tablespoons juice
	Juice of one lemon	3 tablespoons bottled lemon juice
Lettuce	1 pound	6¼ cups, torn
Lime	1 medium	2 tablespoons juice
Marshmallows	1 large	1 cup
	1 large	10 small
Milk/Cream		
Buttermilk	1 cup	1 cup sweet milk + 1 tablespoon lemon juice or vinegar, let stand 5 minutes
	1 cup	1 cup sweet milk + 1 ¾ teaspoons cream of tartar
	1 cup	1 cup yogurt
Cream, Heavy	1 cup	⅓ cup butter + ¾ cup milk
Cream, Light	1 cup	⅞ cup milk + 3 tablespoons butter
Sour Cream	1 cup	⅓ cup butter and ⅔ cup sour milk
Whole Milk	1 cup	¼ cup dry whole milk + 1 cup water
	1 cup	1 cup buttermilk + 1 teaspoon baking soda
	1 cup	¾ cup dry non-fat milk + 1 cup water and 3 tablespoons butter
	1 cup	½ cup evaporated milk + ½ cup water
Yogurt	1 cup	1 cup sour milk or buttermilk
Mushrooms	8 ounces	3 cups, sliced
	1 pound	6 ounces canned mushrooms
Nuts, shelled		
Almonds (Whole)	½ pound	1 ½ cups
Peanuts	½ pound	1 ½ cups
Pecans	½ pound	2 cups
Walnuts	½ pound	2 cups

FOOD EQUIVALENTS AND SUBSTITUTIONS

Onion
  Green — 5 green onions — ½ cup, sliced
  White — 2 medium — 1 cup, chopped

Orange — 1 medium — ⅓ cup juice
  Juice of one orange — ⅓ - ½ cup orange juice

Peaches — 1 pound — 2 cups sliced

Pears — 1 pound — 2 cups sliced

Potatoes — 1 medium — ½ cup cooked
  3 medium — 1 pound
  1 pound — 2¼ cooked

Rice
  Brown (raw) — 1 cup — 4 cups cooked
  Uncooked — 1 cup — 3 cups, cooked
  Instant — 1 cup — 2 cups, cooked

Spices and Seasonings
  Allspice — 1 tablespoon — 1 tablespoon equal parts cinnamon, clove, and nutmeg
  Basil — 1 tablespoon — 1 tablespoon oregano
  Caraway — 1 teaspoon — 1 teaspoon anise
  Cayenne — 1 teaspoon — 1 teaspoon chili peppers
  Garlic Powder — ⅛ teaspoon — 1 small garlic clove
  Herbs (dried) — 1 teaspoon — 1 tablespoon fresh herbs
  Mustard (dry) — 1 teaspoon — 1 tablespoon prepared mustard
  Nutmeg — 1 teaspoon — 1 teaspoon mace
  Onion, (minced, dehydrated) — 1 tablespoon — 1 small onion
  Onion powder — 1 tablespoon — 1 medium onion
  Oregano — 1 teaspoon — 1 teaspoon marjoram
  Sage — 1 teaspoon — 1 teaspoon thyme

Strawberries — 1 quart — 4 cups sliced

Sugar and Sweeteners
  Sugar (reduce liquid in recipe by ¼ cup) — 1 cup — 1 cup molasses + ½ teaspoon baking soda
  1 cup — 1 cup honey + ½ teaspoon baking soda
  1 cup — 1 cup maple syrup + ¼ teaspoon baking soda
  Brown sugar — 1 cup — 1 cup white sugar + ¼ cup molasses
  Corn Syrup — 1 cup — 1 cup sugar + additional ¼ cup of any liquid in recipe
  Honey — 1 cup — 1¼ cups sugar + additional ¼ cup of any liquid in recipe

Thickening Agents
  Flour — 2 tablespoons — 3½ eggs
  2 tablespoons — 7 egg yolks
  2 tablespoons — 1 tablespoon cornstarch

FOOD EQUIVALENTS AND SUBSTITUTIONS

Thickening Agents
Flour	2 tablespoons	¾ ounce bread crumbs
	2 tablespoons	1 tablespoon tapioca

Tomato
Fresh	1 pound	3-4 medium
	2 medium	2 cups, chopped
	1 cup, chopped	½ cup puree
Tomato Juice	1 cup	½ cup tomato sauce + ½ cup water
Tomato Sauce	1 15-ounce can	6-ounce can tomato paste + 1 cup water

Yeast
Active dry	1 package (2 teaspoons)	1 cake compressed yeast

FOOD PRESENTATION

Just as the true beauty of a quilt is not fully realized until it has been taken off the frame, "trimmed" and "bound"...a dish is not complete until the final touches have been placed upon it. The beauty of a quilt and the presentation of a dish is in the gift of turning the ordinary into the extraordinary, the plain into the pretty. With a quilt this is obtained through the design and care of the stitch; with the food presentation it is accomplished through imagination, creativity and practice. We hope the following pages will encourage your adventure within.

WHY GARNISH FOODS?

Garnishes give food that final flair that turns the ordinary into something special!

Garnished soups look prettier than plain ones, and they usually taste a bit more interesting, too. The following list of items are great for soups:

almonds, sliced	eggs, hard-cooked	parsley
avocado slices	fennel	peppers, diced
bacon bits	green onions	pimiento
basil	herb butters	radishes
caraway	lemon rind or slices	scallions
carrots, grated	onion slices	shrimp, tiny
celery, diced	orange rind or slices	sour cream
cheese, grated	parsley, minced	sunflower seeds
chervil	poppy seeds	tarragon
chili powder	pumpkin seeds	tomatoes
chives, snipped	mint springs	tortilla strips
croutons	mushrooms, sliced	watercress
cucumber, sliced	nuts	whipped cream
curry powder	olives, ripe or green	dollops
dill	Parmesan cheese	

Use some garnishes below to give your salads extraordinary eye appeal!

avocado slices	curly cabbage leaves	nuts
bacon, crumbled	dried fruits	onion rings
broccoli florets	eggs, hard-cooked	raisins
cheese, grated	fresh flowers	red bell peppers
coconut	golden bell pepper	sausage
croutons	green pepper rings	sesame seeds
		sunflower seeds

Desserts should look as yummy as they taste. The list below can make your dessert sensational!:

cinnamon sprinkles
cinnamon sticks
chocolate curls
chocolate leaves
chocolate shavings
confectioners' sugar
edible flowers

drizzled creams and
   sauces
ginger, candied
ice cream
kiwi slices
lemon twists
lime slices

Maraschino cherries
mint sprigs
nuts, toasted
pineapple slice
raspberries
strawberries
whipped cream,
   dollop

Containers for Dip, Sauces and Salads

apples
artichokes
avocado
bread, hollowed
cabbage
eggplant

grapefruit
lemon
lime
melons
onion
orange

peppers
pineapple
pumpkins
squash
tomato
watermelon

HORS D'OEUVRES TIPS:

Apples, pineapples, potatoes, grapefruits can be used as a base studded with a display of delicacies on picks. Combine the flavors and colors of some of the following items for a tasty display:

Ideas for Delicious Cold Skewered Tidbits:

apple pieces, celery pieces, cheese squares, cocktail sausages, cream cheese balls, dates, gherkins, grapefruits sections, green onions, ham, honeydew melon, pickled onions, ripe olives, stuffed olives, small onions, pickle slices, prunes stuffed with almonds, shrimp, smoked turkey, watermelon.

Attractive Hot Skewered Tidbits:

bacon, cherry tomato, chicken liver, cocktail sausage, diced cucumber, diced eggplant, lobster pieces, mushroom, mussel, olive, onion section, smoked oyster, scallop, shrimp, diced squash.

■ ■ ■ *"Handy-Andy" Tip: Remember the **Law of Light and Dark** when trying to make foods look pretty; top light with dark items, and dark with light items.*

KITCHEN GLOSSARY

Al dente - tender but slightly firm cooked pasta

Amandine - made or served with almonds

Au gratin - dish, usually topped with cheese or bread crumbs, and browned in the oven or broiler

Barbecue - to roast or broil over hot coals and baste with a seasoned sauce

Baste - to brush or spoon liquids over food while cooking to keep the surface moist and flavorful

Batter - a thick, yet pourable, uncooked mixture

Beat - to stir or mix rapidly with a whisk, spoon or beater

Bisque - creamy, thick soup

Blend - to thoroughly combine ingredients until smooth in texture

Bone - to remove bones from meat

Bouquet garni - a small bundle of herbs used for flavoring soups and stews, usually bound together or wrapped in cheesecloth

Bread - to coat food with crumbs before cooking

Broth - liquid in which meat or vegetables have been cooked

Brown - to cook at a high heat on top of stove or in oven or broiler to seal in juices

Brule - foods glazed with caramelized sugar

Caramelize - to melt sugar over low heat until brown in color

Caviar - salted roe (eggs) of large fish and usually served as an appetizer

Chowder - thick soup usually made with seafood or fish.

Clove - one small section of a segmented bulb

Coat - to cover food's surface with a substance

Combine - to mix ingredients together until blended

Compote - fruits, fresh or dried, cooked and served in sweetened, flavored syrup

Condiment - seasoning, sauce, spice or relish added to or eaten with food to enhance the flavor

Consommé - clear soup made by boiling meat and bones slowly

Cream - to beat butter with sugar or other ingredients until smooth and fluffy

Creole - dish usually served over rice and made with tomatoes and peppers

Croutons - hard cooked pieces of bread used for garnishment

Cube - cut in small squares

Deglaze - to loosen drippings from pan by adding liquid and heating gently

Devein - to remove black and white veins along the back of a shrimp

Dice - cut into very small pieces

Dilute - add liquid in order to thin or weaken

Dredge - to coat food with a dry mixture

Drippings - juices and melted fats of meats that emerge during cooking

Drizzle - to pour liquid over the surface of food in a fine stream

Dust - to lightly sprinkle the surface of food with a dry ingredient

Essence, extract - concentrated flavoring

Filet, fillet - a boneless strip of meat

Fold - to combine two mixtures, using a gentle over and over motion

Garnish - to decorate food by adding small pieces of other colorful food

Gel - to form a jellylike substance using gelatin

Glaze - a mixture applied to food which hardens, adding flavor and a glossy appearance

Grill - to cook over embers or under a broiler

Jelly-roll style - to roll a flat piece of cake or meat around a filling

Julienne - foods cut in match-like strips

Knead - to work dough with the heel of the hand until texture is smooth and satiny

Marinate - to allow food to stand in a liquid to tenderize and enhance flavor

Mash - to soften and reduce to pulp

Meringue - combination of sugar and beaten egg whites

Mince - to cut or chop ingredients into very small pieces

Mix - to combine ingredients until evenly combined

Mold - to cook, chill or freeze food in a container so that when done the food takes on the shape of the container

Mousse - delicate mixture comprised of whipped cream or beaten egg whites

Paella - a Spanish dish, flavored with saffron, or rice and meat(s)

Partially Set - to chill gelatin until the consistency of egg whites

Pit - to remove seeds and stones from foods

Puree - a thick liquid resulting from mashing foods

Quiche - a custard poured in a pie shell and baked

Ragout - thick, highly seasoned stew of meat

Red Bell Pepper - a more mature green bell pepper.

Reduce - to lessen the amount of liquid thereby concentrating and intensifying the flavors

Roux - mixture of flour and fat, used commonly as a thickening agent

Sauté - to brown or cook food in a small amount of fat

Sear - to brown the surface of food quickly with intense heat

Soft peaks - to beat egg whites or whipping cream until peaks are formed with tips that curl over

Soufflé - a puffy egg dish

Stewing - which means cook by simmering slowly, will tenderize the meat as well as create a delicious blend of flavors called a stew and commonly containing a meat or fish, vegetables and a thick broth.

Stiff peaks - to beat egg whites or whipping cream until peaks are formed that stand straight

Stir - to mix using a round and round motion

Stir fry - Oriental method of cooking using high heat and rapid stirring

Stroganoff - thinly sliced meat cooked within a sauce

Tart - small individual pie

Vinaigrette - a sauce made with vinegar

Whip - to beat rapidly until stiff

Zest - the colored part of a citrus rind

FREEZER STORAGE INFORMATION SAMPLER

BASIC INFORMATION

1. Wrap food in airtight, moisture proof/vapor proof material. This will keep odors from penetrating the freezer and foods.
2. Date and label the contents of all frozen foods.
3. Allow enough time to defrost frozen foods in refrigerator.
4. Do not refreeze food after it has been thawed.

"HOW TO'S"

Freeze baked bread: Let the bread cool completely. Wrap each loaf airtight in foil, then package in a plastic bag, label the contents and date, and place in the freezer. To serve, unwrap and let the bread thaw completely at room temperature. To reheat, place thawed bread on a baking sheet in a 350° oven. Rolls and small loaves should be heated for about 10 minutes, large loaves for 15 minutes.

Freeze Casseroles: Casseroles should be slightly undercooked.

A Real Dish Saving Hint: With heavy foil, line casserole dish and pour in partially cooked casserole. Cool and then freeze casserole. When frozen, remove foil wrapped casserole from dish. Tightly wrap casserole, remembering to label and date and return to freezer. When ready to cook the casserole, unwrap and place in original dish to cook.

Freeze Vegetables: Wash vegetables completely. Blanch vegetables briefly, the time is dependent on the type of vegetable. After blanching, submerge immediately in very cold water for 4-5 minutes. Drain the vegetables and place in appropriate container. Never freeze unblanched vegetables.

Veggie Tip: Green peppers and chives are examples of vegetables that may be chopped and frozen in small portions and used later for cooking.

NOT SUITABLE FOR FREEZING:

cabbage	mayonnaise	salad greens
celery	onions	tomatoes
cucumbers	pears	
hard-cooked egg	processed meats	
whites	radishes	

FREEZER STORAGE OF COMMON FOODS

Beef
Ground meat	2-3 months
Roasts and steaks	6-12 months
Stew	2-3 months

Breads	2-3 months
Butter or margarine	4-6 months

Cakes
Cheesecake	1 month
Coffeecake	1 month
Frosted	2-3 months
Unfrosted	2-6 months

Cheese	3-4 months
Cookies	6-8 months
Fruits	8-12 months
Game	6-8 months
Hot Dogs	2 months
Nuts, shelled	6-12 months
Pies	6-8 months
Pizza	3-5 months

Pork
Bacon	1 month
Ham	2 months
Pork chops	3-4 months
Pork Roast	4-6 months

Poultry
Chicken, cooked	3-4 months
Chicken, raw	4-9 months

Seafood
Crab, scallops, lobster	1-2 months
Fish	2-3 months
Shellfish	3-4 months

Soups	8-12 month

TO REMOVE STAINS FROM WASHABLES

ALCOHOLIC BEVERAGES/WINE
Immediately sponge or pour cold water through stain until it disappears, follow with water and glycerin. Rinse with vinegar for a few seconds if stain remains. These stains may turn brown with age. If wine stain remains, rub with concentrated detergent; wait 15 minutes; rinse. Repeat if necessary. Wash with detergent in hottest water safe for fabric.

HINT: If wine is spilled during a meal, pour salt directly on stain and remain there until the meal is over. After meal, begin stain removal measures.

BLOOD
Pre-soak in cold or warm water at least 30 minutes. If stain remains, soak in lukewarm ammonia water (3 tablespoons ammonia per gallon water). Rinse. If stain remains, work in detergent, and wash, using bleach safe for fabric.

BUTTER, GREASE OR OIL
Place dry cloth under stain and rub with hot sudsy water. Blot with a non-flammable dry cleaning solvent. Wash in detergent in the hottest water safe for fabric.

CANDLEWAX
Use a dull knife to scrape off as much wax as possible. Place fabric between two blotters or facial tissues and press with warm iron. Remove color stain with non-flammable dry cleaning solvent. Wash with detergent in the hottest water safe for fabric.

CHEWING GUM
Rub area with ice, then scrape off with dull blade. Sponge with dry cleaning solvent; allow to air dry. Wash in detergent and hottest water safe for fabric.

CHOCOLATE AND COCOA
Pre-soak stain in cold or warm water. Wash in hot water with detergent. Remove any grease stains with dry cleaning solvent. If color remains, sponge with hydrogen peroxide, wash again.

COFFEE
Sponge or soak with cold water as soon as possible. Wash, using detergent and bleach safe for fabric. Remove cream grease stain with non-flammable dry cleaning solvent. Wash again.

CRAYON

Scrape with dull blade. Wash in hottest water safe for fabric, with detergent and 1-2 cups of baking soda.

HINT: If full load is crayon stained, take to cleaners or coin-op dry cleaning machines.

DEODORANTS

Sponge area with white vinegar. If stain remains, soak with denatured alcohol. Wash with detergent in hottest water safe for fabric.

DYE

If dye transfers from a non-colorfast item during washing, immediately bleach discolored items. Repeat as necessary BEFORE drying. On whites use color remover.

CAUTION: Do not use color remover in washer, or around washer and dryer as it may damage the finish.

EGG

Scrape with dull blade. Pre-soak in cold or warm water for at least 30 minutes. Remove grease with dry cleaning solvent. Wash in hottest water safe for fabric, with detergent.

FRUIT AND FRUIT JUICES

Sponge with cold water. Pre-soak in cold or warm water for at least 30 minutes. Wash with detergent and bleach safe for fabric.

GRASS

Pre-soak in cold water for at least 30 minutes. Rinse. Pre-treat with detergent. Wash using detergent, hot water, and bleach safe for fabric. On acetate and colored fabrics, use one part denatured alcohol to two parts water.

GREASE, OIL, TAR

Method 1: Use powder or chalk absorbents to remove as much grease as possible. Pre-treat with detergent or non-flammable dry cleaning solvent, or liquid shampoo. Wash in hottest water safe for fabric, using plenty of detergent.

Method 2: Rub spot with lard and sponge with a non-flammable dry cleaning solvent. Wash in hottest water and detergent safe for fabric.

INK—BALL POINT PEN

Pour denatured alcohol through stain. Rub in petroleum jelly. Sponge with non-flammable dry cleaning solvent. Soak in detergent solution. Wash with detergent and bleach safe for fabric.

INK—FOUNTAIN PEN

Run cold water through stain until no more color will come out. Rub in lemon juice and detergent. Let stand 5 minutes. Wash. If a yellow stain remains, use a commercial rust remover or oxalic acid, as for rust stains.

CAUTION: Handle poisonous rust removers carefully. Keep out of reach of children. Never use oxalic acid or any rust remover around washer and dryer as it can damage the finish. Such chemicals may also remove permanent press fabric finishes.

JELLY

Rinse in cold water, rub with mild soap, rinse and launder.

LIPSTICK

Loosen stain with a non-flammable dry cleaning solvent. Rub detergent in until stain outline is gone. Wash in hottest water and detergent safe for fabric.

MEAT JUICES & GRAVIES

Scrape with dull blade. Pre-soak in cold or warm water for 30 minutes. Wash with detergent and bleach safe for fabric.

MILDEW

Pre-treat as soon as possible with detergent. Wash. If stain remains, sponge with lemon juice and salt. Dry in sun. Wash, using hottest water, detergent and bleach safe for fabric. If stain is persistent, blot with buttermilk, rinse. Dry in sun.

NOTE: Mildew is very hard to remove; treat promptly.

MILK, CREAM, ICE CREAM

Pre-soak in cold or warm water for 30 minutes. Wash. Sponge any grease spots with non-flammable dry cleaning solvent. Wash again.

NAIL POLISH

Sponge with polish remover or banana oil. Wash. If stain remains, sponge with denatured alcohol to which a few drops of ammonia have been added. Wash again. Do not use polish remover on acetate or triacetate fabrics.

PAINT—OIL BASE

Sponge stains with turpentine, cleaning fluid or paint remover. Pre-treat and wash in hot water. For old stains, sponge with banana oil and then with non-flammable dry cleaning solvent. Wash again.

PAINT—WATER BASE

Scrape off paint with dull blade. Wash with detergent in water as hot as is safe for fabric.

PERSPIRATION
Sponge fresh stain with ammonia; old stain with vinegar. Pre-soak in cold or warm water. Rinse. Wash in hottest water safe for fabric. If fabric is yellowed, use bleach. If stain still remains, dampen and sprinkle with meat tenderizer, or pepsin. Let stand one hour. Brush off and wash. For persistent odor, sponge with colorless mouthwash.

RUST
Soak in lemon juice and salt or oxalic solution (3 tablespoons oxalic acid to 1 pint warm water). A commercial rust remover must be used.
CAUTION: Handle poisonous rust removers carefully. Keep out of reach of children. Never use oxalic acid or any rust remover around washer or dryer as it can damage the finish. Such chemicals may also remove permanent press fabric finishes.

SCORCH
Wash with detergent and bleach safe for fabric. On heavier scorching, cover stain with cloth dampened with hydrogen peroxide. Cover this with dry cloth and press with hot iron. Rinse well.
CAUTION: Severe scorching cannot be removed because of fabric damage.

SOFT DRINKS
Sponge immediately with cold water and alcohol. Heat and detergent may set stain.

TEA
Sponge or soak with cold water as soon as possible. Wash using detergent and bleach safe for fabric.

TOMATO
Rinse with cold water. Use an enzyme presoak and soak at least 30 minutes. Wash using detergent and bleach safe for fabric.

Index

Index

The Junior League of Richardson
1131 Rockingham Rd. Suite # 1121
Richardson, TX 75080

Please send ____ copies of **Texas Sampler** @ $16.95 each _____
Postage and handling @ $3.50 each _____
Texas residents add sales tax @ $1.68 each _____

Name _____

Address _____

City _____ State _____ Zip _____

Make checks payable to: *The Junior League of Richardson*

- -

The Junior League of Richardson
1131 Rockingham Rd. Suite # 1121
Richardson, TX 75080

Please send ____ copies of **Texas Sampler** @ $16.95 each _____
Postage and handling @ $3.50 each _____
Texas residents add sales tax @ $1.68 each _____

Name _____

Address _____

City _____ State _____ Zip _____

Make checks payable to: *The Junior League of Richardson*

- -

The Junior League of Richardson
1131 Rockingham Rd. Suite # 1121
Richardson, TX 75080

Please send ____ copies of **Texas Sampler** @ $16.95 each _____
Postage and handling @ $3.50 each _____
Texas residents add sales tax @ $1.68each _____

Name _____

Address _____

City _____ State _____ Zip _____

Make checks payable to: *The Junior League of Richardson*